"The moment that will never leave my mind is when I walked up on the Navy landing and saw the *Arizona*. The Japanese were overhead, the *Arizona* was down and burning, the *Nevada* was under way, and I stood there and watched her go aground. The *Oklahoma* was upside down. I still see it."

—Ralph D. Byard, Chief Commissary Steward

PRAISE FOR
THE USS ARIZONA

"This book provides the human story of the tragedy in a most compelling way."

—*Publishers Weekly*

"The first-person accounts and the authors' lucid reconstruction of the *Arizona*'s final hours are vividly cinematic and wholly absorbing . . . A revealing glimpse into that other day that shook the world."

—Edward Morris, *Bookpage*

THE USS ARIZONA

THE SHIP, THE MEN, THE PEARL HARBOR ATTACK, AND THE SYMBOL THAT AROUSED AMERICA

Joy Waldron Jasper

James P. Delgado

Jim Adams

St. Martin's Paperbacks

THE USS ARIZONA

Copyright © 2001 by Joy Waldron Jasper, James P. Delgado,
and Jim Adams

Cover photograph © Bettman/Corbis.

Library of Congress Catalog Card Number: 2001041954

ISBN: 0-312-99351-X

Printed in the United States of America

St. Martin's Press hardcover edition / December 2001
St. Martin's Paperbacks edition / November 2003

St. Martin's Paperbacks are published by St. Martin's Press,
175 Fifth Avenue, New York, NY 10010.

10 9 8 7 6 5 4 3 2 1

To the men of the *Arizona*
and all their comrades at Pearl Harbor
who inspired America to fight for victory

To Gordon E. Waldron, uncle and godfather,
shot on his birthday during the Battle of the Bulge
and died the following day

_____

Aloha pumehana, mahalo nui loa

CONTENTS

PREFACE

The battleship *Arizona* exploded under heavy attack, a thunderclap that rocked the skies. Debris and parts of bodies rained all over Ford Island. The devastation stunned Hawaii and the nation, for the battleship *Arizona*—the greatest casualty of a terrible day—had been destroyed.

The facts were seemingly simple: a bomb, hundreds dead, burning seas, a ship sunk in Pearl Harbor. But it was so much greater, for in that moment more than a battleship perished: the hopes and dreams of thousands of families went up in the oily smoke that blanketed the waters around the ship. Yet the courage and high emotion aroused that day across the United States led to a renewed pride in country and a fervent campaign for freedom across the world.

This is a story of people, of some who died and some who lived to talk of that day. It is a story of a nation's fascination and reverence for the ship that was larger than life, a ship that sparked an intense interest and loyalty in all who encountered it in the following years. Overnight the USS *Arizona* became a compelling symbol of the Japanese attack. "Remember the *Arizona*!" rang through the battlefields of the Pacific, and the ship began its transition to a great and lasting image of war.

I fear we will awaken a sleeping giant and fill him with a terrible resolve.

—FROM THE DIARY OF ADMIRAL ISOROKU YAMAMOTO, COMMANDER OF JAPANESE NAVAL FORCES, JANUARY 1941, ON BEING APPRISED OF AN ATTACK TO BE LAUNCHED LATER IN THE YEAR ON PEARL HARBOR

THE USS ARIZONA

INTRODUCTION

THE *ARIZONA* ENCOUNTER

We were all born after the USS *Arizona* was destroyed. It was years before we learned of the unspeakable tragedy of December 7, 1941, that had flung the United States into World War II.

On that day—the day forever after to be remembered as the Day of Infamy—American forces in the Pacific were devastated and an entire fleet of fighting ships was crippled. In headlines three inches high, Americans elsewhere learned the news: "JAPANESE BOMB PEARL HARBOR." Of all the battleships in the harbor, the battleship USS *Arizona* had suffered the greatest loss of life. Newspapers across the world screamed the Pearl Harbor story in hundred-point headlines, their front pages emblazoned with photos of the *Arizona*'s smoking, horribly twisted wreckage. No one who saw those pictures ever forgot the sight of the *Arizona*'s masts tilted crazily askew and engulfed with billowing black smoke and flames.

Probably every American alive that day could remember precisely when and where the horrible news became known to them, whether they were listening to the radio or watching the Dodgers play the Giants in a late-season football game in New York.

We three first read about the *Arizona* in history books.

After that, the way we met the battleship unraveled differently. Our backgrounds were disparate—a journalist, a historian, and a Marine—and we came from different places in the United States, but the *Arizona* gripped us all intensely and alike.

Joy Waldron Jasper, a news and feature writer, never dreamed that fate would bring her face-to-face with the legendary battleship now underwater, nor that she would crisscross the country nearly fifty years after the event to talk with the survivors. Historian James P. Delgado didn't imagine that his interest in John Steinbeck and the California gold rush would pale when he visited the *Arizona*. And Jim Adams, a proud Marine, developed an unshakable connection to the battleship that his own father, perched in a radio tower, had witnessed in its death throes.

From a distance, the *Arizona* started as a speck in our lives and grew very large. At different times and places, before any of us met, we perused historical documents about the 1941 Pearl Harbor attack and the story of the *Arizona*'s extraordinary demise.

The attack broke out at 7:55 in the morning, just as the ships anchored in Battleship Row were hoisting their flags for colors. Japanese fighter planes blacked out the sky like a locust plague. They loosed their bombs on the battleships, and strafed the decks and surrounding waters where men were frantically swimming to shore. After twenty minutes of unrelenting bombing runs, the *Arizona* took a mortal blow as a bomb pierced its teakwood deck. Thousands of pounds of munitions in the ship's bow exploded. The *Arizona* sank to the harbor bottom, its decks awash with ocean water laced with burning oil. Most of the sailors and Marines on board died that day. Both the *Arizona*'s captain and Battleship Division One's admiral, who had lived on board, went down with the ship. Less than three hundred of the officers and crew survived.

That day around the world, tales of heroism and death abounded. The sheer numbers of the dead—more than eleven hundred men from the *Arizona* alone—etched in the nation's mind the merciless cruelty of war.

The moment of truth for each of us was the first time we dove on the *Arizona*. We couldn't have guessed that the rusting old battleship lying in the silt of Pearl Harbor could change our lives, but it did.

In 1981 Jasper certainly didn't know of the watershed to come. As a feature writer for magazines and newspapers, she chiefly profiled artists and scientists. But that year she had met a team of underwater archaeologists who worked for the National Park Service as the Submerged Cultural Resources Unit (SCR). Fascinated by their focus on ship-wreck documentation and preservation, she began to cover their work for various publications. Shipwrecks—and div-ing—took prominence in her life. Visiting national parks in far-flung places like Isle Royale, Michigan, and St. John, U.S. Virgin Islands, she witnessed the archaeologists as they mapped, photographed, videotaped, and illustrated the ghosts of the maritime past.

Then came the *Arizona*. When the superintendent of the USS *Arizona* Memorial in Pearl Harbor requested that the SCR team evaluate the battleship in 1983, it sounded like an unusual story to the journalist. The archaeologists' task would be multifaceted: to assess the present condition of the *Arizona*, to map and document it, and to determine if the ship was in danger of rolling over or rusting away. And the controversy still continued about how the ship had met its doom—by a torpedo, a bomb down the stack, or a bomb crashing through the decks. Another task for the team would be to find the answer. Who knew what surprises lay in store? No one had dived on the *Arizona* since the days right after World War II.

In search of the story, Jasper accompanied the team to Hawaii.

On that plane flight from San Francisco to Hawaii she gleaned snippets about the survivors of December 7, 1941. Across the decades, a distance that felt closer than a heartbeat, she learned their stories from interviews they rendered in the days after the attack. A small sampling of the few survivors—289, or one-sixth of the officers and crew—were quoted in patches here and there in a few overview books, their eyewitness accounts filled with fresh, cutting words that breathed life into historical statistics.

The tales the survivors told in the days and years that followed disclosed a powerful attachment to the *Arizona*. As she read their comments forty-two years after the event, she was gripped by their intense emotion for the aging battleship they called home. By the time the team had landed in Honolulu that September day in 1983 she was hooked. The *Arizona* had already made an indelible impression on her.

Those exploratory Park Service dives to the USS *Arizona* were considered big news to the world. The archaeological team visited the battleship in three major expeditions, the first in 1983, and twice, more intensively, in 1984 and 1986. When the TV networks and the newspapers found out about the project, it instantly became national news. That first year the big three TV networks carried the theme of the "*Arizona* Revisited" as the number one news story for two days in a row. Every time the diver-archaeologists set foot in Hawaii, reporters would ride out to the dock to watch the divers suit up on the *Arizona* Memorial. When they returned from the dive, journalists would pepper them with questions.

In 1986 the British Broadcasting Company would send a documentary crew of cameramen to Hawaii, where they interviewed the archaeologists of the Submerged Cultural Resources team and other project participants. The BBC production unit, an efficient, good-humored, high-intensity crew under director Derek Towers, shot footage of the battleship underwater. Their USS *Arizona* segment appeared in both the United Kingdom and the United States in 1987 as part of an eight-part documentary titled "Discoveries Underwater."

But in 1983, exploration of the *Arizona* was all just beginning. No one had dived on the ship since shortly after the war. No one knew its condition underwater. Jasper was still grappling with her newfound attachment to the legendary ship that represented America's entry into World War II.

The USS *Arizona* Memorial is a graceful white structure arching over the battleship. Twenty-one hexagonal windows are open to the sea and sky. The memorial was built in 1962 by Alfred Preis, and its architectural shape—a depressed hollow in the middle with the ends sweeping upward to the sky—is said to symbolize both the initial loss at the time of the attack and the ultimate Allied victory in World War II.

Leaning out through an unglassed window to glimpse the *Arizona,* every Memorial tourist sees a shadowy silhouette lying on the bottom, completely submerged but for one rusted barbette that once held gun turret No. 3. The rest of the ship's superstructure has long ago been cut away. Peering down at the ghostly outlines of the massive ship, the bow and forward guns are lost to sight in the dark water. All that remains of tangible goods are the debris on the galley deck and the empty crater of a rusted barbette that once held big guns.

Out there in the blazing sun at the *Arizona* Memorial, December 7 never seems very far away. Somewhere in the air, just outside the edge of vision, is a lone plane flying over the ship, dropping the fatal bomb that pierced the *Arizona*'s decks and exploded the stored munitions. Seconds later, the *Arizona* had erupted in flames and smoke. Cracked through the hull, it broke in half and sank down to the harbor bottom, its decks awash and masts tilted over the water.

"Remember the *Arizona*!" ran the slogan for recruits and soldiers in battle all through the war. Today tourists gaze down on the *Arizona*'s dark shadow and ponder that hellish day. Remember death on a Sunday morning. Remember the ship broken and battered by bombs, a noble ship reduced to a sunken hulk.

Jasper first saw the ship in its underwater grave on a hot July day. Diving on the *Arizona* was a journalist's dream. No one is allowed to dive it except on official business, since it still holds the remains of its dead sailors and is regarded as a shrine. But as a working reporter, she accompanied the reconnaissance team of underwater archaeologists from the National Park Service and Navy divers who were mapping and photographing the ship.

They moved through the cloudy waters of Pearl Harbor. Divers fanned out in a curve heading toward the ship, their silvery tanks fading fast in the gloom. Laden with loops of black-and-yellow line, the divers prepared to lay a baseline on the ship. To assist the scientific illustrator, a host of other divers carried the requisite clipboards with mylar paper for making sketches. With the help of hundreds of Navy Reserve divers on dozens of dives, the *Arizona* would be measured from bow to stern, every square meter recorded and illustrated. Items lying on deck would be plotted for their exact positioning.

For a few moments there was nothing to see but green. Sediment, washed down from the Koolau Mountains in Hawaii's furious tropical rains, obscured everything beyond ten feet. Jasper was eager to see the ship's remains, having dived on wooden shipwrecks but never on a modern metal one. And nothing the size of a battleship. What would it look like to see a 608-foot behemoth sleeping beneath the waves?

She spotted the mooring chain that went out to the battleship, and wondered for a perverse moment what purpose it served, since the ship wasn't going anywhere. They fin-kicked through a dusky twilight searching for the ship. Ghostly and vague in the cloudy green water, the algae-ridden haze blotted out the ship from view until she was a few feet away.

The ship's immense hull suddenly appeared, looming high over her, an apparition in the mist. The sight of that monstrous ship lying alone in the deep, its blackness shrouded by a green curtain of algae, evoked a sharp gut response she hadn't anticipated. This was no sport dive, nay, not an ordinary historic ship. This was the *Arizona*— the symbol of American loss and American courage, the driving and inspiring force for military forces fighting the war in the Pacific. Pictures of the *Arizona* had filled re-cruiting offices and pulled men and women in off the streets to sign up to fight the enemy who had wrought such havoc in Hawaii.

The bomb that broke the *Arizona*'s back and slammed it into the mud left a path of destruction. Metal, wood, dishes, bits of debris lay scattered everywhere. The current wig-gled the algae on angled pipes. Time seemed to have stopped. But the fish swam gaily over the wreck, as obliv-ious to the dead as robins preening in a country cemetery.

To know the ship was a tomb added tremendously to the emotional impact of diving on it. In the days after the attack some bodies had been retrieved for burial elsewhere, but as war preoccupied the military command and the difficulty of recovering the other victims became clear, the Navy abandoned the task of body recovery. Today more than nine hundred men still sleep aboard the *Arizona*.

Starting at the ship's stern, they planned to swim slowly forward over the deck, all the way scrutinizing the traces of men and guns and war. They'd end their tour at the bow, where the ship had taken the deathblow.

Over a period of several weeks the team of Park Ser-vice specialists would evaluate the overall condition of the ship, studying the cracks in the hull to figure out if it was hazardous, searching for torpedo damage and any other evidence of the attack. They'd take water samples and begin to assess the rate of metal corrosion. And they'd take photographs, videotapes, and with Navy divers would measure every section of the battleship. Was the ship really cracked in two? Would it roll over someday? Was it a hazard?

Jasper had other questions to ask of the *Arizona*. Remembering the survivors' stories she'd read, here she was now in the magical twilight of the underwater, looking at their ship as they'd never seen it. Before her in rusty desolation lay the remains of the legendary vessel that had been the rallying cry for enlistment in World War II. Recruiting posters across the nation showed the *Arizona*'s toppling masts shrouded in huge plumes of smoke. Many sailors had signed up just to avenge the *Arizona*. The object of their loyalty now rested in the mud.

Lying on the harbor bottom, the ship stretches out more than six hundred feet from bow to stern, but the harbor water is dimmed with silt, and nowhere can a diver swim far enough away to view it in one piece. Instead, the battleship reveals itself in parts, a massive wall of steel rising upward, portholes casting a dull glint in the gloom.

Seeing the *Arizona* under the waves feels all wrong. A battleship is supposed to float on the surface of the water, proud and strong, sunlight glinting off its big guns. There is something incomprehensible about seeing its massive shape sunk in the mud and shrouded with green algae, away from sun and wind. In a way, it feels like an intrusion, a violation of privacy, to witness this final resting place.

The hull reaches upward in a vast black wall from the harbor floor, disappearing in the waters brightening near the surface. Except for the rasping sound of bubbles tearing out of a diver's regulator, it is terribly quiet.

A school of Moorish idols darts past in yellow and gold flashes. The tiny fish slip away over the stern railing, picking at little pieces of algae on the deck as they feather past. The *Arizona*'s hull is cool to the touch, a little spongy, rough in patches. The steel metal hull plates, some blackened and breaking apart along the river lines, rise up from the muddy silt of the harbor. Marine organisms of various browns and reds shroud the hull, lending a neglected, battered look.

Despite the poignancy of the sunken ship, it's not hard to picture what the *Arizona* must have looked like in its heyday, when the tremendous hull rose in an elegant sweep high above the waterline.

The battleship's beginnings had reflected high hopes for the newest addition to the U.S. fleet, but the ship passed a mostly uneventful career. In World War I it had stayed in Atlantic waters and missed fighting action. The ship served briefly with the British Grand Fleet in 1918 and even escorted President Woodrow Wilson to the 1919 Paris Peace Conference. But during the twenty-seven years the *Arizona* sailed before its sinking, it never once fired its long guns in combat. All the sailors' drills for the battle readiness never came to fruition, except as an impassioned defense on its last day.

Designed to fight as a "ship of the line," as warships had fought in Lord Nelson's day, the *Arizona* was the last vestige of the pre–World War I approach to naval battles. The philosophy of naval warfare was a Victorian sort of notion, of an era when generals assumed that wars would be fought in a gentlemanly manner, each side taking time to line up its battleships and commence firing at a decent moment, mutually agreed upon and usually in broad daylight.

But as Europe and America discovered in the twentieth century, war was never again to be gentlemanly. World War I saw treachery and savage bloodshed in the trenches of Gallipoli and all across Europe. War was no longer a flashing of colors or a wave of an officer's gloved hand, it was stealth and night maneuvers, espionage and betrayal. Nothing was sacred, as in the U-boat sinking of the *Lusitania* with civilians aboard. No, war wasn't for gentlemen. Certainly not at Pearl Harbor in the flower-scented dawn.

Jasper stroked the ship's hull. The metal was cold and unyielding and slightly slimy with a feathery green algae smudge. Touching the ship that had once been the sailor's home, she reflected that now it was their tomb. Knowing they were still inside, trapped wherever they had happened to be at 8:20 on that long-ago Sunday morning, gave her chills despite the warm tropical waters.

The public, supersensitive to the idea of scientist-divers working around the sacred ship, had already been assured that no one would penetrate the hull and disturb the dead. But the dead seemed to be all around in the gloom. She felt their presence, their voices rising and falling on the waves.

She swam back out from the hull to see how much more of the overall structure she could see. Not much. The mammoth ship faded away to small patches and lines that were lost in the distance. In the murky water it seemed even more mysterious.

A porthole beckoned, the glass reflecting ambient light. Most were blacked out inside by metal porthole covers, but this one was not. Dive mask pressed to the glass, she had a secret look into the *Arizona*. The ship's interior, lighted by a distant sun, revealed metal shapes and jagged wires that shimmered and danced.

She tried to imagine the sound of voices. She wondered about life on the *Arizona* in the months before December 7, when the battleship was a floating city, the home of fifteen hundred men who worked, played football, kept watch, fired guns, and prepared for a war they hoped would never come.

The *Arizona* clutches the heartstrings of everyone who comes out to the memorial, and James P. Delgado, formerly the maritime historian of the National Park Service, was no exception. His dive notes from his first *Arizona* dive reveal the powerful impressions he carried away, much the same sentiments the ship instills in all who come to Pearl Harbor.

That day, as always, the water was too warm for a wet-suit, but bare skin is no protection against rusted metal or barnacles, so he donned a pair of coveralls. Next came the weight belt, tanks, and gear. A quick check of the gear, and the divers strode off the dock, leaving the bright sun and blue skies behind as they hit the water and sank into darkness. As they reached the muddy bottom, they could see only a few feet ahead in the dense water, so they followed their compasses toward the wreck.

Delgado's subconscious mind registered the looming presence of the hulk before he realized he had glimpsed it. His heart started to pound, and his breath grew shallow for a moment. The bright oranges, reds, and yellows of marine life and corrosion covered the hull and blazed beneath the dive light. As he rose, he encountered the first port-hole, an empty, dark aperture. He felt the presence of the ship and the dead, and although he knew it was only in his mind, he couldn't bring himself to look within. At some primitive and superstitious level, he was afraid someone would look back.

He swam along the port side, moving aft toward the stern, until rational thought flooded in. He paused, took his light, and approached an empty port. Inside, he saw what looked like collapsed furniture on the deck, and amazingly, a telephone still attached to a rusted bulkhead. He fantasized that it might be the cabin of Rear Admiral Isaac C. Kidd, killed on that long-ago December morning. As he peered inside, he thought of Kidd and his naval Academy class ring that had been discovered by salvage crews in a pile of ash partially melded to the steel top of the *Arizona*'s conning tower. Kidd's body had apparently been blown there by the blast and consumed by the flames, leaving only his ring, which the salvage crews removed from the steel and sent to his widow. The ring was one of a very few traces left aboard the ship of Admiral Kidd, the former captain who had later become an appointed admiral and was back aboard his old command at the end.

The divers rose up to the deck, and followed it to the rim of the open mount for the No. 4 turret. They dropped down into the darkness, stopping at the soft silt and quietly looking, for a second, at the collection of urns—the interred remains of *Arizona* survivors who have chosen to spend eternity with their shipmates. After a respectful moment, they rose again, back to the deck and aft to the stern. The empty socket of the jack staff reminded Delgado of what he'd read of the last evening aboard the still burning battleship, on December 7, when Lieutenant Kleber Masterson and Ensign Leon Grabowsky took down the *Arizona*'s oil-stained flag as it hung down from here into the water.

Moving aft, off the ship, he looked back and saw that the chain from the buoy that delineates to passing boats that the *Arizona*'s stern had shifted and dragged back and forth across the hull, scraping off corrosion and growth.

The thick letters that spell "ARIZONA" are still bright and shiny, and they reflected some of the light that drifts down from the sun above.

Back to the deck, they followed it along the starboard side, coming up to an open hatch near the No. 3 turret. He hovered, looking down into the darkness, his light picking up tangled debris that blocks it. Then, to his surprise, he saw something rising toward him—a bubble of oil. As it passed the edge of the hatch and floated toward the surface, he watched its slow rise until it transmuted into an oily slick on the surface above. Six seconds later another globule of oil followed. Like so many others, Delgado was struck by the still-bleeding wounds of the *Arizona*.

The light, warm waters on the shallowly submerged deck give way to darkness as they pass beneath the Memorial. He looked up, and through the water saw visitors staring down, some watching him, others gazing out, and a few tossing their offerings of flower leis into the sea. The divers paused here to drop over the ship's side, past the empty mount for a 5-inch gun, and drop down to the top of the torpedo blister. Hatches that line its top are open, but what they were looking for—a burial urn—should rest atop the blister. Just before their dive, the widow of an *Arizona* survivor had dropped the urn with her husband's ashes onto the wreck, but the burial at sea had left the urn visible. A decision was made, with her permission, to move and place it inside the No. 4 turret with the other urns. Delgado saw the urn, but it lay inside a corroded section of plate that cut deep into his thumb as he tried to pull it free. He left the urn there for other divers and, clasping his bloody thumb cut nearly to the bone, he continued the dive.

They moved forward, past patches of teak decking, lines

of fire hose, dropped by the crew as they desperately fought to extinguish the *Arizona*'s fires, and then over the base of the stack. No bomb fell inside it—both the Navy's divers in 1942 and 1943 and the NPS team had found that the stack gratings are intact. But forward of the stack, the deck drops away dramatically, and as they fell into the darkness, they suddenly came up to the top of the No. 1 turret. Angled down, slightly tilted, the three barrels of the 14-inch guns guide the divers forward. He stopped, gazed into the muzzles, and thought about the crew who lay beneath them, crushed and burned into the collapsed decks.

Then, as he turned, a wall of steel—a twisted "flower garden" of thick steel, confronted him. Armored decks, once horizontal, now vertical, and sheared supports. He rose along this wall and reached the gaping maw of the hawse pipes, then turned back to swim along the port side. The huge crack in the side of the hull is, as author Ed Raymer reported, both wide and "jagged as hell." He found the description apt, for on December 7 the explosion that had erupted from within the ship and out of that crack must have seemed like the unleashing of hell itself. Everywhere the effects of the blast and the heat are evident.

Moving further aft, he saw a porthole with its deadlight in place, the blast cover sealed shut behind it. The thick corrosion does not obscure the glass, and inside he could see that the space between cover and glass was only half flooded with oily water. The lack of oxygen has perfectly preserved the paint on the cover. For a moment, time seemed not only to stand still but almost to go in reverse. He fancied that the death wounds of this ship were brand-new.

Delgado passed again under the Memorial, pausing for a second at the stub of the mainmast. Looking up, he saw the American flag flying from the staff welded to it. He swam to the dock and surfaced. As he climbed out he was silent. Looking down, he saw he was smeared with oil: face, hands, hair all thick with it, coveralls stained. The blood from his thumb dripped with the seawater onto the clean concrete.

He knew that while other dives would follow, he would never forget this first visit to the *Arizona*. From firsthand experience he now knew that the *Arizona* was more than a name in a history book, more than an image captured on film.

Jim Adams was only one step removed from the disaster at Pearl harbor. His father, Val Adams Jr., served as a Radioman 3rd Class (RM3c), U.S. Naval Reserve (USNR), and on the day of the attack he was working in the yard signal tower on Oahu overlooking the harbor. From his vantage point he saw the *Arizona* as it blew up and sank. The image stayed with him the rest of his life—and his stories made an indelible impression on his young son. After the war the Pearl Harbor survivor became a journalist with the *New York Times* and the *New York Daily News.*

Young Jim's first real memories of the *Arizona* story go back to 1966, when he was twelve years old, the year of the twenty-fifth anniversary of the Pearl Harbor attack. That event prompted his father to return to Pearl Harbor for the first time since the war's end. Val Adams had casually mentioned in earlier years that he would someday bring Jim to "Pearl," but now he was bothered that due to the boy's "great interest in the excitement and adventure of war and guns and military matters" he might be contributing to the glorification of war in a young and malleable mind.

On that vacation Jim Adams accompanied his father to the *Arizona* Memorial, a visit that elicited painful memories for the former Navy teletype operator. As Val Adams went aboard the memorial built over the sunken *Arizona*, he was shocked at the effect it had. It was all the more surprising, because he remembered that for more than a year after the war started he had remained on duty at Pearl, and the wrecked *Arizona* came to be a common sight to Navy men. Nothing could have prepared him for the experience of seeing the sunken *Arizona* up close.

The back wall of the shrine room is covered with marble. On the vast expanse are inscribed the names of all Navy and Marine Corps personnel killed aboard the ship on December 7, 1941. He scanned the names reluctantly for confirmation of something he'd really known in his gut for a quarter of a century. Despite the years, it was still a shock when his eyes raked through the *W*s and he saw the familiar name: B. M. Wilson RM3c. It was his friend Willie, a radioman third class. Val Adams cried as he read Willie's name on the crowded marble wall. There were others he knew, too, but Willie had been a real buddy.

He'd gone to radio school with Willie. The night before the attack, the two young men had run into each other while both were on liberty in Honolulu. When they parted later that night in a restaurant, Val Adams remembered saying, "So long, Willie." Now he thought of Willie just a few feet below, still aboard the ship underneath the Memorial.

Young Jim Adams saw something different in his father at that moment, an emotion he'd never seen before. That moment stuck in his mind for life.

Later on the same visit the father and son visited Honolulu's National Memorial Cemetery, where many of the

Pearl Harbor dead are buried. They walked along row after row of graves, reading the markers, some with the simplest marking of all: "Unknown. December 7, 1941."

Jim was visibly moved. It was the first intimation Val Adams had that his son had begun to think about war without the glory and excitement. He felt that alone was worth the trip back to Pearl Harbor.

Eleven years later, when Jim Adams was twenty-three, he sailed into Pearl Harbor as a Marine Corps lieutenant commanding a rifle platoon. Having served overseas for a year, he was returning to the United States aboard a U.S. Navy amphibious transport. Passing the *Arizona* Memorial, the sailors and Marines stood in formation and saluted. He remembered how honored he felt to be standing in front of his platoon paying tribute and remembering those who had fought and died on December 7. The next morning he departed Pearl Harbor on the way to San Diego, again passing the *Arizona*. He looked one last time at the Memorial and then at the signal tower where his father had been.

He couldn't know then that, years later when he'd retired from the Marines, he would take the job as cultural resources manager at the *Arizona*. One of his chief functions would be overseeing burials of *Arizona* survivors' ashes on the ship they once called home. Diving the *Arizona,* he felt close to the men interred within.

"I can't imagine how anyone with any sense of history would not be totally enthralled with the experience of diving on the *Arizona* and recognize its significance," Adams says. "No matter how many times I swim around the *Arizona*'s forward section I'm stunned as I look at the broken, wrenched jagged metal blasted out from her sides, the result of the fatal explosion in the forward magazines that sent the Arizona to her death." He often recalls his father's description of the "raging inferno"—perhaps the most terrifying sight of that morning—as he watched the rapidly spreading fire fed by oil from the forward tanks. When the fire reached the powder magazines, he had witnessed as the thunderous explosion sent the Arizona's bow out of the water and flames leapt a hundred feet into the air. The ship's wounds bled heavy, black smoke for days afterward.

Adams holds deep inside the memory of his father's friend Willie, last seen on December 6. On one occasion Adams was assisting in a service at the Memorial. Visitors were given a flower and a slip of paper with the name of one of the men who had died at Pearl Harbor. They were asked to think about the name as they took the flower out to the memorial and cast it into the water over the sunken Arizona. His slip, which he had arranged for, held the name of Willie Wilson.

"I always thought about Willie while diving on his ship— was he still there in the radio room when I swam by it? Or in the crew's mess? I always wondered where he was and how it happened for him. I go to the wall every time I visit the Memorial, and I find his name. Since he was my father's friend, I thought it only right that I remember Willie."

Willie was one of hundreds of names on the marble wall. Each man had left a life behind, a life where someone knew and loved him. Robert Leopold left a mother, sister, and a fiancée back in Kentucky. Lester Mayfield left a grieving family in the Rockies. Delbert Anderson perished, leaving his twin brother, John, also an Arizona sailor. Admiral Isaac

Kidd left a wife and family and a distinguished caree
Quiet-spoken Captain Franklin Van Valkenburgh left a fam
ily and a host of friends. Treating officer and enlisted alike
fate, in the morning hours of December 7, stole a lot from
humanity.

As a journalist, Joy Jasper couldn't get the stories of th
Arizona out of her mind. She wanted to meet some o
the survivors in person, to hear the story firsthand from th
men who had manned their stations as the battleship wa
bombed. She thirsted to hear eyewitness accounts of th
attack on Pearl Harbor from the men who had lived throug
one of the greatest wartime horrors ever known.

After her first encounter with the battleship underwater
she received a list of *Arizona* survivors from Fred Kukonu
a Park Service employee at the Memorial. Kukonu ha
since died. A soft-spoken Hawaiian, he had loved the *Ar
izona* even though he'd never sailed on it. For his years o
working to memorialize the battleship, he'd been dubbe
an honorary survivor in the seventies.

Jasper left Hawaii a week later with a passion to fin
Arizona survivors. For the next eight years she journeye
across the United States from Connecticut to Florida t
Texas, tracing her way down the survivors' list, calling o
writing men who'd once sailed the *Arizona*.

The list was short. When the count was taken after th
1941 devastation, only about 289 *Arizona* men were sti
living; 1,177 were killed on the *Arizona* on December 7—
more than half the casualties at Pearl Harbor. Some ha
died in the ensuing war years, and many more had passe
on in the decades afterward. By 1983 the living had dwin
dled to less than a hundred. She located a few who wer
on the list, a few others referred by other survivors. Som

had relocated and just weren't to be found. But she contacted perhaps twenty living *Arizona* men who had been assigned to the ship at the time of the attack. Carrying tape recorder, camera, and notebook, she asked them to talk about the *Arizona*.

Most of the men had already told their stories at least once, either to their wives and families or their local newspapers on some anniversary of Pearl Harbor Day. A few had visited the *Arizona* Memorial and told the historians there about the day of heroism and fear. But some of the survivors had been so traumatized by the ship's destruction they had never spoken of the *Arizona* after its loss. Although some were still hesitant to speak of the day they could never forget, most were eager to unlock the silence of the decades.

One by one they told their stories, some with anger, some with tears. One officer said he wanted to arrange an interview when his wife was not at home, "because I know I'll cry when I talk about the *Arizona*." He did. They all did. Not a man spoke of the *Arizona* without glistening eyes and choked voice. A few were embarrassed about their emotion, until they heard that other sailors got just as choked up. And even fifty years later they, to a man, still considered December 7, 1941, to be the day that changed their lives more than any other ever would.

The events of history are made meaningful through the eyes and voices of the people who witness those turning points in time. Hundreds of writers and historians have recorded accounts of the Pearl Harbor attack and the military-political buildup to World War II, yet little has been written of the life on board the peacetime *Arizona* and the intense connection *Arizona* sailors felt to their ship. As the survivors provided eyewitness accounts of events on the most famous battleship in American history, it was clear that parts of the *Arizona*'s story had never been told.

This is the story of a ship that never died, and of the men who never forgot. The survivors tell what really happened, and their stories reveal why the *Arizona* has become a symbol of the best and the worst of humankind.

CHAPTER 1

A BATTLESHIP IS BORN

The construction of the USS *Arizona* was the result of naval arms race that began in the last decades of the nineteenth century. The Industrial Revolution, beginning in the late eighteenth century, rapidly introduced steam engines, shell-firing guns, steel, and thick armor to conduct wars afloat rather than on land. The results were dramatic. Ten years after Nelson's victory at Trafalgar in 1805, Britain launched the world's first steam-powered warship. Nearly fifty years later, the famous battle between the ironclads *Monitor* and *Virginia* in 1861 made wooden warships obsolete. By the end of the nineteenth century, steel-armored battleships with their guns mounted in rotating turrets had replaced the huge wooden ships-of-the-line with their guns mounted in rows, deck after deck, that had secured Britain's rule of the seas a century before.

As late as 1900 Britain was still the world's greatest naval power. But the contenders were building up their fleets and grabbing colonial possessions around the world, possessions that required stronger navies of their own. The new contenders included Britain's traditional rival, France, as well as the recently created German empire (1871) and two non-European contenders: Japan and the United States. Nationalism and imperialistic desires by all of these rivals spurred the naval arms race.

While Britain, France, and Germany focused on one another's navies as their potential foes, the United States and Japan used their growing naval power to expand beyond their coasts. Spain's overseas empire in the Caribbean and the Far East fell to the United States in 1898, and while Cuba gained its independence as a result of that war, the new American possessions in Puerto Rico and the Philippines made the United States an imperial power.

The American Philippines ultimately proved a challenge to the growing power of Japan. An isolated feudal nation, Japan had been forcibly "opened" by American warships in 1853. The resultant changes in Japan brought an end to the dictatorship of the shogun and propelled the emperor, until then a figurehead, to real power in 1868. Under the Meiji emperor, Japan built a modern navy and embarked on a campaign to expand Japanese control to neighboring islands.

China, once the strongest power in the region, had increasingly weakened over the last few centuries. Unable to resist the incursions of foreign powers arriving in Asian waters starting in the early sixteenth century, China suffered a humiliating defeat dealt by Britain in the Opium Wars of 1839–40. In the 1890s the Japanese decided to seize control of nearby Korea, then a nominal vassal state of China. The Imperial Japanese Navy and Army landed in Korea, defeated the Chinese navy in two decisive battles in September 1894 and February 1895, and pushed into China and Manchuria before the war ended in April at the request of the United States and other colonial powers with an interest in the region. The Sino-Japanese War ended with

Korea now "independent" but under close Japanese scrutiny. Other territories, such as Taiwan, fell into Japanese hands.

European colonial powers were quick to exploit China's even greater weakness after the war with Japan. Germany seized control of Tsingtao, and Russia extorted a "lease" of Port Arthur as well as some of Manchuria. The Czar's government also built up the Siberian port of Vladivostok as a naval base. Finally, in 1904, Japan acted to forestall further Russian gains in the region. A surprise attack by Japanese destroyers hit the Russian fleet at anchor at Port Arthur on February 8, 1904. Two days later, Japan declared war on Russia. The Imperial Japanese Navy defeated the Russian fleet twice, first in August 1904 when it neutralized Russia's Pacific Fleet. The second and decisive battle, in May 1905, caught another Russian fleet that had rushed from the Baltic, in an ambush in the narrow Straits of Tsushima between Japan and Korea. In a matter of several hours, the Japanese sank eighteen Russian ships, killing 4,830 men, at a cost of three torpedo boats and a hundred lives. Tsushima, the first major battle between the century's new and "modern" warships, reinforced not only Japan's power but also the rise of the battleship.

The naval arms race accelerated. Britain built a new, all-big-gun battleship, the HMS *Dreadnought*, in 1906. Powered by huge steam turbines that gave it an incredible (for its time) twenty-one-knot speed, and armed with ten huge, heavy-hitting 12-inch guns in turrets, the *Dreadnought* was the world's most formidable warship. It steamed five knots faster than America's most modern battleship, and outgunned it. The disparity of other nations' fleets without "dreadnoughts"—when matched against Britain's latest ship and her sisters—was not lost on naval planners. Soon the other navies of the world were building their own fleets of the new battleship. Congress authorized the first American dreadnought, the USS *Delaware,* in 1906. To build up national pride in the Navy, and send a message to the world about America's intentions, President Theodore Roosevelt sent sixteen ships—the "Great White Fleet"—on a global tour in 1908. The tour also encouraged Congress to authorize more dreadnoughts to meet the needs of a "two-ocean Navy" on both the Atlantic and the Pacific, linked by the Panama Canal, another great American achievement then under construction.

March 16, 1914, was a historic day in Brooklyn, New York. Cranes whirred and turned in the Brooklyn Navy Yard as the keel was laid of the USS *Arizona,* a new battleship authorized by an Act of Congress. As politicians and newsmen gaped and cheered, and workers stood by in a cold northeast wind, cranes lifted the giant steel hull plates onto the shipway. Cries of "Bravo!" rang to the skies as the sun poked out briefly from the clouds. The *Arizona*'s construction was officially under way.

It almost hadn't been built at all. Two years earlier the Navy's General Board had selected one battleship design from a variety of sketches. Adding more guns than the earlier battleships *Nevada* and *Oklahoma,* the new plans allowed for variations in speed and hull form. Though an anticipated four ships were to be built in this class in 1913, only one ship emerged from the bureaucratic wrangling—the *Pennsylvania.*

But in the Act of 4 March 1913, Congress authorized one more battleship, specifying that it be built in a government yard. The ship would be named the *Arizona,* after the state. The word derived from the Spanish "Arizonac," meaning "arid, dry land." The *Arizona* was the second and last of the *Pennsylvania* class of battleships.

By the time the *Arizona*'s keel was laid in March 1914, the Navy envisioned it as one of a new line of "super dreadnoughts." After the 1914 opening ceremony, engineers riveted the plates together. In the days that followed, they fitted the ship's frames in place, 150 enormous curved forms spaced 4 feet apart. Within a few weeks the backbone and ribs of the massive ship stood like a stark metal skeleton, ready to take on the bulkheads. Armed with a battery of 14-inch guns, the *Arizona,* like its sister ships, was evidence of how the naval arms race called for bigger ships, more guns, and larger caliber. Where ships once had carried 12-, 14-, and then 16-inch guns, the world's battleships were becoming armed with weapons of increasing range and firepower, culminating in Japan's 18-inch guns on the super battleships *Yamato* and *Musashi.* Ironically, the progeny of the *Dreadnought* was always vulnerable, not to guns but to other new weapons that would in time signal the end of the battleship. Those weapons were the aircraft and the torpedo.

Slightly more than a year later, the ship was officially finished on the nineteenth of June, 1915. On that day Esther Ross, an Arizona pioneer's daughter, christened the ship's bow with a bottle of champagne. But when the *Arizona* was launched from the Brooklyn Navy Yard as the third United States warship to bear that name, the new battleship slid down the ways with much of its construction not yet completed. Fitting out the ship took time, and it was not until October 17, 1916, that the Navy commissioned it as the USS *Arizona* (BB-39).

The 608-foot-long steel hull swelled to a maximum breadth of 97 feet, and the ship drew nearly 30 feet of water. Displacing 33,000 tons, the *Arizona* and its sister ship *Pennsylvania* carried two more guns than the just completed USS *Nevada* and USS *Oklahoma*. Four turrets, each mounting three 14-inch guns, made up the *Arizona*'s principal armament. In addition to the big guns, the battleship also carried twenty-two 5-inch/51-caliber guns, four 3-inch/50-caliber antiaircraft guns, thirty-nine 45-caliber machine guns, and two 21-inch torpedo tubes.

While more powerfully armed than the *Dreadnought,* the *Arizona* was no faster. Its four paired Parsons turbines and twelve Babcock and Wilcox boilers, which developed 33,375 horsepower, drove the *Arizona*'s four shafts to a maximum speed of twenty-one knots. The battleship's propulsion and engineering systems remained basically unaltered throughout its career. But unlike its predecessors, all of which fired their boilers with coal, the *Arizona*'s fuel was oil. This "modern" development kept it out of the European Theater during World War I, since oil was a limited and precious commodity for the fleet out there. Instead, the *Arizona* remained behind as a gunnery training ship on Chesapeake Bay. Not until the cessation of hostilities in November 1918 did the *Arizona* depart for Britain.

From Portsmouth, England, the *Arizona* steamed forth on December 12, 1918, bound for Brest, France, as part of the escort for President Woodrow Wilson, who was aboard the *George Washington* and intent on peace treaty negotiations. Following this duty, the *Arizona* returned to the United States, crossing the Atlantic once again in early 1919 when the Navy sent it to the Mediterranean on a few months' cruise. Returning to the United States in July of hat year, the *Arizona* served in an uneventful career with he Atlantic Fleet, cruising the Atlantic coast of the United States and the Caribbean. In 1921 the battleship was sent nto the Pacific to join the United States Pacific Fleet, with only a three-year break in service when it returned to the Atlantic coast in 1929 to be refitted in the shipyard after Congress approved its modernization. Before reentering ervice in 1931, the *Arizona* received extensive modifications.

Torpedo bulges were added to the battleship's sides, increasing its beam to 106 feet. These reinforced compartments protected the hull by absorbing torpedo hits. The engines were upgraded, and the original boilers were replaced with six Bureau Express, 3-drum boilers. The *Arizona*'s fuel capacity was increased from 2,332 to 4,630 tons of oil, which increased its range. Extra armor was added o the turret tops and decks; along with the torpedo bulges, this increased the *Arizona*'s protection. The battleship's armament was also improved during the 1929–31 modernization. The 14-inch guns, when installed in 1915, elevated 15 degrees, giving them a range of ten miles. The modernization allowed the guns to elevate to 30 degrees, nearly doubling their range.

Before rejoining the Pacific Fleet in 1931, the *Arizona* carried President Herbert C. Hoover on a cruise to the West Indies. The battleship then transited the Panama Canal and in August reached San Pedro, California, its new home port. The *Arizona* remained with the Pacific Fleet for the remainder of its career, moving with the other vessels of the fleet to Pearl Harbor on Oahu when it was decided to shift the home port there in June 1940 in response to increasing tensions with Japan.

Prior to World War I the gentlemanly "ship of the line" attitude toward battleships had expected two lines of battleships steaming on parallel courses, shelling each other in hopes of inflicting mortal damage. Airpower changed all that. Once the war in the Pacific began, the astonishing growth of airpower guaranteed that battleships would never face off in a surface battle again, the way the British and Germans had in the Great War's Battle of Jutland. Battleships yielded their striking force to the aircraft carriers who had moved into first place as the "queens of the fleet."

Despite the shift to modern warfare and new weapons and technology that took place after World War I, joining the navy—any navy—placed a man in a world as ancient as Roman times. Ships may be made of wood or steel, powered by sail or steam, but the common factor is captain and crew—they are sailed in wind, storm, peace, and war by people whose emotions, intelligence, and personal or professional desires can alter the outcome of a cruise or battle.

Over the centuries, shipboard life had evolved into rigid protocols that, even when their origins had long been forgotten, were still binding and sometimes life-threatening if broken. Ancient rules set up by Viking marauders still dictate today where a twenty-first-century admiral will take his walk on a battleship, where Marines sleep in relation to officers and enlisted sailors, where the sick bay can be located, and a host of other restrictions. Before ships switched from sail to steam, military rules called for striking the sail and taking in the flag when a ship of superior class was encountered. Today the vestiges of that practice remain in determining which flags shall be flown at sea and at anchor.

The very language of the sea was acquired gradually, taking many words from Old English and Anglo-Saxon. The word *ship* itself was, in the Anglo-Saxon, "Scip," and the various parts of a vessel were named after the parts of the human body. The eyes of a ship are forward, and even into this century China and other nations have painted eyes on the bows of their ships. Amidships one finds the waist, and farther aft the quarter and the stern.

Sailors have seemingly always been ambivalent about the role of women aboard ship. From Anglo-Saxon and Viking times, at least, ships carried figureheads on their bows of buxom women with flowing hair, perhaps to encourage the men to stay the course through the long years at sea in order to return to a loved one. Some say the sirens of the deep needed to be appeased, and that a woman was the mediator between the sailors and Neptune.

Yet despite the love of a figurehead, sailors at sea didn't want the real thing, considering it terribly bad luck for a woman to be on board. For centuries women were essentially banned from coming aboard a capital ship.

In yet another contradiction, ships have been referred to as "she" since Roman times, when Latin ascribed a gender to all nouns. That tradition carried on into the Romance languages, which also split words into genders of masculine or feminine, so it is understandable that *la barca* in Spanish or *la barque* in French might come across to an English sailor as a "she." At any rate, Her Majesty's Navy called its ships "she" and its sailors spoke of "breaking her back," "dragging her stays," and other such phrases.

Lieutenant Commander R. G. Lowry of the Royal Navy, in his book *Origins of Some Naval Terms and Customs*, said that a ship is "always feminine (the cynical say because she is sometimes difficult to handle)." So it may be that gender in language caused a ship to be "she," or it may be that men indeed saw a ship as an errant woman needing a strong hand. In these days of political correctness, the *New York Times Style Book* has one brief entry regarding "she," to the effect: Ships and cities will not be referred to as she. No further explanation is needed, since it is clear to most people. Still, to this day sailors often refer to a ship as "she."

At least the days of banning women from coming aboard shifted to an acceptance prompted primarily by ship captains. Commerce frequently took men away from their homelands for two to three years on long cruises, and the separations from their wives and children were simply too long to tolerate. Even more common for the family man was the type of commerce that necessitated sailing a packet ship from port to port around his own country peddling goods, a life on the water that could last for most of one's adult life. By the nineteenth century, many an Irish, English, or American ship's captain had his entire family living on board. Children were schooled by their mother, if at all, and her lying-in was frequently on board to avoid an unnecessary stop in a harbor. Midwives and maids could live aboard ship, too.

In the twentieth century, families of military personnel were allowed to visit their men on board, as did the family of Admiral Isaac Kidd on the USS *Arizona,* and presumably Captain Franklin Van Valkenburgh. And of course, as women have joined the Navy, ships are now open to those women of qualified rank and skills, both officers and enlisted.

But back in the years before December 1941, sailing was

still a man's world, and the men of the *Arizona* were a brotherhood. In a wonderful expression of American pluck, *Arizona* men referred to their ship as the At 'em Maru, a combination of "up and at 'em" and the Japanese generic word for ship. At 'Em Arizona became the name of the ship's newsletter. The *Arizona* survivors continued to publish the newsletter at least through 2001.

A battleship was the place to be—powerful, impressive, impervious to the winds. In a battle it was considered far better to be on a battleship than a destroyer or smaller craft. As one *Arizona* midshipman wrote back home in December 1940, "Well, Mother, a battleship is about as safe a vessel as you can find in a fleet, so you don't have to worry about my well-being!"

CHAPTER 2

ORCHIDS AND STEEL

May 1940 in Pearl Harbor, Hawaii. A young Navy sailor just out of boot camp in San Diego stood on the dock waiting for the first glimpse of his ship. Golden finches twittered, their feathers bright flashes of scarlet and yellow in the oleander thicket near the water's edge. A gentle breeze perfumed the air with plumeria and wild orchids as James Lawson, seaman 2nd class, peered across the water to the harbor mouth. He had come to Pearl, as the sailors all called their port, on a supply ship to Hawaii.

His first billet would be the USS *Arizona,* a battleship that carried the flag and the admiral of Battleship Division One. For a moment his eye caught a swiggle of movement in the dusky waters of Pearl Harbor, cloudy with sediment washed down from the flower-laden Koolau Mountains. When he looked up he was dazzled. Rounding the turn was an enormous ship, its crow's nests tilting at the sky. Those stark lines etched against the horizon could only be a battleship. Enormous black letters on the bow pronounced it the USS *Arizona.* Lawson's heart pounded.

Four massive gun turrets trained their three-fingered long-range guns at the horizon. Rows of second-battery guns flanked the gun turrets. Deck above deck rose to the sky, open spaces crawling with more than a thousand sailors scrambling to make ready to land.

The battleship sailed to its berth on the east side of Ford Island, a small military outpost in Pearl Harbor, and tied up on quay Fox 8. When all the lines were tied and the ship was anchored, Lawson took the shore patrol launch out to the quay. He stepped on board the ship, but in his awe he completely forgot the protocol.

"I was just overwhelmed by the size of it," he said. "New sailors are like that. You go up that gangway for the first time, and you've been trained to ask permission to come aboard and salute the flag at the stern, but the new seamen 2nd come aboard and right away they forget. Of course, the officer of the deck or the seaman on the gangway watch says, 'Hold on, you're supposed to salute.' In those days it was a tough Navy."

Lawson was a typical USS *Arizona* sailor—eighteen years old, fresh out of school, and looking for a way to beat the Depression. He'd grown up in Chicago and San Antonio, Texas, the son of a World War I vet. A football player in high school, he wasn't big enough to go for athletic scholarships, and in 1940 jobs were scarce. The Navy was the way out for him, as it was for so many other young men. He volunteered on February 13, 1940, thirteen days after his eighteenth birthday.

Every seaman 2nd class was assigned straightaway to a deck division, and he first drew Deck Division 4, whose men lived in and maintained the ship's stern section that included the port quarterdeck and turret No. 4. Months later he would serve as a gunner's mate on turret 4, but for now he had deck duty. DD4 also included the No. 2 catapult on the ship's fantail, which would mount spotter planes to seek out enemy ships and relay their positions back to the *Arizona*'s control deck. Lawson had a stint on the catapult, too.

His first duty was just plain hard physical work. Life as a seaman 2nd class was sweat work: chipping paint, polishing brass, airing mattresses, whatever the boatswain's mate ordered. Seamen ran the gauntlet through a hierarchy of jobs. One of the earliest in their deck career was swabbing down and holystoning the *Arizona*'s teakwood deck.

Holystoning was a sailor's penance, a task left over from the days of wooden sailing ships and an endless supply of deck hands. The original holystones were pieces of cut stone left over from building medieval churches, but by modern times they had been replaced by bricks with a small hole in the center. A sailor would press a broom handle into the hole and push it back and forth across the wooden deck, while other swabbies threw sand on the deck and flooded the space with running water. The holystoners pushed the bricks over the teakwood until the deck glistened or the boatswain's mate said it was good enough.

"Holystoning was the world's toughest job. I still have a sore back from that," Lawson said. "I was a seaman 2nd as short a time as possible—something like six months. Deck duty was all it was, all day long from breakfast to dinnertime, with lunch off. Chip and paint. It was just seamen's busywork, shine and bright work: polish in one hand, a rag in the other."

When a seaman 2nd was moving up to seaman 1st, he nearly always caught the job of messcooking. The duty meant setting up tables for other sailors three times a day, and running to the galley to haul large aluminum tureens of potatoes, vegetables, and meat back to the tables.

"Messcooking duty was an all-day and half-the-night affair," Lawson said. "You had to set up the table, go to the scullery, get food, get the dishes and the silverware, set up the mess table, get it off the overhead, and set the places, just like home cooking. When it was ready to serve, you had to go up to the galley to get the big tureens full of food. You'd previously gone to the bakery to get whatever they were having for baked goods that day. So you were a waiter, that's exactly what it was.

"When everybody was through eating, you had to clean up. That meant semi-wash the dishes, hang the table back up on the overhead, put the dishes on the dish racks and take them back to the scullery so they could be run through the dishwashing machines, and go back and swab down the deck area."

A messcook also was responsible for the dry stores. "In the holds, in the same general vicinity as turrets 3 and 4 but off to the side, we had to go into the dry stores and get one-hundred-pound sacks of flour, fifty-pound sacks of onions, and the like. Carton after carton, case after case, we'd shoulder 'em and go up the ladders, in this case, the rungs built into the side of the hull. You'd have to carry them up either to the bakery on the boat deck, or the casement deck. It was midships. So you'd get stores from back near the turrets and at least three decks down and carry them up to the galley on the second deck, the boat deck. And the baker's was forward of that another deck up. That's a long way."

Besides serving the meals and hauling stores, a sailor

with messcooking duty also spent time working in the galley, rotating jobs with other division messcooks. A typical messcook would spend a week carrying stores, then a week peeling spuds in the galley, then a week working with the butchers. Messcooking usually lasted three months.

Lawson's mess duty began when the *Arizona* left the Navy yard at Bremerton, Washington, where it had spent the winter months of 1940–41 in drydock. While he was learning the drill of readying the tables and serving the food, his battleship headed for California. Stopping in San Diego for a couple of days in February 1941, the ship headed west for Hawaii, where the U.S. Pacific Fleet would now be based. Lawson wouldn't set foot Stateside again until the war was over.

Three months later he was promoted to gunner's mate 3rd, where his next shipboard duty was working the No. 2 catapult, one of the two catapults aboard the *Arizona* that launched spotter planes into the sky. During maneuvers the spotters would fly out and radio back positions for the gunners to shoot. In wartime it would be the real thing: The spotters would fly over enemy fleets and call back the positions to American gunners.

The launching catapults employed a 5-inch cartridge called a powder can, consisting of a brass cartridge case and the powder case.

"All that went into the firing mechanism," Lawson said. "As the plane was sitting back here on the catapult, we put the can into the chamber and fired it. It released the pressure and shot that plane down the catapult into the air."

Deck Division 4 oversaw the No. 2 catapult on the fantail, and DD3 held the No. 3 catapult, which was located right on top of turret No. 3. Whenever a commanding officer decided he wanted one of the two-winged seaplanes to go out on patrol or get mail, turret 3 or turret 4 personnel rotated the duty. If the officer of the deck (OD) chose the No. 2 catapult, Lawson and his mates were the ones that fired the plane off.

"The plane sat on top of the catapult on a cradle, with a long cable that ran along the tracks of the catapult," Lawson said. "Usually the plane went off the port side. As the ship turned and faced into the wind, we'd get the word to fire. We'd hit the firing key, and it was just like firing a gun. The firing mechanism would fire off that 5-inch cartridge, basically a can full of powder, and when that charge expanded the gas it fired the plane, and it would run on the cradle all the way to the end of the catapult. By the time it hit the catapult it was at takeoff speed.

"We had trained to rotate the catapult so that when planes left the ship they'd be headed into the wind, which was takeoff position for aircraft. When they would come back in, the ship would have to swing around to make a slick. That big ship turning this way or that way would flatten out the waves enough for the aircraft to sit down in the water. The plane would taxi up close to where the boatswain's mates could swing the crane out to hook onto the plane to hoist it back aboard and over onto the catapult."

At the same time he joined the turret, Lawson also qualified as a helmsman, standing wheel watches every other day in four-hour shifts on the bridge. As the nerve center of the ship, the bridge is where all commands are implemented. The captain passes on his decisions to the OD.

Normal steering and course changes during a particular watch are the specific duty of the OD. Everyone on the bridge is subservient to the officer of the deck, who must follow whatever steaming orders he's given by the captain and admiral. As the man in charge of the ship's safety, the officer of the deck keeps the helmsmen on course, the lookouts alert, and the engine room at proper speed.

"The normal steering for day-to-day sailing was done with a controller—a long brass bar with a handle sticking up," Lawson said. "We stood or sat, some of each in a four-hour shift, beside this pedestal. On the pedestal was a grid that was operated electrically, and it was graduated for the degrees of turn."

The controller was very touchy, he recalled. "It wouldn't take much to move that huge ship. So when the officer of the deck would say 'come right 10 degrees' you'd go 10 degrees on that grid in front of you, and electrically it would move the rudder. You'd think it would take a lot, but just a little turn of the wrist and you're moving 10 degrees."

The electrical system's controller was the modern way of steering the *Arizona*. But at 0700 the ship changed over from electric steering to steam, which was the backup system for emergencies in case the electrical power failed. Down in the fire rooms the crews shifted to operating boilers, whose steam coming back from the boiler rooms turned the huge rudder. At the same time up on the bridge, the helmsman would let go of the controller on the pedestal and reach for the enormous ship's steering wheel right beside it.

"This was a big brass wheel that came to about my chest," Lawson said. "That's really when I found out how much it takes to turn that big ship, because it'd be round and round and round and round to come 10 degrees. They'd run that for 30 minutes, and it's a real workout."

There was yet a third steering system, called the auxiliary steering. If electric and steam power failed, the battleship could actually be steered by hand. Military preparedness meant routinely operating this system to ensure that all was functioning properly. Most helmsmen dreaded one particular wheel watch, the one that fell between four and eight o'clock in the morning, for that was when, in order to test all systems, the *Arizona* would shift its steering from electric to steam, and then to the auxiliary system. Lawson knew the system intimately, having pulled that watch countless times.

It took many sailors to supply the manpower. Down in the curve of the hull was a room about fifteen feet long, with two huge wheels with spokes that ran horizontal to the deck. This auxiliary steering station was the very first battle station for green, newly come-aboard seamen from all of the deck divisions, and somebody always had to be there. "You'd run down a long hallway and grab one of those big spokes and ride that sucker down," Lawson said. "Somebody'd go right behind you and ride the next one down. It was a constant run, one man at a time. You'd drag one and there was a guy coming up to get another one. They'd run that for thirty minutes, and then they'd switch back to normal steering again for the last hour of the watch."

On the *Arizona*, the steering drill was done every day. Lawson and the seamen took some comfort in that knowledge. "If for some reason the ship lost electric power, they knew—'cause it was done today—that they could, if necessary, operate under steam conditions and we wouldn't be lying dead in the water in the Pacific somewhere."

Lawson took great pride in holding the wheel of the *Ar-*

izona. The ship hadn't yet won its place in legend, but the men aboard considered themselves "more equal than equal," because a battleship was a special place to be. "Battleship sailors were unique. We were the kingpins of the Navy in those days," he said. "We looked down on the destroyer sailors. I'd be up on the bridge standing those wheel watches far out on the Pacific, and we'd be taking spray on the bridge. I'd be sitting up there taking 'em as they go, you know, just keeping it on a steady course as best I could, and seeing just the tops of the masts on these destroyer escorts, the rest sunk in the waves. How in the world could those people live on those ships when all you could see was the tops of the masts?"

Despite living in the midst of fifteen hundred men, Lawson and the other seamen befriended only a few other sailors and seldom spoke with anyone else, except on duty. Opportunities for making friends depended mostly on who lived in the same quarters, not who stood the same watch.

"I'd go up on the bridge and take a wheel watch," Lawson said. "The guy I relieved probably didn't know me. I'd get up on the bridge and say, 'You're relieved,' he'd give me what was happening on the bridge at that time, I'd say, 'Fine,' and I'd take ahold of the control.

"You didn't know people. It was like living in a big city. We kept constantly getting new people aboard in the deck division. We all had our own work to do. They went to their crew's quarters for meals, we'd go to our crew's quarters for meals. They slept in their turret, we slept in ours. Hell, it was very secular kind of living. Of course we'd see each other, and we might know them by a nickname: Hi, Red. If you didn't know him and he was rated [as a gunner's mate], you'd call him Guns. Everybody was Guns."

Lawson knew only the men who lived and worked closely with him every day, the ones who used nearby lockers or sat next to him in the turret. In the peacetime Navy after World War I, enlisted men were almost all regular Navy—six-year enlisted men. Regular Navy sailors considered themselves above the Reserve sailors, who began entering the service in droves in January 1941 when the Navy began to overcomplement its ships.

"Regular Navy made you more equal than equal," Lawson felt. "You wouldn't get much money because the Navy paid very little money, but with the Regulars you could leave your locker wide open, put your money, wrist watch, billfold there, and nobody would touch it. It was safe."

That trusting attitude changed when Reserve sailors started coming on board, a change Lawson and many others hated to see. "Once the Reservists started coming aboard—all the riffraff they were taking in—everybody had to lock their lockers," he said.

Later his duty changed to gunner's mate in turret No. 4. "Now, in the turret it was something else again, because it was a close-knit group," he said with pride. "We never locked anything because nobody came to the turret except us. Except that we had an exercise when the seamen came down there to haul powder out to put it in the hoist. But they were too busy to go snooping in somebody's locker."

One of the few ways sailors could reduce tension was to take part in athletics aboard ship. Lawson and three other turret members—Clarence Otterman, Louis Pacitti, and a man remembered only as Rocky—played football on the *Arizona*'s team. Running plays on the boat deck, the foursome got stoked up for the games to come in Oahu at the end of every cruise, where they'd play against other battleship teams or Army teams. In those days it was the old single-wing formation. No face masks, minimal padding. Lawson, a defensive back, liked the practices almost as much as the games.

"We never got to play much in the way of games, but we had fun getting ready to. And it got us out of some work," he added.

By this time Lawson had made seaman 1st class, and he wanted to get out of the deck division. Applying for a transfer, he hoped to be located in the ship's forward compartments where the storekeepers lived. His request was denied. Instead he was invited to join turret No. 4, where as a gunner's mate he became a pointer for turret 4's three 50-foot-long-range guns that could fire twenty miles over the horizon. Whenever the call came for general quarters—alerting men to race to their battle stations—Lawson now headed for the turret.

His job as pointer was to aim the guns up or down, based on coordinates that were relayed from the control room. His counterpart, the trainer, moved the three big guns horizontally in an arc. Like most battleships of the day, the *Arizona* had no radar, so the spotter planes launched off the catapult were the source of information for the fire control director in the ship's control room, who passed on the coordinates to the turret gunners.

"I sat in the left-hand seat and the trainer sat in the right-hand seat," he recalled. "We each had a periscope, just a little slit in the turret, so if our ship had any visual contact with something, you could see it through the periscope. We had a set of wheels in front of us, and mine had a trigger guard and a trigger. My wheel elevated the three guns to whatever firing angle we wanted. He'd roll the wheel that turns the turret horizontally. The turret was mounted so it could travel roughly two-thirds of a 360-degree arc."

Working together, the pointer and trainer could aim the turret guns to fire and hit a ship up to twenty miles away, even one that was out of sight past the horizon's curve. If the big guns found their target, the sailors who fired them wouldn't know until the spotter planes radioed back the news—or in war, if a smudge of smoke blackened the horizon.

"It was a thrill: pulling the trigger and knowing it was going after somebody a cross the horizon with another 2,500 to 3,000 pounds of high explosives," Lawson said happily.

A gunner's life was constant work of loading and shooting the guns, then cleaning them. The turret guns were 14-inch/45-caliber giants. In handguns, caliber refers to the bore diameter, but in capital guns—guns of war—it describes the length of the barrel times the bore diameter. Since the turret guns measured 14 inches as the inner diameter of the bore, the gun's barrel length was 45 times 14 inches—more than 50 feet long. Those massive jaws of death spewed out projectiles that weighed about 1,500 pounds.

Gunners might have been higher up the chain than mess-cooks or the lowly swabbies, but they were still a world apart from the officers. A sailor's world of friends was limited by circumstance, but protocol issued a powerful dictum: Sailors don't mix with officers. Most sailors never even talked to officers except to take on duties or to salute and say "Good morning, sir." Lawson was one of the few enlisted men who actually got a glimpse of the officers' inner thoughts, for during his wheel watches he often stood side by side with the ship's captain, Franklin Van Valken-burgh. He liked what he saw.

"He was a gentleman of the old school," the sailor said. "A fine man, patrician is the word I would use. He treated everybody like people. He got to know all the helmsmen, called us by name when he was on the bridge. Coming off the watch he'd say, 'Come on and have a smoke.' He was the only captain I ever served with that did this. He'd call me Jim or Seaman Lawson. After I made gunner's mate he'd call me Guns. We'd go out and chew the fat. He wondered how things were going. We'd stand on the wing of the bridge, if it was pleasant weather."

Van Valkenburgh, tall with thinning white hair, was look-ing forward to retirement in a year or so. "He told me on more than one occasion how thrilled he was to be in com-mand of a battleship at the end of his naval career," Lawson recalled. "It was the culmination of all his hopes and dreams."

Lawson didn't know if the skipper was married or single, nor did he know anything about his likes and dislikes, for asking personal questions of a superior was out of line. "A gunner's mate 3rd is not going be that chummy with a four-stripe. The captain tells you what he wants to tell you and asks you what he wants to know, and that's it. But he wasn't like some of these guys—'Get out of my face, sailor.' He was a gentleman. And he was only aboard six months or so."

By contrast, Lawson disliked having an admiral live on board. The *Arizona*, as the Division One flagship, was home to the division commander, Rear Admiral Isaac C. Kidd. Battleship Division One included the USS *Arizona*,

USS *Nevada,* and USS *Pennsylvania.* (The *Pennsylvania* had been designated the flagship of the entire Pacific Fleet, and carried the fleet commander on board.)

Life on board an admiral's ship created a blend of pride and irritation in the sailors. Though some sailors felt it was a privilege to serve on an admiral's ship, Lawson and many others hated the extra ceremony. "He might have been the salt of the earth, but it was still a nuisance. Anytime you carried an admiral's flag you get more unnecessary activity, which makes more work for the sea dogs."

Every day if the weather was pleasant the admiral chose a section of the deck to take his daily walk, usually on the port quarterdeck. Whether he wore full military dress or the summer uniform of shorts and shirt, he always wore his admiral's hat with "the big scrambled eggs all over it," Lawson said.

"The admiral didn't ever talk with the sailors. He had nothing to do with anybody. The admiral was the admiral—next door to God himself," he added.

Surrounded by fifteen hundred other souls, the admiral was a man as alone as a human could possibly be, or so Lawson felt. "They are very solitary, because they're supposed to keep separate. They'd have absolutely nothing to do with anybody. He might invite the captain and executive officer to have dinner with him sometimes or consult with him about maneuvers at sea, but an admiral's responsibility aboard an individual ship is null and void—he has none. His responsibility is a group of ships, a task force, or a division."

As the head of Battleship Division One, Kidd was in full charge of all battle practices and maneuvers. At sea, then, he was in command. Even though operating the ship was Captain Van Valkenburgh's task, all other shipboard activities revolved around the invisible person of the admiral.

Lawson found the whole scene unpleasant. "Whenever you did have to be around him," he said, "like standing the gangway watch when the admiral was coming aboard or leaving the ship, you'd think it was God leaving or coming aboard. Bang! The walls came down. Nobody liked it. This solitary individual carrying this awesome responsibility has gotta be at a specific place at a specific time and nothing by God better disturb it. Everything else was cut off at that point until he cleared the area. Like when he took his walks, nobody was allowed out on the deck. It didn't make any difference if you had work to do. If we were cleaning the guns, for example, we had to quit cleaning the guns if the admiral was going to take his walk. A Marine would come by and say, 'The admiral is going for his walk. Clear the deck.' We'd go back into the turret till it was all clear."

Captain Van Valkenburgh, though, talked of many things to the men on wheel watches, but never of his thoughts on the war building in the Pacific. Even so, Lawson said, most of the battleship sailors sensed it coming. "As many rounds as we pumped out of those 14-inch barrels that summer, we knew it would happen. It was just a question of when or where. We got the news by radio and newspaper, and the internal newsletter that the radio shack put out. So we knew what was going on in the East Indies, and when the Japs were making a run down the Malay Peninsula and into New Guinea."

Even late in 1941 officers and men of the United States Navy continued to hope that war would come, if it came at all, out on the open sea. "We envisioned, if you will, what we practiced for," Lawson said, "which was the standard naval procedure at the time: a line of ships training their guns at a line of other ships. We figured we'd meet up with them out in the broad expanse of the Pacific or near the Philippines. And every time I'd press the firing key in that turret and hear those big bullets going *shreeeeeeeeeooooooooooo* twenty miles across the water, I was thinking, here's another one for TOJO—that was what the head honchos called the Japanese in those days. We figured that, with our superior forces, our superior ships, our superior gunnery, we'd take 'em. Nobody in their right mind would have thought it might happen at Pearl Harbor."

CHAPTER 3

RITES OF PASSAGE

Some of Jim Lawson's shipmates came away with a very different perspective on shipboard life. Take John Rampley.

Twenty-two when he joined the Navy in 1939, the North Carolina boy had attended boot camp in Norfolk, Virginia, then qualified for hospital school. One day he read a notice on the Norfolk bulletin board that changed his life.

"It said the Navy wanted men for the fleet out in California," he said. "Ever since I was big enough to know there was a West I had wanted to go that way. So my buddies and I went into the hospital corps and got assigned to the Pacific Fleet. We were shipped across the country to San Diego, where the men were distributed to various ships. According to the last names in the alphabet, myself and twenty-four fellows were put on the *Arizona*."

Rampley went aboard his ship in February 1940 as a seaman 2nd class. He remembered his deck duty as "a form of slavery. You'd get up at five in the morning and swab decks. We'd scrub that teakwood, and when it dried it was a brilliant white. It made the beans and cornbread taste wonderful."

Two or three months after Rampley joined the *Arizona*, the Pacific Fleet was moved to Hawaii, where maneuvers at sea were high on the list of priorities. Later in the summer the fleet returned to the West Coast to make an appearance at the World's Fair in San Francisco.

Rampley was messcooking at the time. Every mealtime he set up three tables of twenty-four men each, served the food from the galley, and cleaned up when the meal was done. "If you did a good job, the guys would put a bowl on the table and throw in a buck, which was a lot of money in those days."

Seaman Rampley was aboard the *Arizona* when it sailed up to Washington State in the fall of 1940 to get refitted in the Navy yard at Bremerton. There, while loading catapult ammunition, he slipped and fractured his ankle. It was New Year's Eve. He spent the next three months in the Navy hospital at Bremerton, while his ship sailed to California and then Hawaii without him. When the ankle was fully mended, he rode out to Hawaii on the battleship *Colorado* to rejoin the *Arizona*.

He soon got transferred out of the deck force and into gun turret No. 3, where he joined a crew of twenty men. It was a coup, because getting into a turret wasn't easy. "A man's name was presented by the senior petty officer to the whole gun crew," he said. "If any of them didn't like him or thought he wouldn't be compatible, you didn't get in. So if you did make it, you felt that you were part of a select crew."

On the day he was told he'd been accepted into the turret, the officer of the deck told Rampley he could take the whole day off—a signal honor—and move his belongings into the turret. "In my whole Navy stint I'd never had a day off before," Rampley said wonderingly. He ensconced himself in the base, or bottom, deck of the turret where the turret men made their living quarters. "Life then was pretty good."

When on duty in the turret, gunner's mate 3rd class Rampley was a control telephone talker. His job was to receive and transmit information to the fire control director on the bridge, who was the liaison between the spotter planes and the gunners. Sitting in the turret with headphones on, Rampley would speak to the director and relay orders to the other members of the turret crew.

He also transmitted messages between the different levels of the turret. Each gun turret had four or five levels, and in maneuvers or war it was essential to communicate between the levels in order to get ammunition up to the gun deck. On command, the ammunition—the large shells for the 14-inch/45-caliber guns—was loaded onto hoists to raise it up to the gun deck level.

Rampley was surprised that, despite the threat of Japanese attack, the fleet didn't operate under emergency or wartime conditions and allow easy access to ammunition. "The ammunition was padlocked and the guns were padlocked," he said starkly. "Only so many fellows would have keys to the ammo lockers, and if anything happened to them, the lockers remained locked."

The Pacific Fleet's three battleship divisions each contained three battleships, and their whereabouts reflected the growing tension. "We had a routine: Two divisions were out of Pearl Harbor, one was in. We'd go out scouting around a routine part of the ocean. We'd go just off Maui and anchor in the area called Lahaina Roads. Everybody knew why we were there—so we wouldn't be bottled up in Pearl Harbor," Rampley said.

"Maybe the enemy would come, but you just didn't think it would ever happen," he added. "That was the feeling that most of the fellows had. The possibility seemed so far away."

James Foster was another sailor who found the likelihood of war "unthinkable." Unlike the small and slender John Rampley, Foster was tall, well over six feet, and he loomed over his shipmates. The curly-haired Texan, better suited for football than war, was born in 1920. As a young man he decided to go into the Navy simply because it was "the thing to do" in those days when Hitler was storming through Europe and the Japanese were creeping over the Pacific islands. In October 1939 he traveled up from his Corpus Christi home to enlist at Houston. Spending an uneventful boot camp at Long Beach, California, he was then assigned to the USS *Arizona* as a seaman 2nd.

He liked the battleships, but he was especially pleased to live on board a flagship. "It seemed to me the *Arizona* was in a class by itself because of the admiral on board. I felt proud of that," he said.

He moved through the chain of deck force duty and sailor's busywork, finally assigned to be a gunner on one of the 5-inch/25-caliber antiaircraft guns. His gun was located on the starboard boat deck, forward of the admiral's living quarters. Sixteen men worked each antiaircraft gun, and Foster eventually became the pointer on his gun, the man who pulled the trigger.

The Navy's decision to move the U.S. Pacific Fleet to Hawaii in 1941 was thrilling to the inland Texas boy who'd never traveled to the idyllic tropical islands. The lacy palm trees and strikingly cobalt-blue waters made Hawaii seem like an enchanted place. He loved "going over on the beach and rattling around," whether it was to listen to island music at one of the hotels or walk the beach with a buddy.

Although sailors train for war, it was truly unimaginable to Foster. Although they'd all heard rumors that the Japanese were planning something, most sailors found it hard to believe a thing like that could happen after twenty years of peace.

Peace was something William Goshen expected. His reason for joining the Navy was not to fight but to see the world, and what he best remembered about the peacetime *Arizona* were movies and ice cream.

Born on April 22, 1919, he was raised in Harlan, Kentucky, on the southeast corner near Tennessee. "There was nothing to do in Harlan," he said, "except get into trouble. I had a brother-in-law in the Navy, and he talked about it some. That was my dream—I wanted to join the Navy and see the world."

He joined the Navy in March 1940, and shipped aboard the *Arizona*, his first assignment, in early July. During watches the work was hard, but the life was also enjoyable, as the men found their own ways of coping with being offshore and away from civilian life for months at a time. They forged friendships that, in many cases, lasted for decades.

"Life on board wasn't too hard in peacetime," Goshen said. "It depended on where you were and what your uniform was, what you could do. It wasn't too bad a life. We'd go down to the ice cream parlor and get a geedunk—a pint of ice cream—and go to the movies."

Goshen got more than he bargained for in the Navy, having to endure the ceremonies of crossing the equator.

The rites of passage on a capital ship were almost as

old as the sea itself. For hundreds of years sailors around the world had celebrated their sailing over the equator into the Southern Hemisphere, a sort of coming of age. Centuries ago, the equator rites in some navies held brutal, strange experiences involving exorcisms of demons, beatings, and humiliation for the junior sailors. But in the United States Navy in 1940, the event had metamorphosed into good-natured repartee, with seasoned veterans dunking new sailors in tubs of water and maybe giving a friendly hair-washing with raw eggs.

Whenever a sailor crossed the equator for the first time, in Navy parlance he went from being a "softback" or "polliwog" to a "shellback." At the end of the festivities each new shellback would receive a "Shellback Certificate" stating the ship's name, the date, and the coordinates where he had officially entered King Neptune's domain.

In those days a capital ship could not cross the international dateline, so American military vessels steamed west close to the dateline, turned south and crossed the equator instead to hold their ritual. About two weeks after William Goshen joined the *Arizona*'s crew, the battleship headed southward and was preparing to cross the equator. Along with Seamen Lawson and Rampley and a hundred other sailors, that day Goshen was handed a summons, a legal-looking document that read:

Subpoena and Summons Extraordinary

THE ROYAL HIGH COURT OF THE RAGING MAIN
REGION OF THE SOUTH SEAS
DOMAIN OF NEPTUNE REX

To All Who Shall See These Presents,
Greetings:

Whereas, The good ship ARIZONA, bound southward, is about to enter our domain; and whereas aforesaid ship carries a large and loathsome cargo of landlubbers, beach-combers, guardo-rats, sea-lawyers, lounge-lizards, parlor-dunnigans, plow-deserters, chicken-chasers, four-flushers, dance-hall sheiks, drug-store cowboys, asphalt arabs, and other living creatures of the land, masquerading as seamen, of which low scum you are a member, having never appeared before us; and

Whereas, THE ROYAL HIGH COURT OF THE RAGING MAIN will convene on board the good ship ARIZONA on the 24th of July, 1940 in Latitude 0 0'0", and whereas, an inspection of our *ROYAL ROSTER* shows that it is high time your sad and wandering nautical soul appeared before Our August Presence:

Be it Known, That we hereby summon and command you

GOSHEN, W.E. SEA2C, U.S. NAVY

to appear before the *ROYAL HIGH COURT* to be examined into your fitness to be taken into the citizenship of the deep and to hear your defense on the following charges:

CHARGE I: In that you have hitherto willfully and maliciously failed to show reverence and allegiance to our *ROYAL PERSON,* and are therein and thereby a vile landlubber and polliwog.

CHARGE II: In that you have plotted and connived with certain parties in seeking a way to escape your just punishment.

Given under our hand and seal,

Davy Jones, SCRIBE   *Neptunus Rex,* SUPREME RULER

In the ensuing ceremonies, Goshen was symbolically transformed from a softback to a shellback. So were Jim Lawson, John Rampley, and Galen Ballard.

"There was a lot of ritual," Goshen recalled. "They did a little of everything. The people who stood watches were dressed up like Neptune and all of those people. First you went down through the line and got the shillelagh. Next you went down the water chute and everybody was pounding you then. It was all in fun. Nobody got hurt. Nobody got mad. They'd sit you down in a chair and take rotten eggs and rub them on your face to shave you. Then they'd dump you backwards in a tub of water. I became a shellback then—I was a polliwog before."

The certificate recorded the date: July 16, 1940. Only a few certificates would survive the conflagration, like Goshen's, and Jim Lawson's, which he had mailed home to his mother.

At the time William Goshen joined the *Arizona* sailors, Van Valkenburgh was captain and Kidd was the admiral. Goshen was one sailor who liked having Admiral Kidd live aboard the *Arizona*. "Kidd was always around," he recalled. "He was very nice. He'd stop and talk to you just like he'd known you all of his life."

Goshen remembered Kidd as a gray-haired and more formal officer. "In peacetime you had to be pretty old to be an admiral. See, he made admiral off the *Arizona*. He had been the *Arizona*'s captain, and then he went back to school—war school in Washington—and when he came out he came back to the *Arizona* as admiral."

Since enlisted men didn't socialize with officers, Goshen didn't know Kidd personally. "You didn't get to know the officers too well. You'd see them, speak to them and salute them. There's a few people that had close contact with them, but my duty didn't call for it—I was a deck-hand. If the captain came by on Saturday morning for inspection, maybe the admiral would be with him, and they'd check the compartments. If you happened to have a cleaning station other than in the vicinity of where your living quarters was, you had to go down there—you didn't stand inspection on topside. You'd have to go down to your cleaning station and be there when they came through."

Goshen's cleaning station was on the fifth level below-decks, comprised of two compartments about a hundred feet long and eight feet wide. Located down in the bowels of the ship, the compartments enclosed the ammunition conveyor belts that ran through it and on to other compartments. It was Goshen's duty to keep the area dust-free and shipshape.

Like others on the deck force, he holystoned the decks, "a hated chore," he remembered. "We'd start scrubbing every morning till the boatswain's mate would come around and say, OK that's good enough, fellows." He thought the *Arizona*'s food was as good as anywhere, except that a sailor couldn't order what he desired but had to take whatever the messcooks brought out from the gallery. Goshen himself messcooked, too, for all of nine months, a duty that paid five dollars a month more than a seaman's pay of forty dollars a month. Best of all, it paid tips.

As the months wore on, Goshen, still in the 7th division, was reassigned to become a pointer on the No. 3 turret's 5-inch antiaircraft gun. His battle station then was located straight across the deck from another sailor, Vernon Olsen, whom he would come to know years later, long after the *Arizona* was gone.

————

Unlike Goshen and most of his shipmates, Vern Olsen did indeed believe that war was coming, and he didn't want to get drafted into the Army, feeling that he'd rather die in the ocean than be trapped in a foxhole. He very nearly did at Pearl Harbor.

Built small and tight like a fighter, dark-haired Olsen came from Rockford, Illinois, to join the Navy on October 8, 1940. Just over twenty years old, he hadn't finished high school. He signed for a six-year hitch, the obligatory stint for anyone choosing regular Navy over Reserves. He spent boot camp at the Great Lakes, then went out to Bremerton to pick up the Arizona in drydock. He remembers his first duty as scraping barnacles off the ship's bottom.

He started his tour of duty as an apprentice seaman assigned to the *Arizona*'s 6th deck division. In the buildup just before the war, the Navy shipped a bunch of Reserves on board and split the 6th into the 5th and 6th divisions.

Olsen's post during at-sea maneuvers was the crow's nest on the *Arizona*'s after mast. An aerie of weaponry aloft in the steel masts, Olsen's post held four 50-caliber machine guns that he and his mates manned during the mock skirmishes at sea.

"They'd put targets up in the air and we'd fire at them in order to become accustomed how to use the machine gun," he said.

Ralph Byard didn't work with the gunners, since his job was in payroll. By 1941 he'd already spent nine years aboard the *Arizona* and had qualified to be a warrant officer. The *Arizona* had been home to Byard since July 4, 1932. The years aboard, the friendships he forged, and the strong feeling of comradeship bound him to the ship, creating emotional ties more binding than Navy duty.

"There were a lot of men who were on that ship for years," he said. "You couldn't live and work so closely with that many people without forming strong friendships with many of them. One good friend of mine was Estelle Birdsell, a machinist's mate who worked in the pump room, which has to do with the distribution of water in the boilers, and control of the flow and the salinity. The two of us, even though we were in different divisions—he was in the engineering force and his working station was way down in the ship and my working station was on the deck above the main deck—we met each other and liked each other."

Byard, tall and soft-spoken, was a seaman 1st class who turned twenty-seven in 1941. He remembered years of living aboard the battleship, details big and small, including the task of polishing the teak decks. "I remember standing in a row of seamen, pushing that little brick back and forth. It did make the beans and gravy taste good, but I tell you, I still think that we fed very well on the *Arizona*."

He recalled the admiral's presence on board ship. "The admiral and the captain used to come out in the evening and walk up and down the starboard side of the quarterdeck on the after portion of the ship. That was the admiral's home. You did not go over there unless you had duty."

As a junior officer by 1941, he was privy to more news than the seamen, and he learned of the disparity between Washington's assessment of Pearl Harbor and that of the military commanders stationed there. One event caused him deep concern.

"After we'd been there in Hawaii for quite a while, Admiral [James O.] Richardson flew back to Washington and—now this is hearsay but I believe it—it was said he went up through the chain of command to the Chief of Naval Operations, and finally wound up in President Roosevelt's office.

He pounded on Roosevelt's desk and said he would not be a party to keeping the fleet in this horribly unsafe situation. He wanted to take the fleet back and be operative off the West Coast. And Roosevelt said, 'You won't be a party to staying in Pearl Harbor? So you won't be commander in chief of the Pacific Fleet.' And he relieved him of his duties. Within a few weeks after Admiral Richardson arrived back in Pearl Harbor, he was relieved of his command, way ahead of time, and Admiral Kimmel was appointed to replace him.

"That was April 1941, that is my memory. This story has more or less been documented, and all the Pearl Harbor veterans believe it. Of course, we figure that, after all, the President's the commander in chief, no matter how much he bungles it. I don't argue against it, it's a necessary evil. But it's not good when you get somebody who has the attitude and ego of Roosevelt."

During the late summer and early fall of 1941, Byard and the other *Arizona* officers felt the noose tightening, as Japanese submarines were sighted and officers stopped joking. Like on board tensed, maneuvers increased. Byard's network of friends watched the show, trying to make sense of the signs of war.

Galen Ballard enlisted, not to fight and not to see the world, but to learn a trade. Tired of working on an assembly line at Fisher Body in Detroit, Ballard signed into the Navy in 1935 when he was nineteen years old. "My father said I'd learn a trade and get paid at the same time," he explained. But during the Depression years the Navy was a very selective organization, and it wasn't easy to get in, even after a man had passed the physical and mental tests. Ballard had tried to enlist the year before, and finally made it in

1935. He took a pay cut from thirty-five dollars a month to twenty-one, but he hoped it would pay off.

The *Arizona* was his first ship, and he climbed on board in March 1936. For four years he worked as a sea dog in the First Division's deck force. Ballard's typical day started at 5:30, when a bugler piped reveille over the loudspeaker. "You had until ten to six to put your hammock away, go in and wash up, brush your teeth and hair, come out and have a hot cup of coffee. Very seldom did I get a cup of coffee—I can't move that fast in twenty minutes, even when I'm hurrying."

Ballard then worked at his duty station until 7:30, when he could quit for breakfast. Early-morning duty usually meant polishing brass or holystoning the deck. Ballard's position in the First Division actually affected the workload, because the captain on the bridge looked forward and always noticed what the "First Div" was doing.

"Because the captain looks forward, the boatswains' mates were always in a competition to see who could get their decks whiter. You could see their deck, so they'd holystone it. You were ready for breakfast." Ballard spent the rest of the day on "shine and bright" work assigned by the boatswain's mate.

Sleeping accommodations carried over from medieval times on shipboard. "The first year was a hammock that you hung up six feet over the deck where people could walk underneath it," he said, "where if you're lucky you didn't fall out of it. It rocked nice and put you to sleep but it was very easy to fall out of. You don't roll around much in bed in a hammock—too many times I'd be lying on my side looking at the deck. That's a long way to fall."

The ship was lined on the sides with hammock netting, where men stowed their sleeping gear during the day. Seven half hitches would render the hammock tight, and a sailor would then fold it into the netting and tuck it up out of the way. After that first year Ballard graduated to a cot, "upper crust," he called it. "I bought one from somebody, paid fifty cents for it," he recalled.

Ballard found he liked the peacetime Navy, and formed a close group of friends. Four sailors in particular became his buddies: Riley, Byers, Stanley, and Hughes. On liberty the five used to go ashore together. "We looked out for each other," he said. "Everybody called each other by last names on the *Arizona*. Even Riley—I don't know his first name and he was my buddy for four years. I remember Stanley's because it was so unusual: John Cornelius Aloysius Michael Patrick Stanley Jr." All four buddies were transferred off the *Arizona* before the attack.

Ballard served under several captains on the USS *Arizona*. He remembered a Captain Brown who served in 1937, and another, Captain Alexander. "He was a little short guy. He looked funny when he was leaning over the rail—his head just came up to the [speaker] on the bridge and he'd holler down it to the guys belowdecks. It was just comical."

He recalled Captain Isaac Kidd very clearly, for Kidd was "a physical nut," Ballard said. "I remember he was death on drinking or getting in trouble. He was a stickler." Captain Kidd had been known to slap a man in the brig for disorderly conduct.

Ballard couldn't recall meeting Van Valkenburgh, the *Arizona*'s last captain—"He must have been pretty good, 'cause I don't remember him"—but he noted there was little contact between officers and seamen, and that was fine with him. "As a lowly enlisted man, they were all respected by me," he said. "At that stage in the game the less I had to do with officers the better."

He figured it was better to keep his head low and not attract the attention of an officer. "In those days there wasn't any fraternization between the higher enlisted and the lower enlisted: 2nd class and 1st class didn't pal around with a seaman or a fireman. So it was very much like the chain of command. They just didn't associate with each other, for discipline reasons, I presume. If you went out and palled around with them and got drunk with them, how could they have discipline?"

Despite the rigid protocol, Ballard discovered he liked the Navy well enough, and when his first stint was due to expire, he extended for two more years as an engineer in the B Division, where he became a fireman 1st. His term would end in December 1941, when he could go home.

"I was assigned to the No. 6 fire room," he said. "Although I was a fireman 1st, I was taking the duties of a water tender in my particular water tender watches, which are usually taken by a 2nd class."

B Division was located amidships. The fire rooms had a big blower designed to provide air for the burners in the firebox. "You went and sat under the blowers to get air," he said. "You had so many atomizers that went in there, and you had to change them, because the requirements were different for underway and in port. When we went out below the equator, we put the smaller ones in and decreased the air, because there we didn't need as much."

His work involved constantly opening, closing, and securing valves. The room was hot, and most of the men worked naked from the waist up. "But if you happened to hit your arm on one of those pipes, it'd sear your arm," he said. "It went up to 130 degrees in there when they shut the blowers down and secured it."

Sometimes he would take a short break. "I'd go up the ladder to a little place where you could shut the hatch. You lay there and just made a little puddle of water, you were so hot. I had no trouble keeping my weight there," he said. "I'd spend a four-hour watch in the fire room: four hours on, eight off. But that was your watch—you still worked up on deck."

On regular duty or standby duty, he went to his duty station in the fire room. Otherwise when on board he stayed in his living quarters in B Division. Instead of sleeping in a hammock, he'd finally got a cot. First class and petty officers actually had bunks, but Ballard wouldn't complain about his cot—he preferred it to a hammock.

He saw many changes aboard ship during his *Arizona* stint, including the wave of incoming Reserves. He didn't like what that did to morale among the sailors.

"At first when I came on board," Ballard said, "you had your sea bag hung up on a jackstay, and you'd roll up your immediate clothing, underwear and socks, and hang it in the sea bag. Then we had these little lockers aboard ship where you kept your clothing and personal possessions. Nobody ever locked their locker. But then when the war buildup started and everybody came in, you had to lock your locker."

One thing Ballard especially hated was anchoring in Pearl Harbor on weekends. "It was a bottleneck," he said. "They should have had a way of getting in and a way of getting out, not just one channel in there." Still, he didn't think there'd be a war, but then again, many a sailor never dreamed war would come, especially when the azure sky hung over Honolulu like a burnished pearl.

CHAPTER 4

WAR GAMES

Clint Westbrook was smitten with the azure skies of Hawaii, and like his shipmates Ballard and Lawson, the light-hearted New Yorker didn't think war was looming. Heck, the Navy was a six-year stint strictly to travel around. The drill was learn a trade, have some fun, get discharged, go home and start a family. Even when war did strike with such ferocity, he kept his sense of humor, despite wounds that later, much later, earned him the Purple Heart.

At age twenty-one he joined the Navy from the Bronx. It was 1940. He'd just finished high school, and decided the Navy might take him even though he was skinny. As for war, he never gave it a thought.

"We were somewhat distanced from the European part," he said. "A lot of us were scandalized or disturbed, but we were not concerned as to getting into it. I signed up for a six-year peacetime stint."

He spent two months at boot camp in Newport, Rhode Island. Then taking boot leave, he returned briefly to New York and took his girlfriend to the World's Fair at Flushing. On returning to Newport, he spent two weeks aboard the USS *Constitution*. He was now part of the Sea Division, those who had completed boot camp and were awaiting assignments.

In quick succession, a number of assignments followed for Westbrook. He spent several months at the Philadelphia Navy Yard on the USS *Maddox,* a World War I destroyer the Navy was refurbishing. On the shakedown cruise in September 1940 the ship went to Charleston for repairs, and about that time Westbrook got transferred to the battleship USS *Texas.* He packed his sea bag, wrapped his hammock around it, and walked from the destroyer at one end of the yard to the battleship on the other.

He spent only three days on the *Texas.* "The entire three days they were looking for West Coast volunteers. They finally just simply busted us up and said 'You, you, you, and you. You're volunteers.' " He got picked. Destination: USS *Arizona.*

He took the train to Long Beach, California, to pick up the *Arizona,* where he was assigned to communications. Shortly afterward the battleship went to Bremerton for its last overhaul. Staying in the States for Christmas, the *Arizona* sailed for Hawaii in early 1941. It returned to Bremerton in June for 2 weeks, Westbrook recalled, "but it wasn't enough time to get home."

Attached to the 4th division, one of the deck divisions, by mid-1941 he was helping to man turret 4. "The first four divisions manned the turrets, and the 5th and 6th deck divisions manned the antiaircraft 5-inch guns up on the boat deck. They had a regular division for the aircraft—I don't remember what they called them. We had two float planes. All the battleships did."

Life on the battleship seemed to Westbrook like a crowded city, with almost ninety people in the 4th division alone. "I was the last one sleeping in a hammock. I liked it. It made it nice, especially at sea, 'cause you don't roll.

The hammock stands still and the ship rocks around it. But in a bunk you feel it all the time.

"The others had bunks that they had stove along the sides. It was much easier just to lash my hammock up. But the boatswain finally got tired of hitting his head on it, and told me I had to quit."

Most weekdays, he remembered, sailors were kept busy. "You were always doing something: scraping paint, wash, they always had something." Fridays were special cleaning days. "Every Friday we cleaned the ship inside and out, polished all the brass, holystoned the decks."

He messcooked for six months, and he liked the perks. "Every payday you put a bowl, or two bowls, on the table. I fed the 4th division and the musicians—the band—so I set up six meals a day. It kept you busy: You got extra food, and you had access to the galley and the bakery all the time so you could snack in between. And you'd get tips. The pay varied, depending on the person's rate—when I went in it was twenty-one dollars a month, and as a seamen 2nd I went to thirty-four dollars a month."

Westbrook's living quarters were located on the afterdeck, two compartments forward of the quarterdeck. His bunk was across the ship's girth from the "Admiral's Playground," where Isaac Kidd lived. "He was way up," Westbrook said, referring to Kidd's status, "and he had the Marines to guard him. He had his own staff, cook and steward, the works. When the admiral came aboard to live, he took quite a section. But of course the big ships already had it built into them, so any one of them could become a flag."

When Westbrook went aboard the *Arizona* it was already a flagship, so Kidd's presence was an accepted fact. "You rarely saw him, maybe once a year he might hold an inspection," Westbrook said. "You heard him being piped aboard or piped off, but you didn't want to be around him. Too much gold."

Like other sailors, Westbrook understood that Kidd was not concerned with operating the ship, but rather with the entire group of ships in Battleship Division One. "He had no say [in the *Arizona*] unless he thought the captain was doing something dangerous," he said. "He was always coming and going—they had meetings on the beach."

The admiral traveled in his own gig, a launch that he alone used, escorted by sideboys, or Marine escorts. The rest of the *Arizona* men used one of three boats: a 50-footer, a 37-footer, and a small gig. The three boats sat in boat skids up on the boat deck, nestled like Chinese baskets, one within the other, starting with the big one on the bottom, the next smaller inside it and the next smaller inside of that.

Westbrook's normal day began with reveille, deck work, then breakfast, followed by general quarters at 8 A.M. when boatswains assigned the day's duties. Jobs were rotated, so sometimes a sailor would get general crew duties, sometimes a specific task. The assigned duty often lasted for a week or a month, depending on how long it would take.

Westbrook got assigned to clean the lower deck compartments, a task that lasted for two or three months. "Most of it was scraping and cleaning ladders," he said. "The ladders went down through an opening like a shaft, but fairly large, and different compartments led off that. All I was responsible for was the entire column: ladders, decking, fire hydrants, things like that. Shine all the brass—that got inspected every Friday."

Although Friday was usually "field day," or inspection

day, sometimes even that changed, depending on the duties—or the whimsy—of the captain. "Sometimes if they
were going to have personnel inspection also, then all of
Saturday morning would be inspection day. If they weren't
going to have personnel inspection that Saturday, then Friday afternoon was the field day inspection, and you'd better
have everything spotless."

When Westbrook joined the *Arizona*'s 4th Division, he'd
been assigned to communications. The job didn't last too
long, he said, because he didn't follow the book. "If I
missed a character in receiving radio messages, I would
stop to try to remember it, instead of forget it and go on.
So the division officer finally said, 'Westbrook, you've had
it.' He wouldn't let me keep the job."

Next he was assigned to a turret as the No. 85 powder
man. Each turret had 85 men assigned to it, and they were
each called "powder men" and numbered from 1 to 85. As
No. 85, the turret's newcomer, Westbrook was located deep
down in the turret magazine, and his specific job was to
remove the covers from the powder cans and take out the
powder bags. A powder bag was packed tightly with powder capsules the size of a cigarette filter. Encased in silk,
each powder bag weighed 60 pounds.

Powder man No. 84, beside him, would then carry the
bag and place it on a scuttle in the fireproof door between
the magazine and the bottom handling room. "You dropped
the 60-pound bag in the scuttle and pulled a lever, and the
shuttle would rotate 180 degrees and the next guy out there
would take it out and hand it to somebody to put it in the
mount," he said. "If the mount is maneuvering, then you
increase or decrease the number of men that are handling
a powder bag."

Two hoists, one each at port and starboard, sent the ammunition up to the turrets. At the top of the hoist, men grabbed the powder bags and rolled them into the turret. The last man to handle the powder bag was called the No. 1 powder man. By December 1941, Westbrook had made it all the way through the "powder ranks" to No. 1.

Up in the turret, or gunhouse, sitting above the deck, three men waited beside ramps where the hoists would dump the powder bags. In turn they would supply the No. 1 gun, then No. 3, then the middle gun. The rammer would come down and push it into the gun, and the breech man would close and lock the breech block.

The breech man had to be built on the small side. "He stands in a pit about waist high, and you can't put a fat man in there because of the recoil," Westbrook said. "So he stands back and he signals ready, and when they fire the recoil comes in and he has about 6 inches clearance."

It was an honor to be selected to be the breech man, since the risks were high. Yet it was actually difficult to have accidents, Westbrook said. "You can take that powder, hit it with a sledgehammer or throw it into a fire, but it won't burn. The biggest thing that happens with powder that's not encased with silk is flareback."

In order to prevent flareback, after firing the gunners would blow compressed air through the barrels. When the wisps of smoke had disappeared from the barrels, the gun captain would unlock the breech block and look in to make sure no burning silk remains. If he neglected to check, the next projectile might be rammed in on top of burning silks and fragments and thereby cause a fire. The resulting flareback tends to go back through the turret rather than out the gun. "At that point the breech block is open so it's got no place to go except back into turret," Westbrook explained. "You can't get away from a flareback without killing everybody because it takes all the oxygen."

Success in war depends as much on teamwork as on individual acts. All drills strove to make men work together as a team, and it was especially commendable when a turret team did its job well. The U.S. naval officers had long ago instigated a competition for excellence, where the different battleships of the fleet would try to best each other.

"In gunnery in those days they had engineering, communication, signalmen, all competing for E for excellence," he said. "If the ship got an E it'd go up on the board at the side of the bridge. And you'd keep that, you didn't lose it the next year. If you won your E again you'd get half mark. So you'd see some of the ships with a red E for engineering, a green E was communications, and I think the white E was gunnery. And you'd see them with several half marks."

The *Arizona*'s four turrets competed against each other to be the best aboard ship. "So you worked hard at it," Westbrook said.

The crew within the turret itself numbered thirty to thirty-five men, including the fire control man, the boatswain's mates who were in charge of the people up there, and the division officer, who was the gunnery officer for that turret. On each end of the turret sat the pointer and the trainer. The division officer sat on a small platform raised up in the back, and peered through duplicate sights to watch the pointer's and trainer's targets. His matched pair of sights enabled him to look in and see what his pointer and trainer were seeing at the same time. If the turret was being fired under "local control" rather than from the bridge, the division officer gave the command to fire.

Aside from getting to know his turret mates, Westbrook found living on the enormous battleship almost as anonymous as living in the Bronx. He made a few friends, but didn't know most of the *Arizona* sailors. "It was too big a ship," he explained. "You never got to know anyone enough to decide whether you liked him or not. Except your division officers."

Unlike wartime ships that worked a full crew as a unit, the *Arizona* split its men into divisions with specific tasks. "On the *Arizona* you didn't work except with your eighty-some-odd men. You didn't know anybody else, except occasionally you might make friends with somebody else. But you'd make friends one on one; it wouldn't be a half-dozen people getting together."

Officers were not people Westbrook sought out. "In those days I stayed strictly away from brass as much as possible. So did everyone else if they could. If you ran into them, you just never knew what you'd get. You might get assigned new duties. And when they were around, you had all the formalities you had to take care of, saluting and all this business. If you felt like being a little sloppy, that was fine at other times, but you couldn't do it around them."

He, too, noted the great chasm between officers and enlisted men. "It was pretty much of a division," he said. "The officers were the officers and the enlisted were the enlisted, and you didn't associate with them except businesswise. And you didn't associate ashore, because Navy policy was very strict: Officers and enlisted do not mingle. I guess it's to preserve the chain of command. I would say the basic feeling was that if you got friendly, then you couldn't command—it would be a conflict."

While he enjoyed being on a battleship, Westbrook felt "no special attachment" to the *Arizona*. "I'd much rather be ashore. Of course, you had Cinderella liberty all the time in Hawaii—you had to be back at midnight. There were no overnights, except for married men or people with special permission. A man going ashore had to put it in writing, make a record of it, so if he wasn't aboard at a particular time, they knew where he was."

Like so many sailors, Westbrook didn't think a war was really coming. He was not privy to officers' intelligence, and never heard beforehand of the secret messages going back and forth between Tokyo and Hawaii. "The lowly sailors were too far down the chain—we didn't even hear the rattling," he said.

In 1941 the plan for sea duties for Battleship Division One sometimes kept the fleet out of Pearl Harbor on weekends, but it was an unusual operation that lasted more than two weeks.

"Normally we were out Monday through Friday and in Pearl on weekends, but not always. We had definite operations and depending on the plan, we might stay out over a weekend or not. But basically you wouldn't be gone more than two weeks at the longest."

The times at sea were spent preparing for war, if it ever came. Maneuvers occupied most of the at-sea time, "playing war games," Westbrook called it. General quarters would see the men run drills, each one performing whatever his battle station required. "Your damage control people would play games, and your people with guns would track and train."

The war games at sea employed the long-range turret guns. "We fired them, all right," he said. "They had tows for us to shoot. There'd be a tug out there with a big target on it, and you did short-range and long-range firing on it." Since the tows would be used repeatedly, the gunners did not fire directly on them, but by offsetting the shot a certain number of degrees, they could employ the target for gunnery practice and still not destroy it.

"The short range was within sight, so it could be five to ten miles. Long-range firing was the horizon—fifteen or twenty miles." For short-range firing, two powder bags per shell were required; for long-range it was four "per gun, per barrel, per shell," he said.

In the fall the pace quickened, he recalled, and every sunrise and sunset the men were called to general quarters. They knew then it was serious.

"We weren't playing games at that particular time of the day," he said. "They felt that was the time that an enemy attack would come, if there was any—sunrise or sunset."

In the autumn months, the *Arizona* spent many a day on the high seas two hundred miles off Hawaii testing its long-range and antiaircraft guns. Destroyers towed sleds for the battleships to fire on. The *Arizona* towed its own target sleds one hundred feet long for the spotter planes to dive and practice on.

The catapult planes would fly to a given area where a phantom enemy ship was supposed to be lurking and radio the location back to the ship. Out there in the broad reaches of the Pacific, while the ocean formed swells that would splash on Oregon beaches, Jim Lawson, John Rampley, John Anderson, and their turret mates practiced firing the big guns, shooting at targets they couldn't see.

"They'd tell us how much elevation we needed on the turret guns, what the aiming point would be," Lawson said. "They could actually fire the turret from there, or they could give local control to the man on the turret. That was me. I pulled the trigger on the big guns."

On sea maneuvers, the sailors took part in endless drills of mock casualty. Sometimes they'd pretend that the electrical power had failed, and the turrets would switch over to battery power. Or they'd simulate a situation where radio communication was broken between the turret and the control room, and the turret gunners would have to speak to the fire control director with special independent instruments. Sometimes the drill assumed that the turret commander, who is the division officer, was wounded, so the chief of the turret would take command.

In maneuvers the gunners didn't always fire the turret guns, expensive as they were to use and wretchedly difficult to clean. Lawson remembered that chore of cleaning, which was performed by a little fellow named Harold Oliphant.

"He was the smallest guy on the turret crew, so he got to go through the barrel. And I could get into the chamber, so I cleaned that element of the gun. We'd go in past the powder chamber, the loading chamber. Those guns had to be cleaned and oiled constantly. We used emery cloth. You're laying in there like this, and it's right close to your face inside the gun. When you visualize those big powder bags encased in raw silk stacked end to end in there—it took four or five men to hoist them—you can imagine how far in we'd have to go to the chamber. So after they'd been fired, we would have to rig out and pull through what we called pigs; they were a series of brushes with real heavy sturdy bristles that looked like toothbrushes. We manually pulled them with ropes through the barrels, up and back, up and back. And as they'd go through, they'd follow the grooves, turning as they came through the barrel of the gun."

Signs of war were everywhere, for those who cared to look. One searing event seemed a dark omen.

"During the spring and summer of 1941 we saw a death ship," said Jim Lawson. "There were a number of battle-scarred ships of the British persuasion, French, too, but mostly British and Dutch, who came into Pearl as a stop-over for whatever retrofit they needed to make them sea-worthy. One ship came in while we were between sea duties. It was a British cruiser, and it had just a makeshift bow they had put on in the Philippines. And the ship stunk to high heaven, because they had had to seal off a couple of frames to make the ship seaworthy, but inside those frames was a whole bunch of their crew dead and rotting, and you could smell it all over the harbor. They were dead from a torpedo they took somewhere in the South Pacific."

Other ominous signs of intensifying military activity ap-peared. "We painted the fleet three times that year," he said. "I guess they were trying to find out what color the fleet would look best in during combat conditions, in order to avoid being seen by submarines or aircraft. Coming out of the Navy yard in Bremerton and going back out to Pearl, it was a typical paint job—Navy gray. Sometime during the spring we went to black. Dead black above the water line, red below. The whole Pacific Fleet. Then they decided black was no good, so somewhere along the way they painted the ships with the Atlantic zigzag pattern—the camouflage painting of the Atlantic ships with gray-and-black jagged patterns all over the ship. Then they decided zigzag was no good, so they went to blue. And that's what they stayed—various shades of blue, light blue."

Maneuvers at sea were stepped up in October. Besides firing on targets, the fleet sailed in zigzags, when the battleships threaded their way among one another like ponies at a gymkhana. The officer of the deck presided over the intricacies of at-sea formations.

Zigzags were a timed sequence. "You'd sail so many minutes on such-and-such a degree of the zig," Lawson said, "and so many minutes on the zag. At the appropriate moment the OD would give the orders to so-and-so for the steering of the ship. The lookouts on the ways of the bridge and on the crow's nest would be responsible for feeding information, whatever they could see, back to the bridge. If anything untoward happened, the officer of the deck would have to notify the captain. If the captain thought it was necessary to make an appearance on the bridge, he'd come up and see what was going on."

One day in October 1941, the captain was rudely surprised. During particularly intensive war games as the battleships were practicing steering shifts in the zigzag exercises, a shocking event occurred: The *Arizona* was rammed by another battleship, the *Oklahoma*.

Lawson had just stepped out of the shower in the petty officers' washroom. "There was a smack and I'm sitting on my behind in that washroom. I thought we'd been hit by a torpedo, so I wasted no time getting out of there, and topside I went. I got to my gun station just in time to see the other battleship rounding the fantail.

"Fortunately they had somehow got wind of the fact that they were on a collision course with the *Arizona* and they were on full astern when they hit us. But as they went scraping along the side—you can imagine what that sounded like—they peeled every speck of those blisters off the side of the ship." Blisters, the steel honeycombs ringing the ship at the water line, were designed to absorb the initial impact of a torpedo.

Jim Foster was another sailor who recalled the dramatic moment when the *Oklahoma* rammed the *Arizona*. "It got us right on the bow. We thought we were going to sink that night. It pitched and rolled. We finally took on water on the other side to get it right." He blamed the stepped-up pace for the *Oklahoma* incident. "We had a lot of exercises and the [officers] were really pushing us pretty hard."

Clint Westbrook remembered vividly the *Oklahoma*'s collision with the *Arizona*. "Our division was working at sea in broad daylight, and we were doing maneuvers, changing column, line-of-bearing maneuver, and we were in the third step of the maneuver, when everybody looked out to the port side and there's the [*Oklahoma*] bearing down on us."

Westbrook had been belowdecks at the time, on his way to general quarters. When the collision was imminent, the call went out for general quarters. "I think the collision alarm went off. You manned pretty much the same station you would at general quarters. So everybody was in the process of dashing madly to their post when it hit, 'cause I went off a ladder, I can remember that. I was halfway up the ladder and it knocked me right off it. And the first thing that went through everybody's head that hadn't been out on deck was that we'd just been bombed."

The other battleship had missed a maneuver, he explained. All the battleships had been sailing in line, making starboard turns, ninety degrees at a time. "They were going one step out, and we're steaming this way and she's steaming this way. I guess the other ship was at our port side, and they just missed one turn somewhere or made one turn too many. She ran broadside smack into us, just aft of the bridge. The damage was enough to put us in the yard for a while." The other ship, he added, was "crumpled up pretty good."

The accident displaced the *Arizona* a hundred feet sideways. "You take 33,000 tons and ram it into something that's not going in the same direction! A few of us got bruises—it knocked them off their feet. I think the hole was 30 feet high and probably 18 to 20 feet wide," Westbrook said.

The ship listed 10 degrees or more until water was let in on the opposite side to compensate. Water had entered the gash. "If the bow's high enough it goes in over the armor plate, so it damaged the tanks. The old battlewagons had fuel or water tanks down the sides, and that's what formed the blister all the way around. The blister came out about that high or so out of the water, so you could see that much of it. And the [*Oklahoma*'s] bow hit and went across it, crushed all that and cracked the armor plate."

Westbrook heard later that after an inquiry the *Oklahoma*'s captain was removed. "The captain's ultimately the one, he takes the blame regardless of whether he was in command at that particular moment. Inquiry? Oh yeah, they had a big one."

The *Arizona* limped into Pearl Harbor and went into drydock for about three days to repair the blisters and replace several hull plates. While the ship was out of water, the crew was put to work scraping barnacles off the hull. "All hands evolution" was the order that brought every seaman out to scrape the bottom.

"I don't remember how much damage there was to the hull," Jim Lawson said, "but I think it might have caved in a couple of plates. The main thing I remember was having to get over the side to clean the ship. And when they put the new blisters on, why they didn't paint them first and then hang them to this day I don't understand, but that's the Navy way of doing things. Once they got them attached and welded onto the hull, we had to go in and paint these things inside. Talk about claustrophobic, oh boy—red lead paint in the paintbrush inside a small space!"

During the drydock days the men continued to live on board. "When they put ships in drydock," Westbrook said, "battleships and destroyers even, the men stay aboard. Only if they're going to do extensive alterations do they move you ashore and put you in barracks. But when you go in the yard every three years for 90 or 120 days for overhaul, they'll pull the engines, cut down through the decks, take them out, overhaul them or replace them. Then the men live ashore."

The *Arizona* didn't stay in the yard long, as fast as ships were being pushed in and pulled out. In fact, many other ships never even made it into drydock, being repaired alongside a dock whenever possible. All told, the *Arizona* was out of action only for about two weeks. "You can't hurt a battleship much," Westbrook said with unknowing irony.

Even at that late date he didn't think war was coming. "It still felt like peacetime," he said, "except for general quarters in the morning and the evening, and that was a pain in the neck, as far as we were concerned. It was just part of the security that they were starting at that point."

Out on the high seas and even in close around the Hawaiian Islands, enemy submarines were sighted more and more often. The sailors all felt the tension mounting.

"In November we went to sea for the better part of two weeks, maybe three," Jim Lawson recalled. "I stood many a wheel watch and fired many a bullet. Our submarines and destroyers kept getting sub contacts. I was on the bridge on several occasions during wheel watch time when a report would come in that somebody had a sonar contact. Where we were then I don't know, because we were a couple hundred miles out to sea, and once you clear land the water all looks the same. A helmsman never worked with the charts, you just work by orders: Come right. Come left. Do this. Do that. But the sub contacts were there, which meant that the Japanese were out lurking around, watching what we were doing, reporting back."

On the last cruise the *Arizona* made, leaving port in late November and returning December 5, the war maneuvers turned real. In a bold display of confidence, Japanese submarines followed the fleet in close quarters around the Hawaiian Islands, coming dangerously near at the anchorage of Lahaina Roads off the island of Maui.

"We used to go to what was a sleepy little fishing village, Lahaina. In those days it was so lush that even several miles at sea you could smell the flowers wafting across the water and you knew you were close to Lahaina. If we were going to be there two or three days at anchor—swinging around the hook, as we called it—we'd get to go ashore. There was nothing doing in Lahaina in those days, the town wasn't longer than a street, but we'd go to the beach where the big long Pacific swells used to roll in and crash on the sand."

The fleet pulled into Lahaina that November afternoon, and the ships dropped anchor. Sailors took shore liberty but returned to the ship by midnight and turned in. "Long about one o'clock in the morning the general alarm went off— Man your battle stations! The picket submarines and picket destroyers had detected a bunch of sonar contacts. Every man aboard knew that meant Japanese submarines. They called the special sea detail, which puts the quartermasters on the bridge, ready for battle. The deck force pulled up the anchors, and the whole fleet got under way."

Deciding that the subs were not threatening, the fleet admiral gave orders to sail to the open seas for gunnery practice as planned. But it had been a vulnerable moment for the U.S. Pacific Fleet. "There we were sitting anchored in open water," Lawson said. "The Japs could've hit us there. They wouldn't have had to fly those planes in two weeks later."

On Thursday, December 4, the day before the *Arizona* returned to port, the football team had practice scheduled on the boat deck. They were eagerly preparing for a big game the following Sunday that pitted the *Arizona*'s team against the Army team at Schofield Barracks. But that Thursday on the high seas, while the men called their plays above the roar of the waves and tackled each other under the hot tropical sun, Lawson's division officer came up and said practice was canceled. When the sailors asked why, he replied that Sunday's game was also canceled. Football was over for good. It seemed the top brass expected the war to break out right after the first of the year.

"He told us to take all the gear down," Lawson said

sadly. "To those who were in the turret, he told us to stack our stuff in the turret and they'd pick it up Monday or Tuesday of next week and turn it back in to the athletic locker. We were all disappointed the game was canceled. We'd been practicing hard, as much as you can practice under the circumstances, and we'd really looked forward to it."

On Friday, December 5, the fleet pulled into Pearl Harbor for the weekend. Pulling up to the quay known as Fox 8, the *Arizona* loosed a flood of off-duty sailors headed for "the beach." Aboard the ship that Friday evening, social activities got going, and some men went to the ship's movie. Jim Lawson, disappointed and tired, sacked out early.

On Saturday morning the repair ship *Vestal* came alongside the *Arizona* and tied up, bow to bow, stern to stern. All day the ships in port prepared for at-sea maneuvers the next week. Everywhere sailors oiled guns and cleaned the decks. For hours the *Arizona* took on oil, its enormous tanks sucking in a million gallons in preparation for a long cruise.

Battleships sailing into the harbor were automatically facing toward Oahu. Since the harbor was too small to permit maneuvering of such large ships, they remained at a serious disadvantage, being unable to sail out until the tugs turned them, one by one, to face out and exit. All day Saturday the small boats worked away, ferrying the big ships around, turning their bows from landward to seaward, so they could sail out of the harbor on Monday.

In the early evening, Lawson stood on deck and looked down at the *Vestal* and its crew for a few minutes before leaving the ship for a meal in Pearl City. Some of his buddies stayed for a few hours later to dance at the nightclubs, but Lawson came back to the ship early, eager to see the *Arizona*'s Saturday night movie of *Dr. Jekyll and Mr. Hyde,* starring Spencer Tracy. He wouldn't miss it for anything.

The movie over, he walked the deck alone for a few minutes, feeling not exactly antisocial, but wanting a little quiet time. He fell asleep as the night came down, thinking of the football game that had been scotched.

That same evening, Admiral Kidd held a ceremony to make athletic presentations to the *Arizona* men for awards they'd won in various sports: baseball, rowing, boxing. A good many of the ship's company was assembled, except for the men who'd gone ashore. John Rampley was there.

"He said to us, 'I think I know what all you men want for Christmas, and you're going to get that.' We all wanted leave. After he said that, scuttlebutt started floating around the ship that we were scheduled to leave Monday the eighth for R&R in San Diego."

As John Rampley fell asleep that night, he reflected back on the day. The *Arizona*'s massive tanks had been refueled. Five thousand tons of oil had been pumped into the tanks deep in the hold, in preparation for the long cruise eastward to California. Hawaii was great, he thought, but it would be wonderful to spend Christmas at home in North Carolina. He got a lump in his throat thinking of his family.

That first week of December was a good-feeling time for Galen Ballard, whose Navy stint was nearly up. Only one week of duty remained before he'd be a free man. Told he would be sailing home on the thirteenth, he was eager to spend his last weekend at liberty. He remembered the last weekend on the *Arizona* as being routine. "I don't think any of us had any idea whatsoever that anything was going to happen. We were as happy as larks."

Ballard had been assigned for duty in standby section Saturday night. Now he was looking for someone to stand in his place so he could go ashore. And since the Navy didn't give shore liberty on demand to lowly seamen, he asked a friend to write out an invitation inviting him to dinner so he'd have a reason to ask for shore leave. "You had to have a written invitation to go ashore [overnight], 'cause there wasn't any liberty except for those that were married, or if someone invited you over to their home. No way could they accommodate the fleet over in Honolulu, so all they had was daytime liberty."

The friend wrote the letter, but Ballard still had no one to cover his watch. He spoke to another sailor, Lester Mayfield of Colorado. "He was waiting to see if he'd gotten some money in the mail," Ballard recalled. "If so, he was going ashore. He didn't get it. His name was Mayfield, and he said he'd stand by for me." Mayfield agreed to surrender his pass to his buddy Ballard and cover the watch. For such a trick of fate, his name would later appear on the list of dead men from the *Arizona*.

Ballard walked his request through. "You're supposed to have it in the day before. To walk it through means I had to take it to the engineering log room, take it to the engineering officer and the executive office, by hand. It was only the second overnight liberty I'd had since I'd been there—close to two years." Borrowing some money from another sailor, he took the launch to the beach.

He headed for the dance at the American Legion at the Honolulu Post, where a man named B. E. Jackson signed his pass. The music, soft, smooth, romantic, reminded him of the world outside the Navy. Swaying to the rhythm with his girlfriend, Helen, he passed a pleasant evening. "She was a Hawaiian gal, very nice, and worked for the Navy. She also played the banjo at the Moana Hotel."

Although Ballard had gotten off the ship by sheer luck, he almost went back to it that night. At the Legion dance he became angry with his girlfriend for dancing with other sailors. In a huff he stalked out and began walking along the road to the boat launch, where he now planned to catch the shore patrol's liberty boat.

"That's where I was lucky again. I'd got upset and I walked out and started going back to the ship. She drove up, picked me up." He went home with his date, holding his overnight pass in his breast pocket like a talisman. He would sleep in, he thought, and return to the *Arizona* around noon.

Vern Olsen had spent Friday on board, messcooking and cleaning. His duty lasted till noon on Saturday the sixth, when he was planning to take liberty ashore.

Since the *Arizona* had to be manned at all times, liberty was granted only to certain sections of the ship: port liberty one day for the sailors stationed on the port side, starboard liberty the next day. Olsen had starboard liberty.

In those days enlisted men seldom had overnight liberty in Pearl Harbor. Officers or married men could usually get weekend passes, but Olsen wasn't married, so midnight was the cutoff to get back to the ship. He caught a launch to the dock early Saturday afternoon and headed for Honolulu, planning to return in midevening.

"I drank beer and raised hell," he said. "There was a lot of good friends on the ship, quite a few from right around the Rockford area, so there was quite a few that we knew:

Russ Warriner, Herb Buehl, and Tom Lounsbury of Wood-stock—they were all within a fifty-mile radius. They were all friends. And Dick Folkes, he was from Aurora, Illinois. We used to go on liberty together."

Sometime after eight, Olsen returned to the ship, leaving behind the bright lights of Waikiki and the humming banjos and ukeleles of island bands. He'd heard that the *Arizona*'s band was competing on one of the other ships in the Battle of the Bands, but he didn't go. He skipped Admiral Kidd's presentation of the athletic awards and passed up the Saturday night movie, preferring instead to hang out in his quarters. He went to bed at the regular time, unaware that Kidd had told the *Arizona* men they'd spend Christmas in California.

Clint Westbrook spent Saturday night on duty as shore patrol.

Even after the clock struck midnight on December 6, he was still making night runs with the liberty boat to pick up men returning from downtown Honolulu. "Rotating within your division of ships, you were also assigned shore patrol, and you'd bring the late ones back. And when you're assigned to that type of duty, you don't just get your own crew to come back, you get a mixed bag of people that they picked up on the street—drunk, disorderly, or just plain late—so you might have six ships going around the harbor.

"Our last run was twelve-fifteen, twelve-thirty in the morning, 'cause they were supposed to be back by twelve o'clock, but sometimes guys were late. Usually you were considered there if you were at the pier at twelve o'clock, and that's why the boat hung off a little bit, usually waited about twenty minutes or so before heading back to the ship to catch anybody that was a fraction late."

After the midnight run around the harbor to deposit sailors at their ships, Westbrook and his mates headed back to the Arizona. His duty would officially end at eight in the morning, and after that he planned to go ashore for a flying lesson.

Westbrook fell asleep in his hammock that night thinking of tipping wings and heroic dives in a tiny plane over Oahu's volcanic mountains. The last thing he remembered was an image of reddish trumpet flowers on the hillsides yielding to blackened fingers of lava shoreline.

After nine years of living on the Arizona, Ralph Byard spent his last night on the ship December 5. Saturday he went ashore to Honolulu, where he maintained an off-duty apartment in a building that housed a small group of men who worked up the ship's payroll.

For many years he'd been friends with an Arizona sailor named Paxton Turner Carter, a former ship's storekeeper from California who had risen to the rank of pay clerk, or warrant officer. That Saturday night Byard, Carter, and a woman friend from Honolulu went to the Keawala Inn for dinner and drinks. As happened with so many men, fate pointed its finger that night, keeping Byard ashore and sending Carter back to the Arizona to sleep.

"Later in the evening I asked him to come on back and sleep in my apartment, and he said no, he had to go on back to the ship," Byard said with a shaking voice. "He was going to get up early in the morning and grade some training course exams that some of the men in the division had taken. I couldn't persuade him to stay ashore, so he went on back to the ship, and I went on back to my apartment."

In the clear, cloudless night Byard walked back to his apartment alone. He turned in and slept heavily.

On board the *Arizona,* the bands of all the battleships were competing in the Battle of the Bands, blowing their trumpets and clashing their cymbals in exuberant military marches. After two hours of impassioned playing, the Arizona band was awarded second place. As a reward, they were told they could sleep in on Sunday morning.

Late Saturday night was quiet for Jim Foster, who walked the decks and thought about the wide-open spaces of Texas. Even out here on the *Arizona*'s boat deck, a web of steel and deadly weapons, he could hear the trill of a tropical bird calling through the trees on Ford Island. He thought of owls hooting in the sagebrush back home. The lush, sensuous aroma of orchids floated across the waves from the island hills, but it reminded him of Texas bluebonnets.

Throughout the evening, while other sailors cavorted on the beach and others attended the shipboard festivities and the Battle of the Bands, William Goshen stood watch.

He remembered the time as quiet and uneventful. By nightfall the harbor tugs had turned the battleships around, so the *Arizona* faced the harbor mouth. He noticed the *Vestal* was tied up on the *Arizona*'s port side, shielding the battleship from the channel.

As stars filled the Hawaiian sky with crystal light, it turned 2 A.M. Goshen's watch ended. Heading belowdecks, he turned in, dreaming of taking his day liberty in the morning and visiting the beach at Waikiki.

CHAPTER 5

THE JAPANESE DRAGON

Midnight on the last day of peace. As blackness deepened over Hawaii and the last sailors fell into their bunks, a fleet of thirty-two Japanese ships on the high Pacific steamed toward Hawaii. They would sail just far enough to provide a launching spot for planes targeting the U.S. fleet, locked in Pearl Harbor. An unthinkable destiny awaited the men on Battleship Row.

The attack on Pearl Harbor was a brilliant and bold military operation, but it was hardly an impetuous gamble. Although most United States politicians and many high-ranking military personnel had disdained the possibility of an air raid at Hawaii, Japanese strategists had speculated on such an event for years.

Following their defeat of the Russians in 1905, the Japanese had continued to build up their military forces. In 1914 when war broke out in Europe, Japan joined the Allies. This allowed the Imperial Japanese Navy to strike out at another European colonial power in the Far East, Germany. Germany's East Asiatic Fleet, outgunned by the Imperial Japanese Navy, left the region, allowing Japan to occupy Germany's colonial possessions. The Treaty of Versailles, signed in 1919, ceded this group of islands, including the Gilberts, Marianas, and Marshalls, to Japan.

Japan had become both an extensive overseas empire and a military power, and it continued to arm itself, building more ships, including *Nagato* and *Mutsu,* the first battleships in the world equipped with 16-inch naval guns. But the rapid pace of Japanese industrialization and militarization slowed in the 1920s as the island nation's resources dwindled. To continue to feed its people and its industry, Japan needed to import more raw materials, including steel, rubber, and oil from abroad. As the depression settled across Europe in the 1930s, Japan had enjoyed a dynamic climate of industrial competition, bolstered by big business and a strong army and navy, but now the depression that had begun in 1929 spread and hurt Japan's economy, and helped a growing cadre of militaristic politicians and soldiers take control of the government. By 1931, the militarists successfully staged an invasion of China, seizing Manchuria in 1931.

In July 1937, the Japanese military staged an "incident" with a Chinese border patrol and used it as an excuse to launch a bloody invasion of China. The war that followed was marked by unparalleled savagery against Chinese civilians, with the world watching in horror as Japanese atrocities mounted. The United States, with a nominal force in China, helped other colonial powers patrol the Yalu River.

Five months later, in December 1937, Japanese forces "accidentally" attacked and sank the U.S. gunboat *Panay,* killing some of the crew. Although the Japanese apologized and paid reparations, it was clear that war between the two nations was not too far off. The next blow was China's capitulation to Japanese aggression, a move that greatly alarmed the United States, particularly since the Pacific events held parallels to the European theater. As America built its military strength in Guam, Hawaii, the Philippines, and Midway and Wake Islands, it inadvertently positioned itself as the first priority for a warmongering Japan.

In the spring of 1940 Hitler wreaked havoc on Europe, while Japan stationed troops in northern French Indochina.

War grew closer to the United States in 1940 as Japan allied itself with Nazi Germany and Fascist Italy. Outraged by Japanese aggression in China, President Franklin D. Roosevelt in July 1940 had placed an embargo on strategic materials bound for Japan. At the same time he lobbied Congress for a stronger Navy, and shifted the Pacific Fleet further out into the Pacific by relocating it to Pearl Harbor. Japanese assets in the United States were frozen. Within a few months the embargo, initially covering only scrap steel and raw materials headed for Japan, was enlarged to include oil and high-octane gasoline, very critical materials in wartime.

Following Japan's signing the Tripartite Pact with the Germans and Italians in September, American preparations for war accelerated, although in Roosevelt's mind the greater threat lay in Europe, where Hitler's blitzkrieg had resulted in the quick conquest of Poland and the fall of France. The downfall of France led the Japanese to bolder advances in the Far East as they occupied French Indochina, wresting it from Hitler's puppet state of Vichy France in the summer of 1941. Roosevelt's response was to complete the freeze of Japanese assets in the United States and strictly enforce the embargo on oil. Japan imported 80 percent of its oil from the United States. War was now only months away.

Japanese military planners decided to seize the raw materials they needed by invading Southeast Asia, which was largely a series of British, Dutch, and American colonies, and adding them to the empire. The United States Pacific Fleet at Pearl Harbor was an obstacle to conquest, but the Japanese were emboldened by the U.S. relocation of some of the fleet to the Atlantic. Hitler's U-boat war in the North Atlantic had already led the United States to augment its naval forces in those waters. Japan's military leaders carefully watched these developments. Realizing that the warships then under construction in the States would out-number their own forces by 1944, in the summer of 1941 Japan decided to strike while they had the numerical advantage of nearly twice as many warships, including ten aircraft carriers to the United States' three carriers in the Pacific.

The larger Japanese plan, the "Southern Operation," called for a quick sweep south, seizing the American Philippines and Singapore, the capital of British Malaya. Hong Kong, Thailand, and Burma's conquest would add Southeast Asia to the Japanese Empire, while additional southern strikes into Borneo, the Celebes, Timor, Sumatra, and finally Java would conquer the oil-rich Dutch East Indies. The key to success was the destruction of American and British military forces in the region. Best of all would be a decisive blow at Pearl Harbor that the Japanese hoped would not only devastate the fleet but also American public morale, thus keeping the United States out of a war and leaving Japan the master of the Pacific.

The assault on Pearl Harbor, in order to be successful, was to be a surprise attack in the longstanding Japanese tradition. The architect of the attack, Admiral Isoroku Yamamoto, who had been recently appointed commander-in-chief of the Combined Fleet, advocated an aerial assault from carrier-based aircraft. Yamamoto had studied an earlier U.S. Navy fleet exercise that successfully simulated a carrier attack on Pearl Harbor. He and some of his officers had also learned lessons from a British raid on the Italian fleet at Taranto, where a group of Swordfish biplane torpedo bombers from the carrier HMS *Illustrious* attacked the Italians on the evening of November 11, 1940, sinking the battleships *Littorio, Conte di Cavour,* and *Caio Duilio,* and two fleet auxiliaries. Yamamoto turned the tactical planning over to Commander Minoru Genda another advocate of air power.

To successfully neutralize the Pacific Fleet, Genda envisioned a carrier strike force, the Kido Butai. Comprised of thirty-one ships, including six carriers, the Kido Butai would carry 355 aircraft, including high-altitude bombers and torpedo and dive bombers, to within 230 miles of Oahu. The principal target was the three American carriers, as well as the battleships. A screen of fleet submarines would lie in wait off the harbor entrance to torpedo any ships that fled the holocaust. A critical part of the planning was the development of a successful technique for torpedo attacks. The Nakajima B5N2 "Kate" torpedo bomber, when it launched its weapon, needed deep water. The torpedo would plunge to about a hundred feet, and then rise to attack depth as it ran toward the target. But Pearl Harbor was only, on average, forty-five feet deep. Technicians fitted large wooden fins to the torpedoes to assist the pilots in a new maneuver that had them fly close to the water, and then bank sharply as they dropped the "fish" into the water. Rather than dive deep, these torpedoes ran shallow and true into their targets.

Another modified weapon was a special 1,750-lb. bomb

made from a 16-inch naval shell. Taken from the ordnance stores for *Nagato* and *Mutsu*, these shells were reshaped and tapered with a lathe and fitted with fins to become aerial bombs that high-flying "Kates" would drop. Aichi D3A1 "Val" dive-bombers fitted with a 550-lb. bomb, and Mitsubishi A6M2 "Zero" fighters, armed with 20mm cannon and 7.7mm machine guns, would strafe American aircraft on the ground and take on any defending planes that made it into the air. Planning for the attack began in January 1941 and continued through November, while the aircrews trained in secrecy. The Kido Butai sailed from Hittokapu Bay in the Kuril Islands, north of Japan, on November 25, even as Japanese diplomats continued negotiations with their American counterparts.

Possessing a mere six-month supply of fuel for its armed forces, Japan felt it must conquer Southeast Asia, a move that would certainly trigger war with the United States, Great Britain, and Holland. As the Nazi conquest of Europe appeared to gain the upper hand, Hitler's military feats dazzled the Japanese, who signed the Tripartite Pact with Germany and Italy on September 27, 1940, wherein the three partners pledged to assist one another "with all political, economic and military means when one of the three Contracting Parties is attacked by a power at present not involved in the European War or in the Sino-Japanese conflict."

Japan was primed to go to war with the United States. Admiral Isoroku Yamamoto, the commander in chief of the Japanese Combined Fleet, assessed the U.S. Pacific Fleet as a formidable obstacle to Japanese victory in Asia. He visualized a surprise attack—in the best tradition of Bushido, feudal Japan's code of honor—as the fleet lay at anchor in Pearl Harbor. Indeed, strategists from America, England, and Japan had theorized about a Pearl Harbor raid over the years.

In 1925 British author Hector C. Bywater, naval correspondent for the *London Daily Telegraph,* had published *The Great Pacific War,* a description of a Japanese attack on the U.S. fleet in Pearl Harbor occurring simultaneously with assaults on Guam and the Philippines. The *New York Times Book Review* carried the review on its front page, headlined "If War Comes in the Pacific," at the same time Isoroku Yamamoto was serving as a naval attaché in Washington.

Seven years later, in 1932, American naval officials staged a military exercise in Hawaii, simulating an air raid that was to "determine the effectiveness of an air, surface and land attack against Hawaii and the adequacy of the air, surface, sub-surface and land defenses of Hawaii to repel such an attack."

The commander of the attack force, Admiral H. E. Yarnell, left his battleships and cruisers behind in California while he hastened to Hawaii with the carriers *Saratoga* and *Lexington* and their destroyers. Yarnell launched 152 planes a half hour before dawn, confusing the defenders, who expected a traditional naval attack. As planes swooped down in the early-morning darkness from Kahuku Point, they charged across Army airfields and the harbor as the defenders shook their heads in surprise, their planes still on the ground. Yarnell had won complete air supremacy in the mock battle. And yet the military conclusion stated: "It is doubtful if air attacks can be launched against Oahu in the face of strong defensive aviation without subjecting carriers to the danger of material damage and consequent great losses to the attacking air force."

In the spring of 1940 while Hitler advanced in Scandinavia and France, the Japanese air force conducted aerial torpedo exercises that were closely monitored by Yamamoto and Admiral Shigeru Fukudome, head of the first division of the naval general staff. In the midst of one maneuver, Yamamoto said softly to Fukudome, "I wonder if an aerial attack can't be made at Pearl Harbor."

Japan—and the United States—had tacitly assumed that a harbor attack was nearly impossible, due to the workings of conventional torpedoes, which required depths of one hundred feet and long horizontal distances in order to arm themselves. But for a year after Japan's development of the wooden-finned "fish" torpedoes, which featured altered arming devices that could arm and explode in short depths and short distances, the Japanese First Air Fleet trained with the new weapons in simulated conditions. The results were promising.

Without knowing for certain how intensely Japan was scrutinizing Hawaii, American military men were feeling increasingly vulnerable there. In the summer of 1940 the U.S. Pacific Fleet had begun to base operations in Hawaii, an unnerving strategy for the naval commanders, who knew that the small harbor with only one way out could be a death trap for the fleet.

Roosevelt removed as commander in chief of the U.S. Pacific Fleet (CinCUS) Admiral James O. Richardson after, as Navy legend has it, Richardson complained to naval superiors of the fleet's exposure. The President seemed not to consider the possibility of an assault on Pearl Harbor, a peculiar oversight, since even his trusted confidants speculated on that very idea. Joseph Clark Grew, the U.S. ambassador in Tokyo and a friend of Roosevelt's, had reported in January 1941 that the Japanese might "attempt a surprise attack on Pearl Harbor using all their military facilities."

Five months later, in June, the new fleet commander, Admiral Husband E. Kimmel, told Roosevelt the same unpalatable truth. "Pearl Harbor is a damned mousetrap," he said. "If they sank one ship in the entrance of the harbor they have the whole Fleet bottled up and it can't get out. The only place for the Fleet to be if the Japanese should attack is at sea, and not in port."

As the U.S. embargo tightened the noose around Japan's military activities, diplomatic efforts in Washington grew increasingly frustrated. In November Japanese emissaries made overtures that were refused by Roosevelt's cabinet, and a series of "war warning" telegrams went out from Washington to U.S. armed forces indicating an imminent attack, perhaps in the Philippines.

Attack was indeed imminent, even earlier than "the first of the New Year" that analysts in Washington predicted, but the target wasn't the Philippines. Following a strategy laid out months before, a strike force of thirty-one Japanese vessels, the Kido Butai, sailed easterly from Japan on November 25. Commanded by Admiral Chuichi Nagumo, the strike force included six aircraft carriers: *Akagi, Hiryu, Soryu, Kaga, Zuikaku,* and *Shokaku,* holding a full complement of dive-bombers and torpedo bombers. Admiral Nagumo chose to sail the northern route to Hawaii, knowing the rough winter storms would mask the ships' journey and also lessen the chance of encountering U.S. ships. A screening force of submarines traveled two hundred miles ahead of the fleet and picketed around the Hawaiian Islands. As Kido Butai steamed closer, Japanese submarines from Hawaii radioed back the positions and maneuvers of the U.S. Pacific Fleet, including maneuvers-at-sea off Lahaina Roads, Maui.

If all went as usual, agents on Oahu reported, the fleet would be in Pearl Harbor on the weekend of December 6 and 7, and many men would be granted shore leave. The fleet still operated on a peacetime basis and did not appear to be on the alert. The cluster of ships presented an appealing target: eight battleships, numerous destroyers and tenders, submarines and minesweepers. Unfortunately, the spies reported, the carriers *Lexington* and *Saratoga* were not in port and were presumed headed to Wake Island.

As Japanese tacticians refined the attack plans, American naval advisors to Roosevelt realized the Japanese strike force was missing, and discussed the possibility that Japan was preparing to attack the Philippines. Admiral Kimmel in Hawaii was uneasy over Kido Butai's disappearance and quizzed his officers for further intelligence. While Washington cryptographers raced to decode the "Magic" messages sent between Japanese diplomats and military strategists, naval officials decided not to inform Admiral Kimmel and his Army counterpart in Hawaii, Lieutenant General Walter C. Short, of those highly volatile communiqués.

However, as war seemed truly imminent and the diplomatic talks appeared stalled, the U.S. Chief of Naval Operations, Admiral Harold R. Stark, and his Army counterpart sent a so-called "war warning" telegram to General Douglas MacArthur in Manila:

Negotiations with the Japanese appear to be terminated to all practical purposes with only the barest possibilities that the Japanese government might come back and offer to continue period IF HOSTILITIES CANNOT, REPEAT CANNOT, BE AVOIDED THE UNITED STATES DESIRES THAT JAPAN COMMIT THE FIRST OVERT ACT PERIOD THIS POLICY SHOULD NOT, REPEAT NOT, BE CONSTRUED AS RESTRICTING YOU TO A COURSE OF ACTION THAT MIGHT JEOPARDIZE YOUR DEFENSE ...

A similar message was sent to Lieutenant General Walter C. Short, Commander of the Hawaiian Department, but it also ordered him to do nothing "to alarm civil population or disclose intent." He misunderstood and believed he should institute only a sabotage alert. He informed Washington of this action but apparently nobody there read his reply carefully: He was never told he had missed the import of the instructions.

On November 27 Stark sent a message to Rear Admiral Husband E. Kimmel in Hawaii and also to Admiral Thomas C. Hart, Commander of the Asiatic Fleet in the Philippines:

THIS DISPATCH IS TO BE CONSIDERED A WAR WARNING X NEGOTIATIONS WITH JAPAN LOOKING TOWARD STABILIZATION OF CONDITIONS IN THE PACIFIC HAVE CEASED AND AN AGGRESSIVE MOVE BY JAPAN IS EXPECTED IN THE NEXT FEW DAYS X THE NUMBER AND EQUIPMENT OF JAPANESE TROOPS AND THE ORGANIZATION OF NAVAL TASK FORCES INDICATES AN AMPHIBIOUS EXPEDITION AGAINST EITHER THE PHILIPPINES THAI OR KRA

PENINSULA OR POSSIBLY BORNEO X EXECUTE AN
APPROPRIATE DEFENSIVE DEPLOYMENT PREPARA-
TORY TO CARRYING OUT THE TASKS ASSIGNED IN
WPL [WAR PLAN] 46 X . . .

Out at sea around the Hawaiian Islands, Kimmel was
apprehensive, yet it appeared the attack would happen farther west than Hawaii. He planned to bring the fleet into
Pearl Harbor as usual for the December 6–7 weekend.

On December 2 in Tokyo, Rear Admiral Matome Ugaki
confirmed that the U.S. fleet was scheduled to be in port
at Pearl Harbor. Diplomacy with Washington was ended,
and war was to begin. He dispatched a short telegram to
the Japanese Combined Fleet in the vast reaches of the
Pacific Ocean that simply said, "Climb Mt. Niitaka, 1208."

Kido Butai had received its orders. The telegram was the
go-ahead Admiral Nagumo was waiting for: Attack Pearl
Harbor on December 8, Tokyo time.

In Hawaii it would be December 7.

CHAPTER 6

ATTACK! THE VIEW FROM BELOWDECKS

In the early dawn on December 7 as the rosy sky paled to a soft tropical glow, the Japanese strike force lay 230 miles north of Hawaii. At 6:00 A.M., after a reconnaissance flight by seaplane scouts, the carriers *Akagi, Hiryu, Soryu, Kaga, Zuikaku,* and *Shokaku* swung into the wind and launched the first wave of 183 planes, their wings displaying the blood-red symbol of the Rising Sun. Flocked in deadly formation were dive-bombers, Zero fighters, and the Nakajima B5 N2s called "Kates" that served as torpedo bombers in the first part of the mission. By 6:20 they had massed together in the sky and headed south. It would take ninety minutes to reach Pearl Harbor.

Just then in Hawaii the destroyer USS *Ward* sighted a submarine a short distance outside the entrance to Pearl Harbor. The ship fired and depth-charged the submarine, and sank it within the defensive sea area. It took more than an hour of bureaucratic wrangling to get a report of the sinking over to Fleet Admiral Husband Kimmel.

Half an hour later, at 7:02, two Army radar operators at Opana station on Oahu's north shore registered a large formation of planes on the radar screens. They checked and rechecked the equipment, then radioed the Fort Shafter watch officer. Remembering that the American carrier *En-*

terprise was due to arrive that day with a contingent of planes, and noting also that B-17s were expected from California, the watch relaxed.

At 7:15, while *Arizona* band members still slept after their Saturday night second-place victory, a second wave of 170 Japanese planes rose off the aircraft carriers far out in the ocean, bringing the total planes in the air to 353. As the sky lightened over the Pacific, more Nakajima Kates flew with Mitsubishi AGV12 Reissen Zero fighters and Aichi D3A1 Val dive-bombers. They would mingle with the first wave so precisely that Pearl Harbor sailors couldn't tell where one stopped and the next began.

By 7:57 A.M. the skies were dark over Oahu and the planes sped in from the mountains as thick as locusts, so thick they blocked out the sun. The wave of torpedo bombers split into two attacking groups and approached Battleship Row, launching their "fish" just before the battleships prepared for colors. Splashing into the water, the torpedoes slammed into the sides of several ships. Five torpedoes exploded into the *Oklahoma*, and seven ripped into the *West Virginia*. The *California* took two torpedoes, and another two hit and capsized the *Utah*. The cruisers *Raleigh* and *Helena* and the battleship *Nevada* were also hit.

At 8:05, ten groups of high-altitude bombers approached from the south, dropping their 1,760-lb. bombs in formation, as dive-bombers and fighters swooped in, strafing and bombing a fleet engulfed in fire and smoke. Then a huge shock wave shook the aircraft overhead and the harbor below, as a pillar of smoke and fire climbed into the sky and pieces of debris—and bodies—rained over Battleship Row and Ford Island. The USS *Arizona* had exploded.

For *Arizona* sailors, December 7 on Battleship Row had

started out like most other Sundays, with men sleeping late, others preparing for colors or finishing breakfast, and off-duty sailors preparing to spend time ashore.

Jim Lawson, happy as a lark to be back in port, had finished breakfast that idyllic Sunday morning on board the *Arizona* and walked over to the executive officer's office just inside the main deck hatchway to buy a newspaper. He continued on three spaces forward to his deck division's quarters and settled in with a fresh cup of coffee to read the paper. He was chuckling over *Flash Gordon* when he heard a thump.

For a moment he didn't think much of it, because on Friday and Saturday the Army explosives men had been blasting over at Merry Point to put in a new ferry slip. But Lawson wondered why anyone would be working on a Sunday morning before church.

"After a couple more of these whumps," he said, "I looked out the porthole just in time to see the airplane drop a torpedo into the battleship ahead of us. I think it was the *California*. I could see the red meatballs on his wings."

Just then the general quarters alarm went off. Over the loudspeaker the boatswain shouted: "This is no drill. This is no drill. General quarters. All hands. General quarters. We're under attack. This is no drill."

"The newspaper went one way, the coffee went the other and I went out the hatch," Lawson said. Trained to go to his battle station, he raced for turret 4. When he got there he dropped to his hands and knees to crawl through the hatch, but it was dogged down, locked from the inside with the hatch dogs fastened tight. For a moment he had nowhere to go.

He looked up at the continual rush of planes strafing the decks and he swallowed hard. Fighting down his fear, he wondered how else he might help, since he couldn't get inside to his turret position. He thought the *Arizona* might want to get under way and go to sea, but he knew there was a major obstacle: It was still tied up to the repair ship *Vestal*. "I realized there was no way the *Arizona* could get under way with the *Vestal* there," he recalled.

He doesn't remember grabbing the fire ax off the turret 3 bulkhead, but wielding the tool he raced to each of the mooring bitts twenty yards apart, and sliced through the giant hawser ropes as if they were butter. "To this day I do not know how, I don't even remember getting the ax, but I cut the *Vestal* loose. In a month of Sundays you couldn't break those hawsers with the blow of an ax, but I did it. It took me fifteen seconds."

The freed *Vestal* quickly backed off and got under way, but battleships take hours to build enough power to sail, so the *Arizona* remained in place and continued to take punishing blows from dive-bombers and torpedo planes. Casting off the *Vestal*'s mooring lines, Lawson raced back down the ladder near the executive office and ran to the third deck to get aft of the turret. He met up with some sailors trying to put loading trays together for the turret guns.

"They were so flustered, and they were scared," he said simply. "Naturally. They were trying to muscle this aluminum tray, but they were doing it backwards. So I took it from this one guy who was trying to do it, turned it around and slapped it together, and kept on going down into the turret."

He got only as far as the turret's lower handling room when he was thrown to his knees. One of the Aichi dive bombers had just hit the *Arizona*'s teakwood deck with an armor-piercing bomb that burrowed into the forward magazine between turrets 1 and 2. As a million pounds of ammunition blew skyward, the ship bolted on its anchor lines and broke in the center. Men on deck were blown into the water, and Admiral Kidd and Captain Van Valkenburgh on the ship's bridge vaporized. The entire ship's band was concussed to death belowdecks, as were the firemen, the storekeepers, and anyone whose battle station was on the forward section of the ship.

"As far back as we were from the explosion, it knocked us down. The lights went out, and the emergency light came on in about ten seconds. Inside the lower handling room of the turret we had four battle lanterns, battery-operated electric lanterns. We put those on. As soon as I got up I realized we'd been hit real bad, but I figured we'd get under way."

When the power failed all communication ceased, and men belowdecks had no idea what was happening topside. Knowing the 14-inch battery guns of the turret were no good in a locked harbor, Lawson didn't know what the gunners could do, but he went up the ladders inside the turret to take his seat in the gun spaces.

He peered out the little periscope and saw a Philippine messboy run by the turret. "I'm not sure, but I think I saw him shot. There was a sea of bullets kicking the wooden deck, so he probably got strafed."

The ship shuddered with repeated bombs, but the men in the turret sat in silence, isolated by massive steel-plated walls from the hellfire outside. Too frightened to leave, they felt somewhat protected in the turret, until they learned of a greater threat than bullets and fire: The *Arizona* was sinking.

"It was just a few minutes when the people down in the lower handling room, where the powder magazines were, started yelling, 'We're hitting water and it's coming pretty fast.' We didn't have any power or any communications whatsoever with the rest of the ship, so we had no idea what condition she was in. The guys there in the lower handling room kept getting water, water up to their knees, water up to their waist. Pretty soon it was up to their chins."

Unable to leave their battle stations, the men in the lower handling room would drown if they remained where they were. The gunners in the turret realized there would be no firing that day from the big guns anyway, and they pleaded with the division officer to release the men. He let them come up to the upper level of the turret, and everyone gathered in the gun positions in the hollowed-out space under the gun barrels.

Water continued to rise. Submerging the lower handling room, it buried the gunners' living quarters and crept up to the next deck. The level above held the batteries, the backup power for the turret in case electricity failed. The battery bank was located just below the shell deck and the first level of the turret, the gunhouse that rotated to train the guns on target. As the men waited in the turret, the seawater below swirled over the wet-cell batteries, releasing a cloud of chlorine gas that filled the shell deck where the bullets were stored. Soon the turret room reeked with lethal fumes.

Water was rising fast, but the gas was deadlier. "The fumes were so bad I was sitting there in the pointer's chair with a T-shirt over my nose saying, what do we do next?" Lawson said. "The division officer was absolutely worthless—he didn't know what to do either. We had no communications with the bridge, we couldn't ask anybody what was going on. We were just sitting there in limbo. We knew we'd been hit bad."

When the men of turret 4 announced they were leaving, the division officer hastily agreed. One by one the men dropped out of the overhang onto the deck. They emerged into a fiery nightmare where they could see that the ship was destroyed. "Then and only then could we see that she was sitting in the water, broken right in half," Lawson said. "And she was on fire past that second mast, the tripod mast. The fire was licking the forward wall to the barbette of turret 3, and those guys were dropping through the fire to get to the deck."

The fire hadn't yet reached back to turret 4. Running downhill on the sloping deck toward the ship's center, the gunners raced for life rafts hung around the turret 3 barbette. Shoving rafts into the water right below the turret, sailors leapt down to them. Normally it was at least fifteen feet from the main deck down to the water, but the Arizona had already settled, and the jump was only four feet. Flames surrounded the ship.

"She was afire all the way back to Fox 8, the big concrete quay that we were tied up to. Guys were screaming and yelling who got trapped on Fox 8. I don't know how many people were trapped out there, but they couldn't get off and nobody could get to them," Lawson said grimly.

As the men waiting on the quay tried to hide from the relentless planes still strafing the battleships, Lawson and his mates noticed the waters were thick with a layer of oil that burned in snapping gusts. "It was deep and there was an awful lot of it," he recalled. "Those rafts immediately started drifting and floating into the burning oil, which was right there even with turret 3. So those were quickly abandoned. I saw what was happening, and I was still trying to get the last one into the water with another couple of guys. We cut them down, threw them in the water, and jumped in. The two or three guys that actually got on one were going right into the fire, so they had to get off immediately The currents were taking them right into the fire."

He noted that the admiral's barge was still in place on the boat deck, and the crew was making ready to launch it. Just then the senior surviving officer on board appeared, First Lt. Samuel Fuqua. "He was the damage control officer, and where he came from I haven't any idea. He just appeared from nowhere, like Jesus Christ. All of a sudden he was there. He appeared right beside me between turrets 3 and 4. And he wanted to see how we were doing. I think he gave the order to abandon the life rafts, 'cause it was obvious they were going into the fire."

As the fire on the burning decks moved closer, a Reserve sailor clung to Lawson, who remembered that the little man seemed lost. He'd come out of the turret from the lower handling room and, patting Lawson's arm, he said in a terrified voice, "Guns, I can't swim."

Lawson couldn't swim very well either, and the flaming waters were a formidable barrier between the sailors on the *Arizona* and the relative safety of Ford Island. "Well, we gotta go," Lawson said, and shoved him over the side. Lawson jumped in after him and held him up in the water.

"I was the second to last man off the ship. Fuqua was the last guy. He went to the boat boom and got down into the barge. I was trying to take this scared sailor in what I could muster as some kind of a swimmer's carry. I was making no progress, just treading water with him, and the breeze and the current were taking us into the fire. I went ahead and let him go," he said sadly.

But in a dramatic moment Fuqua got the barge running, picked up Lawson, and handed him a T-shirt. Lawson tied it to his ankle and handed the other end to the frightened sailor in the water, who was towed behind the boat by the T-shirt. As the barge made its way through the smoke-filled harbor to Ford Island a quarter-mile away, Fuqua stopped to pick up other desperate swimmers while planes strafed the water.

He landed with a full boatload. Lawson stepped onto the dock and realized he was coated with oil, his skin so black it would take two or three months of hard scrubbing to get it white again.

Onshore a terrible specter approached the new arrivals. "There was a guy standing on the dock, how he got there I don't know. He looked like he just got off the grill. He was burned to a crisp. The poor guy, what kept him alive I don't know. He kept asking for help and no one could help. What could you do?"

Marines herded the sailors to one end of the island, where a storage area and a tunnel made a shelter. Lawson and his mates waited out the raid in the tunnel, listening to bombs drop all around.

At ten minutes to eight John Rampley glanced out a porthole of the *Arizona* and saw the sun lifting in the sky over the mountains of Oahu. In the holiday mood of Sunday morning, he was sitting around after breakfast with the men in gun turret No. 3 waiting for the call to church. It never came.

What did come was a messenger, "a young kid from our deck division, who came running down into the turret," Rampley recounted his tale many years later. "He told us that planes were attacking the drydock area a little beyond where we were. But the kid was a clown, made for exaggerating, so we passed it off. No one believed him. Then we heard the explosions."

The turret gunners heard blow after blow of falling

bombs. Seconds later they heard the whine of bullets peppering the decks of their ship. Shortly after, the ship's PA system blatted out a hurried call to general quarters, followed by words no *Arizona* sailor had ever heard before: "This is no drill, this is no drill." Bombs stunned the ship as men ran for their battle stations. Japanese airmen strafed the decks with deadly aim.

Gunner's mate Rampley raced to his turret position, but since the turret guns were for long-range firing, all he could do was wait with his shipmates for the chaos to stop. "There were a lot of explosions, and they were causing rivets to pop out of the metal. Bolts were flying through the air."

Rampley, the control telephone talker, went to his battle position and sat beside the division officer, James D. Miller, who was in charge of the turret. His friend George Grim, a gunner's mate, waited there, too, in the enclosed, dank room of the turret. He put on his headphones and prepared to talk to the fire control director on the ship's bridge. He was shocked to find there was total silence from that command post—no one was alive there. "I was scared to death. There were no communications at all," he said. "I sat with headphones and communicated with other positions in No. 3 turret."

The ship bucked under the rain of bombs, but ten or fifteen minutes after the ordeal started they felt a tremendous shudder. Although they didn't know it then, a bomb had torn through the Arizona's deck and found its way to the stored munitions. It was the death blow to the forward magazines. "I wasn't sure exactly when the main blast hit, but we knew something bad had happened up forward," Rampley said.

The sailors were panic-stricken, so frightened and confused they didn't know what to do next. "We were waiting. There were a lot of explosions. The worst part was you couldn't see anything. You could hear and feel the explosions. You didn't know what was going on. There was no ammo for those guns, but they were long-range anyway."

They waited, for hours it seemed. "We weren't off the ship till maybe eleven o'clock. It was a world of confusion, probably from the explosion that took place on the forward part. There was no communication at all. It wrecked the bridge."

Finally division officer Miller released them from their stations and ordered them out on deck. After the relative safety of the turret, the scene on the open decks seemed like madness to Rampley.

"When I came out of the turret on deck, I couldn't believe the scene. The decks were on fire and covered in oil. I remember as I got to the bottom of the ladder I didn't want to step into that oil. I waited there till somebody was stepping on my hand."

He looked forward and aft. His turret, No. 3, was the only one that appeared intact. No. 4 had taken a direct hit from a bomb that almost melted it. Planes flashed by, still bombing and strafing the row of battleships, when Rampley and his turret mates got the order to go to Ford Island, 125 yards away. "Part of the water was on fire. The boats were too slow for me, so I started swimming. In the water I saw a Texan from the 4th division. He comes swimming by me like I was standing still, passed me and said, 'How you doin', kid?' "

Once Rampley got to Ford Island, Ensign Henry D. Davison of his division took charge. Fate played a hand in the next few minutes. "Planes were still strafing," Rampley recalled. "Ensign Davison, a large man, gathered up a whole bunch of us guys on Ford Island, and we headed into one of these buildings. It must have been a group fifteen or twenty of us. I don't know what it was, but something about the whole situation bothered the ensign. We got inside, and then he said, 'No, I think we should be outside.' We left that building, and just then a bomb went through it and blew it to smithereens."

After that close call, Davison took his men to the south end of the island, where some of the officers had quarters. "I recall something that later that turned out to be one of the funny things," Rampley said. "We were shivering from shock, and one of the officer's wives gave us some clothing and blankets. This one fellow—John Bruce from Kentucky, a little short bowlegged guy in our turret—she gave him a formal captain's coat with the captain's bars, and all these different guys were saluting him because he looked like a four-star."

Soon after, Marines herded Rampley's group into boats and took them across the water to base headquarters, where hundreds of orphaned sailors looked toward the harbor at the wrecked battleships and wondered where they'd sleep that night.

Though he was just a gunner's mate, twenty-one-year-old Jim Burcham was belowdecks in the USS *Arizona*'s wardroom—"officers' country"—doing chores on that bright Sunday morning, when suddenly he realized that something was horribly wrong.

"I saw a deck messenger running down the steps to the captain's quarters," Burcham recalled, looking back at images that were stamped forever on his memory. "He ignored the Marine sentry and just started banging on the door. You don't do that," he said with wonderment in his voice. "You just don't ignore the sentry."

But there was reason to break the rules that day, as Burcham was about to learn. "The captain came running out and went up on deck. I went topside too, and I could see smoke on the island." Then he looked up and saw wave after wave of death-dealing aircraft bearing down on the *Arizona* and all the other vessels in the harbor. Only then did he realize that his ship and his country were under full military attack by the forces of Japan.

The general alarm sounded on the *Arizona*, and all crew members began scrambling to get to their battle stations. Burcham's post was at gun turret No. 3, toward the rear of the ship. He decided to make his way there belowdecks in order to avoid the gunfire above. His pathway almost became a black tomb for him and the fellow sailors scurrying along with him.

"I was moving toward my station," Burcham said. "We were way down in the bowels of the ship. But just then they started hitting us, and all the lights went out. We were in a passageway, and the armored hatch was sprung and closed. We couldn't get through. We banged on the walls, and the men in the handling room heard us and let us in."

The handling room, so called because the men could pass ammunition hand-to-hand up to the gun above for firing, was an open channel to the upper deck, with ladders for quick climbing. "The fresh air was a relief," Burcham recalled. But no sooner had he reached his battle post on the big gun battery when the Japanese bomb detonated the *Arizona*'s munitions, in one of the most awesome explosions ever to send a ship to its doom.

"We were topside at the gun when the main explosion went off," Burcham said. "I don't know many thousands of pounds that gun turret weighed, but the blast just lifted that turret up—and then set it down."

Burcham did not know it at the time, but the explosion had killed most of his shipmates instantly. What he did realize amid the inferno surrounding him was that his ship was mortally wounded and sinking fast. Terribly injured men lay screaming on all sides of him, but every time he tried to go to their aid, strafing and bombing runs would make him run for cover.

"I'd dash back to the turret whenever a plane would strafe the ship," Burcham said, the anger rising in his voice. "I remember I was madder'n hell. There were dive-bombers and strafers. I bet this one plane wasn't fifty feet high. I don't think it was clear of our tripod mast, and that's seventy-five to one hundred feet. You could see their faces. It looked like they were laughing."

By this time, Burcham remembered bitterly, the once-proud flagship's beautiful teakwood decks, which he and his fellow swabbies had often polished with stones for hours on end, "looked like a boneyard," because of the pieces of bodies strewn about. "Everything was in pieces," he added darkly.

The order to abandon ship was given, and somehow Burcham made his way to nearby Ford Island. There for the next twenty-four hours he and the terrified men around him dug in to try to fend off what they imagined was a continuing attack by the Japanese. "We all thought we were being invaded," he said. "I stayed there the balance of that day and night manning a machine gun."

At some point Burcham, who had miraculously escaped injury, looked down at himself and discovered that he was wearing only socks and shorts—he didn't even have on his shoes. "We had tropical shorts for uniforms then," he explained. "I had taken off my undershirt to bandage a wounded man. It didn't help."

At 7:55 in the morning, John Anderson was one of the few men up and about on the sleeping ship. His duty shift had begun early Sunday morning, and when the battle alarms went off, he fled to his battle station as gun captain of the No. 4 turret, where the pointers and trainers sat in semi-darkness waiting for orders.

Anderson's thoughts raced to his twin brother, Delbert, whose post was on the No. 3 turret, the next-forward gun, but the two brothers had no contact as bombs and bullets rained down from above. As gun captain on turret 4, he encouraged all gunners to stick it out, but though they valiantly manned their positions, they never got the chance to fire a shot. Yet till the call came to abandon ship, "every man there stayed as long as he could," Anderson said proudly.

Minutes after the attack began, his battle post was destroyed. "I was standing on gun turret No. 4," he said, "when I saw a bomb hit the side of it. It scooped out the side of the turret. It went right past me, a big mound of molten steel. I got my people out and went to look for my brother."

But he never made it to No. 3, for the way was barred by twisted wreckage, flaming debris, and wounded, dead, and dying men. As he made his way down a ladder, Anderson looked through the rungs and saw a friend named James Green, who was on fire. He reached out for Green and caught him by the hand. At just that moment the fatal bomb slipped through the forward decks and struck the ammunition stored in the magazine. The huge explosion ripped its massive crater through the heart of the *Arizona* and sent concussion waves through the six-hundred-foot length of the ship.

"When the blast went off, we were out for a minute," Anderson remembered. "When I woke up, I still had Green by the hand." He saved the life of his friend, but there was nothing anyone could do for the *Arizona*. As the battleship listed precipitously into the tropical harbor, Anderson recalled, "I could see we were in terrible trouble."

At that point he abandoned the search for his brother. Only later would he learn that Delbert had died while trying to unjam an antiaircraft gun mounted on the No. 3 turret. Seeking an officer to tell him what to do next, Anderson stumbled over the body of his ensign. "He was dead on deck, his back split open like a watermelon." In the maze of smoke and flames he encountered Lt. Cmdr. Samuel Fuqua, who was by then the senior officer on board. Fuqua told everyone to abandon ship.

"By now the ship had settled some in the water," Anderson said. "It was about fifteen feet down to the water from the deck. We were passing down the wounded hand-over-hand into the lifeboats as fast as we could. We weren't any too gentle, as you can imagine."

Ford Island was the nearest land, so the lifeboats all headed there. Once on dry ground, Anderson felt crazed by the sight of row upon row of wounded men. Desperate to help out, he cast around for something to do to aid his shipmates back on the sinking *Arizona*.

"I looked around and saw a boat floating in the water," he said. "I saw a kid named Rose, Chester Clay Rose from Kentucky, and I said, 'Hey, Rose, are you game?' He was a nice-looking kid with curly brown hair. He said yes, so we dived in, got in the lifeboat, and went back to the ship."

As their boat approached the *Arizona,* by now mostly underwater, Anderson saw some of the crew members crawling out along the big lifting cranes that stretched out over the water from the *Arizona*'s deck. Desperate to elude the flaming oil that made the waters surrounding the downed battleship a pool of fire, some of the men remained for torturous minutes on the crane, then dropped off into the smoke and flames and madly swam away, some of them burning. Anderson and Rose couldn't get in close enough to reach them. Searching the oil-slicked burning waters for swimmers farther out where the fire's heat was less intense, the two-man rescue squad did not succeed in saving any of their mates. As they pulled up close to the *Arizona,* Anderson remembers, "all we found was parts."

As the boat slid through the taffeta-stained water, he came on a bizarre sight. The *Arizona*'s cook, a big, burly man who weighed more than 250 pounds, was dead and floating in the water, impaled with one of his cutting knives. "I don't know how he got blown out of the galley to the outside. He was dead, with a kitchen knife stuck in him from the force of the explosion."

Despairing of rescuing any of the men they had served with, Anderson and Rose steered the small boat through the death-filled harbor, pulling aboard anyone who was still alive. They picked up men from other battleships, until finally they could hold no more, and turned back toward Ford Island with their precious cargo. They never made it.

"We moved on into the middle of the stream, got hit by a shell, and lost everybody," Anderson mourned. "I even lost Rose. I was the only survivor."

CHAPTER 7

ATTACK! THE VIEW TOPSIDE

William Goshen had awakened heavily. After only four hours of sleep, he had to shake himself and get some coffee before he could face the day. He'd decided to spend his liberty day ashore. Finishing breakfast by 7:30, he was cleaning up and preparing to go ashore when he heard some unexpected noise.

"I heard BANG! BANG! It sounded like a bomb being dropped," he said. "But I didn't think much of it because we were kind of used to it, because once in a while the Air Force would come by and drop little bombs with little detonators in them. They'd pop. It was a sound like a .45 popping off, or like a little bag of flour hitting the superstructure deck. So we didn't think much about it at first."

The noise grew louder, and Goshen ran up to the boat deck. He saw airplanes so thick they blocked out the sun. "You could see them coming by then, with the Rising Sun on the wings. They were maybe one hundred feet up, just enough to clear the superstructure of the ships."

At that moment the general alarm sounded. He rushed to his battle station at the No. 3 5-inch gun, where he was a pointer, moving the gun in up-and-down line at targets. But today he was helpless, finding no other mates at his station and no ammunition for the guns.

"I got my headphones and put them on," he recalled, "but I couldn't unlock the ammunition hoist because I didn't have the key, the boatswain's mate had it. And I was the only one on the gun at the time of the raid. Maybe some of them didn't make it to battle stations because they were already dead by the time general quarters sounded. 'Cause we'd already been hit by then."

Terrified by the strafing planes, he decided to move to a less vulnerable spot, and went around and stood by a hatch back up against a locker. As luck would have it, his choice of the hatch saved his life, for otherwise he would have hidden up in the protected spot by the boat boom, the area that was devastated by the explosion a few minutes later.

"The boat boom was between the No. 1 and No. 3 5-inch guns, about halfway between them, sticking out the starboard side. The boats were all swung towards forward. I'm lucky they were that way—if they'd been turned the other way I'd have hid on the boat and that would have been the end of me."

Feeling somewhat protected by the hatch with the locker at his back, he looked over toward Ford Island and thought he'd be safer there. The next thing he knew he was in the water.

"The only way I could figure it out was that I was blown off," he said. The force of the *Arizona* blowing apart had picked him up and thrown him into the water, as it did with most of the surviving sailors. The death blow had penetrated at the barbette's base on No. 2 turret, and Goshen's station was only a few yards from that fatal spot. "All that was between me and that bomb was two canvas sheets. Evidently it burnt the canvas off and carried right on into the compartment where I was at, and the concussion happening inside blew me out."

He came to and was swimming for his life, struggling to reach the surface. Eluding bullets that followed him through the water from planes that swarmed like hornets, he thrashed through the smoke and flames and reached Ford Island.

"I looked up at the ship, and I knew there was no need going back there," he said in a choked voice. "I looked up at the boats, and they were all on fire. The *Arizona* was on fire. I heard the buzzing of planes, the cracking of cannons, the machine guns they were strafing with."

Even on Ford the sailors weren't safe. Wounded men and Marine guards alike raced for cover in the nightmare raid. Goshen got up to the beach with two other men and started running. It was only then that he realized he'd been hurt in the *Arizona*'s explosion.

"One guy was running right alongside of me—I don't remember his name, but I told him, don't leave me 'cause my eyes are closed and I can't see very good. He took hold of my arm and we went to an air raid shelter. Who the guy was I don't know, or if he was from my ship or some other ship."

Goshen's body had been 70 percent flash-burned on the *Arizona*. Reaching the air raid shelter, the sailors sat their burned mate down against a wall and wrapped him in a blanket. "Somebody came by with a bottle of vinegar and poured it over my head. Evidently that killed a lot of the fire." The seemingly brutal treatment didn't phase him. "When you're in shock, nothing hurts," he said simply.

After spending about forty-five minutes in the air raid shelter, someone told Goshen he was being moved to the dispensary on the other side of Ford Island. He was helped into a station wagon that set off for the dispensary. Just as the driver started off, planes began bombing both sides of the island. The car, located in between the two zones, escaped injury while buildings collapsed all around. Arriving at the dispensary, Goshen found an empty bed and crawled into it.

Jim Foster, the shy Texan, was an antiaircraft gunner whose duty station was the starboard boat deck's antiaircraft gun. He was off duty amidships at 7:55 when the trouble started.

"I was sitting in the head, and I looked out and saw these men coming down off the fo'c'sle. They seemed like they were concerned. They didn't say a word, they were just pouring down the hatch. Somebody said something on the loudspeaker but I didn't hear it."

Realizing it was an emergency of some kind, Foster dashed out to a deck ladder to go up to his battle station, but the crush of men pouring down the ladder created a stream he could hardly buck. Firemen and other sailors stationed belowdecks were headed for their own stations, and Foster thought for a few minutes he'd never get topside.

"I like to never got off that ladder with those men coming down," he said. "I just had to fight to get up that ladder— they walked on me, fell on me. All those guys while I was going up. I finally got up. Then I had to run about halfway of the ship to the galley deck and I went on to the gun."

Foster's antiaircraft gun was located on the starboard side of the boat deck, and he was the first man to arrive. Two others followed close behind. Although sixteen men were assigned to that gun station, the rest never made it. Right after he got to the gun, Admiral Kidd and Captain Van Valkenburgh came running by the mainmast on their way to the bridge, the ship's command center. The two officers were dressed in full uniform.

Seeing Foster alone on the gun, Admiral Kidd stopped for just a moment to speak to the young sailor. Foster believes he was the last person, other than the captain, to speak to Kidd. "He said, 'Man your battle station, son,' and he hit me on the shoulder. I think he called me son. I don't know why," Foster said with tears many years later. "That was before McCarron got there. Man your battle station—one man on a sixteen-man gun!"

Kidd and Van Valkenburgh realized the seriousness of the attack. "Kidd knew what was going on, I think you could see from his actions," Foster said. As the officers ran on toward the bridge, he turned his attention to the gun.

"Only three of us got there, Ross Lightfoot and John McCarron and me. I don't know much about what went on in the rest of the ship. My part of the ship was only three men. We were the only guys I saw. Except for the admiral and the captain, but I didn't see them after they ran by. They disappeared."

Foster and his two mates were exposed to merciless strafing as they stood around the gun on the boat deck. Ammunition was still locked up, and they felt helpless. Then Lightfoot got a shell. "Lightfoot, I don't know where he got this shell, but he came running up there. McCarron was the gun captain, he told him to put it in the gun. McCarron rammed it in, he had to push it in with his hand. Everything was cut off. Since I was the pointer, I pulled the trigger but it wouldn't fire. I tried to kick it out, but it wouldn't fire," Foster said angrily.

While he struggled with his gun, some of his shipmates on other battle stations managed to fire a few of the 50-

caliber antiaircraft guns. But then, only minutes after the captain and admiral raced to the bridge, the Arizona took a bomb.

"I guess it was five minutes," Foster said. "I don't know for sure. My sense of time was off. It was immediately after, but it could have been three minutes or three years." All he knew was that he was trying to pull the trigger one moment, and the next he was almost knocked out.

"We were blown off the gun. We went over the gunshield and landed on our hats over there. I was on the bottom of the admiral's boat. After we all three got up and looked at each other, we got off the ship." The trio didn't see each other again after the explosion. Lightfoot died two weeks later from his injuries; McCarron survived.

The Arizona's forward magazine had blown sky high. Foster's nose was broken and his legs and feet were badly burned. He looked up at the bridge where Kidd and Van Valkenburgh had been standing and it was aflame. "It was like pouring molten metal in there. It must have been the powder coming up out of the stack on the bridge. They died in that fire," he said sadly.

Explosives were going off in a steady rhythm. Foster walked over to the lifeline. Catching hold of the boat rack that held small boats, he swung down onto the galley deck below, seeking a safe haven. Instead he found trapped and dying men and lethal fumes in the air.

"I stuck my head in and it was full of gas or something. I couldn't breathe. I couldn't see anybody," he recalled, "but I heard them hollering all down below. They were screaming and pounding. Cursing. And the noise of bombs was deafening. Bang! Bang! Boom! Bang! The ship would just jerk and toss every time a bomb hit."

He headed for the water, jumping in so hard he was nearly knocked out. "It seemed like it was slow motion when I hit that water. I went down," he remembered. Dressed in mess shorts and a skivvy shirt, he felt the sea-water sear his already charred legs. He was barefooted, his feet burned so badly it would be months before he could wear shoes.

"When I came up I was gagging. When I come up I was really busting water trying to get away from that thing 'fore it blew up. I wasn't a very good swimmer, but I really busted water for about ten foot and realized I was give out. I was give plum out. I used my last strength to get over on my back and paddled the rest of the way, but I had a heck of a time getting over to the island. The planes were still coming in, and they were strafing all the men in the water," he said.

"That's the first time I saw the planes, when I got on my back. They strafed right close to me. And that's the first other men I saw. When I got in the water I saw some men there on the quay you tie a ship up to. They were just hanging to that thing, and I was struggling to get to Ford Island, and they were down the end of the ship on the thing. I headed for Ford Island and I was just paddling, taking it easy and resting a bit. I heard a lot of guys in the water. One guy come by me and was staring straight ahead and he asked me if I was fine. He asked me if I needed some help. I knew him, but I can't remember his name. He was an *Arizona* man."

The swimmer was Jim Lawson, a fellow Texan, but Foster wouldn't know it until forty years had passed.

Although rescue boats plied the oil-filled waters, Foster

never saw one. It seemed like forever before he reached the edge of Ford Island and clutched the pipeline coming through on the beach. He just barely got to it and hung on for dear life, along with two or three other desperate sailors pressed onto it.

Vernon Olsen had a bird's-eye view of the attack from his battle station. A seaman 1st class in the 6th division, he manned the 50-caliber machine gun in the crow's nest, located on the *Arizona*'s after mast.

He'd started that day messcooking, getting up at 6:00 to set tables in the same compartments where sailors had slept, their cots now folded back against the walls. Then he made interminable journeys to the mess hall to get the food trays and set them out for the hungry men who were ready for breakfast at 6:30. When breakfast ended at 7:30 he folded up all the tables and put them back, then returned to his quarters for a half hour before the 8 o'clock muster for general quarters.

Olsen's compartment was way up on the forward deck where the big No. 1 turret guns engulfed both sides of the ship from starboard to port. He relaxed for a few minutes before quarters, where the officer of the deck would call out a roll to make sure all sailors were on board and give the schedule for the day. General quarters happened every day aboard ship, and Sunday was no different.

"I was just getting ready to go to quarters and the attack started," Olsen said. "We looked outside and saw the planes going by. Then they rang the general alarm. I went up to the crow's nest on the after mast. They were strafing and bombing, but it don't take you long," he said in an ironic understatement. "You crawled up the ladders as fast as you could. I was scared. Everybody was scared. Anybody said they weren't scared were crazy."

The crow's nest, on the very top of the *Arizona,* afforded a great view of the attack. The machine gun nest where Olsen sat was situated even higher than the sky lookout for observing planes, and he could see clearly the *Arizona*'s decks and gun turrets.

Despite the overwhelming fear they all felt, the men manned their battle stations up on the mast and tried to defend their ship. Olsen was proud of them. "Everyone's trained to function automatically—that's what all the battle practice was for. You were almost brainwashed, but it works and you react automatically to the situation."

Like the others, Olsen got into position behind one of the four 50-caliber machine guns. Unfortunately he couldn't fire.

"The ammunition was stored below the platform, but the guy with the key never got there," he said, echoing the words of other *Arizona* gunners. The 50-caliber guns were water-cooled, and they didn't have any hoses hooked up. "When we went out for battle practice," Olsen explained, "they'd pour water in them, just enough to fire so many rounds of ammunition. If you didn't have water in them, the barrels would swell up and burst. If they're not water-cooled they explode from being too hot. We still couldn't have fired them, because the fellow that had the keys to the ammunition [ready locker] never made it up there anyway."

No hoses and no ammunition made Olsen and his mates helpless in the attack, as they watched plane after plane roar down Battleship Row and attack the trapped vessels. It seemed the *Arizona* was a heavily bombed target.

"We just stood there and watched them fly right between the masts and bomb us," Olsen said bitterly. "You could see their faces. You could see them grinning when they were firing at us. They flew right between the two masts. Our machine gun nest must have been two hundred, three hundred feet high, so we had a bird's-eye view of it. We could see them bombing Ford Island. We felt pretty vulnerable."

Olsen watched the scene of carnage below. At some point the senior officials realized the *Arizona* could not get under way, and they announced an order: abandon ship. "You weren't allowed to leave your battle station before they give the word to abandon ship—that would really be something. They had the speakers, and we heard it and came down. I guess I was up there fifteen or twenty minutes."

It all happened fast. As he climbed down the mast from the crow's nest Olsen saw torpedo bombers flying in low between the masts, dropping the "fish" they spewed all over the harbor. He didn't know when the massive explosion ripped the *Arizona* in two, but he thinks he got off the ship before it happened.

"I got off there before the magazines exploded, before the *Arizona* blew, and I got a ride in the admiral's barge over to Ford Island. They strafed us all the way going over, from where the ship was tied up all the way to Ford Island. The Japs strafed the motor launches," he said with anger in his voice.

A badly burned shipmate, Dusty Rhodes, a seaman in the *Arizona*'s deck force, accompanied Olsen in the barge to Ford Island. Rhodes died later of burns received that day. Hardly anyone escaped the brushes with death by fire, for if they eluded the flashburns of the explosion they encountered flames in the burning water. Navigating to Ford Island was dangerous enough with the strafing planes, but the waters themselves were still coated with oil as ship after ship gave up its fuel.

"The oil was pretty bad," Olsen remembered. "I got burned coming down off the mast. The explosions and the heat were so intense, and coming back down to abandon ship I got burned on my arms. Everything was rocking."

On Ford Island the situation wasn't much better. The Japanese were continuously flying over and bombing the island, in part because it was the air station for the U.S. Navy. Olsen found he had left one hell scene for another.

"They were bombing the air station and everything was blowing up. It was absolute turmoil," he said. He looked toward Honolulu, but the city was too far away to see, although he observed activity at Pearl City. He couldn't take his eyes off the battleships in the harbor.

"You could see the *Arizona* and all the battleships under fire. They had them all in a row, two by two, tied to the quays. The *West Virginia* was tied up ahead, and the *Arizona* and the *Nevada* were close behind. The *Nevada* was under way and they beached it, afraid they'd get stuck in the channel. The Japanese had miniature subs going in and out of there," he explained.

"The *Utah* capsized, keeled right over. The *Nevada* they ran aground. There was a hospital ship, the *Solace,* under way. You could see the planes fly in and drop torpedoes. They'd head right in for the ship. Mostly they were torpedo bombers. They'd drop the torpedoes that went down underwater and as they came in they blew up under the waterline."

The *Arizona* was the worst hit. Even after the magazine

erupted in flames, planes kept hitting the battleship. Within minutes after the mortal blow, the ship had sunk forty feet to rest on the harbor floor, its decks awash, cranes tilting crazily out over the water. Japanese fighters and dive bombers repeatedly hit the *Arizona,* while their machine gunners chased down men on decks. "People were hurt and screaming and crying," Olsen said. "The noise was terrible."

After three hours of nearly continuous bombing, there was a lull. No one knew if the Japanese planned to return. Olsen and his mates were still out in the open on Ford Island, after hours of dodging strafing planes, so finally an officer led them to a section of officers' quarters, where they waited out the attack.

In the afternoon they were taken to Aiea Landing, where a big ship's store was located. There the day's task was to paint the ship store windows so the lights wouldn't show, a task Olsen and his buddies set to with trembling hands.

Like so many men, Clint Westbrook would have been safely ashore if the attack had happened an hour later. "I was supposed to have liberty on Sunday," he remembered. "I was learning to fly at John Rogers Airport, a little civilian airport right there on Oahu. I was due to solo that day, and I was scheduled for a nine o'clock flight."

As it was, the attack happened earlier, and as luck would have it, Westbrook was saved from death on the *Arizona* because he was performing a prosaic task elsewhere: taking out the garbage. He'd had duty on Saturday and was going off duty Sunday morning, but he was standby up until 8 A.M., when relief was due.

After his late night fetching sailors off the pier and depositing them on their ships, Westbrook had hoped to sleep in a little, then head for John Rogers Airport for his flying lesson. "Sundays you could sleep in, in those days," he said. "There was no assignment except the duty section. You could eat breakfast anytime you wanted, they had like a breakfast-brunch."

Getting ready for his liberty, he was already up at 7:15 when he got called for a last-minute task at the end of his standby stint. "Normally your ongoing duty crews would take any run from six to seven o'clock in the morning on, even though they're not really officially on duty until 8 o'clock. But they were gone. We weren't happy with the duty, but something had come up and the boat crews were already out someplace, so they had to use the standby boat crew."

He and his fellow standbys showed up at the boat and learned that the detail was to take the garbage out. Westbrook was dismayed. "I thought, this is going to make me late. The honey barge—our name for the garbage scow—was coming early that particular day, so as standby boat crew we had to go get it," he said.

Ships at sea dumped their garbage every day into the ocean, but when in port, all waste had to be transported to the island and dumped on Oahu. "When you were at sea you had big hoppers," he explained, "and they were tremendous. And all the garbage is dumped in that will sink—you can't put cans or official papers or anything like that. You burned those on the fantail. The cans you punctured. Then after sunset they picked the hopper up and tripped it and dumped the garbage overboard every day. But in port you can't do that, so the honey barge would come around to every ship and they would dump the hoppers. But with the tender [the *Vestal*] alongside of us, there was no way they could get to us. So every day a 50-foot motor launch would pull up between the ships, and with a crane they'd lower the hopper down to the boat. And we went back to the Nevada to use their crane to dump it into the scow."

Mooring the *Vestal* bow to stern with the *Arizona* left a wide area between the two ships. A line would run from the stern of a battleship to the frog, or mooring post, and then a line from the bow looped around it. When the 50-footer came into the space between the two ships, Westbrook and the other men on standby clambered aboard. The *Arizona*'s crane lowered down the hopper to the launch, and the driver backed out, went to the *Nevada,* and pulled up alongside to wait for the honey barge to arrive.

Just as Westbrook approached the *Nevada,* the first warning of something wrong occurred. He heard an explosion and saw a column of smoke rise up across the harbor by Ten Ten dock, far off the port bow of the *Nevada.* "I didn't think anything about it," he said ruefully. "And the first couple of planes we saw, we thought, 'Oh, the army guys are out early today,' 'cause they used to make mock attacks against us for practice, and we'd man the antiaircraft guns and manually train them.

"So whenever the Army guys made these raids, that's what we'd do. Everybody that was assigned to gun crews would run up there and man the guns and track them all in. So that was my first comment to the boatswain: 'The Army boys are up early.' "

Westbrook remembered standing on the *Nevada*'s blister top, holding the bow line of the motor launch, looking back at the *Arizona* 250 feet away. The *Nevada*'s crane picked up the hopper and had it ready to dump into the garbage scow, which was bow to bow with the launch and towering over it, facing the same way as the *Nevada.* "And that instant is when it started," he said simply. "So actually the honey barge saved my life. Jap fighters, or might have been fighter bombers, two of them came down the line of battleships, at mast top or lower, strafing. I can remember hearing the slugs bounce off the honey barge and go over us."

He looked up in shock at the plane strafing the *Nevada* and saw a blood-red sun on the wing. He took one look at the coxswain and said, "I'm getting out of here." Seeing two loops of line around a standpipe coming out of the blister top and holding the launch, he grabbed it and went scrambling up the side.

From the blister top, the next deck up was the *Nevada*'s first open deck. Westbrook could just barely reach the scuppers by standing on his tiptoes. "All open decks had three layers of safety chains as standposts. You could knock them down, they were just pinned in, so if you had to do anything alongside the ship you'd just take them away. But they were up," he recalled, "and they had canvas spread. I went up the side of that ship in one leap, I can remember that, and scrambled through the chain and hit the deck. And I remember when I hit the deck facedown I looked over toward Oahu and I could see the mountains. And I rolled."

The *Nevada* had a new gun platform above the deck sitting on a circular centerpiece, waiting for 3-inch guns to be added. When Westbrook rolled, he hit the platform's center column and rolled back. As he moved, his eyes scanning the deck saw little white dots all along the deck. At first he didn't understand what they were.

"I rolled further out to the edge of the platform and looked up and there were two rows of holes in the canvas. That second plane had evidently chased me," he said with wonder. "Not me, particularly, but I just happened to be where he was strafing behind the first guy."

Westbrook's mind went blank. For several minutes he couldn't comprehend the sights and sounds that had changed a peaceful tropical morning in Hawaii to a scene of horror. He didn't know where his shipmates off the launch were, but he was preoccupied with the planes in the sky that raked across the battleships.

It was four minutes to eight, and the color guard was out. As buglers on most ships blew, the battleships went ahead with colors. "The shock really hadn't hit everybody yet. It was such a wide area, and the Japs were hitting the airfields as well as Pearl Harbor itself, so we were only seeing a few of them," he said.

"I can remember one, evidently a dive-bomber, because I could hear the scream as it came down. I don't know where he was, but I scrambled around, down a ladder to the quarterdeck, and I ran up to the officer of the deck, a young ensign. And the bugler was blowing colors. As I rounded the corner to where he was standing, the ensign was trying to get the bugle away from the guy to get his attention, and he's yelling 'General quarters.' So the bugler went back to blowing general quarters over the PA system. Everybody's scrambling around. So I says I'm in the boat crew, what can I do? He says help batten down."

Westbrook raced to the *Nevada*'s starboard side, looking for the portholes with metal covers that could be battened down. He closed one porthole and its hatch and moved to the next porthole. Just then he noticed a red flag fluttering from a nearby launch and his heart nearly stopped.

"It was a red flag, what you call a Baker flag, that designates explosives. As I was looking out the porthole I was staring at this ammunition barge tied up to the *Nevada*. If you're loading or unloading ammunition, you fly the Baker on the ship and the barge—it means 'Caution, no smoking.' I took one look at that and went back to closing portholes." He knew if a bomb found the ammunition barge they'd all be blown sky-high.

The first wave of Japanese planes concentrated on torpedo drops. They flew in over Ten Ten Dock and the submarine area in order to hit the battleships neatly aligned in the harbor. "They came in broadside to the battle wagons," Westbrook said, "and they just laid fish like this. I may have seen one drop a fish, but at this point I was inside the *Nevada* after the initial attack got started. Then she took a torpedo in the bow—it just kind of shuddered. There was so much noise going on, but it knocked out the electrical power from the main deck up on the *Nevada*. And so the hoist stopped to the antiaircraft ammunition."

The hoist out of the magazine and fed ammunition to a conveyor belt that ran all the way down the side of the main deck to each gun position. Each gun had its own hoist and an operator, who would take every fourth shell off, and let the other three go on to other guns. When the conveyor belt quit running, *Nevada* sailors quickly realized they needed to supply the ammo to the 5-inch/25-caliber guns.

"Those of us that weren't doing anything, we started to grab them," Westbrook said, "and we'd take them and throw them on our shoulders, run out to the quarterdeck and up an open ladder to the gun deck and then go to the gun. Normally you'd handle one of these, but practically all of us were carrying two—the adrenaline was running."

By the time Westbrook made his second trip to the guns the gunners were already firing, and he heard the drumming of shrapnel falling back on the deck. Firing straight up at the airplanes, the shell would explode in the air and drop bits of steel on sailors below.

In the constant din and the jerking shudders of the ship as it was hit by torpedoes and bombs, the men were confused and frightened, but also efficient. Just as Vern Olsen had seen in the crow's nest, men who were trained to do their duty had learned it by rote, and they could do their tasks without thinking after having drilled them so many times. Despite horrendous conditions, sailors gave back as good as they could to the mad bombers on high.

Then the *Nevada* decided to sail out, and Westbrook was faced with another dilemma: where to go next? "They decided to get under way, so they passed the word—clear the sides—and that's when we reassembled back at the 50-footer and took off for the *Arizona*," he said. He didn't have the slightest idea what time it was. "I'd say the first three hours went by in five minutes."

The 50-footer cleared the *Nevada* and was en route to the *Arizona*. Westbrook noticed that the Vestal was gone. As his boat crew headed for the gangway, it was clear the *Arizona* was in trouble. "There was a lot of smoke. The *West Virginia* was on fire and the smoke was basically hanging there. There really wasn't enough wind to blow it around too much. I saw a lot of smoke, a lot of it over the land, probably at Hickam Field. And we had a big airfield over behind the hospital, that was probably where that was coming from."

He was looking at the *Arizona* as the boat, riding high with no wake, headed for the ship's gangway about 150 feet away. At that moment his battleship took the mortal blow. The force of the explosion first went upward, and a secondary wave swept along the water and hit Westbrook's launch. "When she blew, it just spun us like a pinwheel, and all four of us ended up in a heap in the bottom. The coxswain almost went overboard. The big motor boats had floorboards so you could take them up to clean the bilges, and they were all loose. It just jumbled them all up. We had to slap them all back in place."

The boat rested in the waves as the men pulled themselves together. They looked up at their ship and tried to assess whether they should go forward or back. "We looked at the *Arizona* and everybody was pouring off the stern, so we knew there wasn't anything there. Everything else was in pieces," he said.

By then the Japanese had hit and ruptured at least one of the pipelines that came in under the harbor to Ford Island and supplied it with water. One was behind the *Nevada,* the other forward of the *Tennessee.*

"Meantime all of the oil tanks on all the battle wagons had been ruptured, most of them," Westbrook added, "and you could just about almost get out and walk on it, it was that thick. And around those ships that had fire it was on fire as well, so a lot of these people jumping off the ships were jumping right into burning oil."

His own ship was fully fueled in preparation for its trip to the States. "We had just loaded the day before 'cause we were going back to the States for Christmas," he said sadly. "The admiral had told us, and we had filled the tanks Saturday. Over a million gallons of oil, if I remember correctly. And she dumped most of hers. So did the *West Vir-*

ginia. About the only two that weren't spilling oil were the *Tennessee* and the *Maryland,* they were inboard."

The burning oil on the water created a dense fog ten feet above the surface, but below that it was clear. In the open patch low down, Westbrook's crew was able to navigate, and they motored over to the *Arizona*'s port side and tied up on the quarterdeck's gangway. They took in the situation from there. Antiaircraft guns fired from battleship decks, and some long-range guns were firing. "Some of the crews were firing their 6-inch guns. They'd just raise it up max, if they see something they could shoot at they would shoot it. It was probably out of frustration more than anything, because they couldn't do much. I can remember seeing an officer standing on one of the ships firing a .45 at a plane going by."

Westbrook's group decided it was futile to go on board, so they started fishing people out of the water. They had to rescue a couple of the 17-footers that couldn't escape the oil slick, so Westbrook's coxswain would run them in to half the length of the 50-footer and he'd throw a bowline over to them, back up, and haul them out of the water. Oil still poured out of the battleships.

Meanwhile the *Nevada,* whose engines had fired up and gotten the ship under way in record time, was steaming through the harbor and heading down the channel to the harbor mouth. Westbrook watched it clear battleship row. "She cleared the row and headed toward the channel, but there she took a bow hit from a dive-bomber, and it went off in the paint locker. There was so much smoke they couldn't see to navigate from the fire. That's when they decided to beach her rather than have it sunk in the channel.

They backed it in and trained all four turrets down the channel, and they lost power shortly after that. They thought there might be a waterborne invasion, that after the air attack there'd be troops coming."

Westbrook's look at the *Nevada* was interrupted as a passing boat stopped near his launch and the coxswain hollered that they were needed at the hospital on Ford Island to move casualties. The 50-footer headed for the pier near the *California* and began carrying the wounded and burned victims across the channel to the hospital landing. He'd unload one boat and dash back for another load.

"I guess we made five, maybe six, trips, and we were strafed during each of those runs. That's when I was hit," he said matter-of-factly. "Eventually we lost the 50-footer. It had enough holes that we couldn't keep the water out, so we had to abandon her. We tied up alongside a barge and she just simply sank to the depth of the two lines we had on her, and that was the last thing I saw of her, half full of water."

Although Westbrook had taken hits from shrapnel in his shoulder and his eye, he scarcely noticed the shoulder wound, and it would be days before his eye hurt. "I didn't know I'd been hit. We had been handling casualties to start with, plus we'd been handling those that had been in the water, so I was black and red." His boat uniform—white duck pants, sneakers, white socks, white undershirt—had absorbed the colors of blood and oil.

Abandoning the boat, Westbrook thought to retrieve his navy blue sweater, the only other piece of clothing he had to wear for the next few days. The foursome found an abandoned pickup truck, complete with keys, and piled into it. Driving along, they spotted a building where people were streaming out, all carrying guns.

"We pulled over and stopped, and went in and got some, too. I thought to myself, I'm going to go Jap-hunting," he said. "I grabbed handguns. I'd love to have had a picture that day, 'cause I had a 30.06 slung over my shoulder, two bandoleers of ammunition crisscrossed, and two .45s strapped on my hips with extra clips. And we found a light machine gun. We set it up in the back of the truck and were prowling Ford Island looking for Japs. We saw one parachute out but he landed out in the water."

In the surreal day it was still morning. By then the second wave of airplanes had attacked, but Westbrook couldn't tell. "I never consciously realized that there was more than one wave, 'cause it never really got quiet enough to think, we're not under attack. It seemed like it was constant." A flat tire on the pickup truck ended that episode and they left the vehicle by the side of the road. It was the last Westbrook saw of the boat crew. Men wandered around, not knowing what they should be doing.

"I'm walking around like a Wild West hero," he said, "and I was heading for the beach side, the harbor side, of Ford Island, when this group of officers saw me. In my whole Navy career it was probably the greatest amount of gold I'd ever seen concentrated in one spot—two admirals, and one had gold that ran from his fingertips to his elbows. I gave a snappy salute."

The admiral, looking for a sailor he could assign as a guard to the other admiral beside him, asked Westbrook a question that was heard all over Hawaii that day: "Son, what ship are you on?" Seaman Westbrook pointed to the harbor and said, "You see that pile of smoke down there? That *was* my ship—the *Arizona*."

CHAPTER 8

GOING TO WAR

Fate has a way of dealing lucky or unlucky cards. Surviving the Pearl Harbor attack—especially for an *Arizona* sailor—was in some cases the sheer luck of the draw. For the men who were on board when the attack came, life and death might depend on the location of a man's bunk or his battle station. The entire *Arizona* band, as the second-place winners in the Battle of the Bands, slept late and were concussed in their sleep on the second deck of the forward bow. Men of the forward turrets No. 1 and 2 suffered the same fate when the forward munitions hold blew. Captain Van Valkenburgh and Admiral Kidd, both standing on the bridge, died that same moment. Kidd's melted wedding ring would be recovered by scuba divers days later.

Some of the 289 USS *Arizona* survivors were spared simply because they weren't on the ship at the time of attack but were "on the beach" on Oahu. Ralph Byard and Galen Ballard both had the good fortune to wake up in Honolulu—not on board ship—on December 7.

Just after 8 o'clock in the morning, Galen Ballard was listening to the Inkspots on a record player. He decided to switch to the radio. He was shocked to find the airwaves filled with military warnings. "They were taking off on the radio about the Japanese planes with the Rising Sun on the wing tips," he said. "Seek cover, they told everybody. Personnel, report to your stations."

Ballard's liberty would have extended until Monday morning, but as the call came to report to duty, he quickly headed out. He was wearing civilian clothes, having changed at the Navy center downtown the night before, leaving his uniform in the locker. Now he raced for the center to change back. When he got there the gate was locked.

"I had to scale a wall to get to my locker and change into uniform and call a cab," he said. "It must have been around 8 because the high-altitude bombers were still going over and doing a lot of firing."

The cab roared down the road and he began to see piles of smoke. "At first I thought from all the smoke they'd hit some oil reserves, but as we got going I realized it was more than that. Going in the cab there was a lot of firing going on. The bombers were going over and there was a lot of antiaircraft fire."

By the time he got to the dock he could see the situation was very bad. "We could see the *Arizona* was up in flames, and the *Oklahoma* was capsized," he said. "All we could see was smoke and flames. I was numb. Frightened. Confused."

He went to the receiving station, "and I remember that we dove under the tables a time or two. I don't know if they were actually strafing us or we just thought they were." He stood in a line waiting for orders, carrying only his billfold. "Everything I owned was on the Arizona—all I had left was what I had on my back."

When warrant officer Ralph Byard first awoke in his bachelor apartment in Honolulu, he remembered it was Sunday morning and he had no special duties to do. Leisurely he got up and made himself some coffee. Then hell broke loose.

"I started hearing explosives from the direction of Pearl Harbor," he recalled. "One of the neighbor women came rushing to my door and said, 'The Japanese are bombing Pearl Harbor.' "

He threw on his uniform and banged on the door of his friend, Estelle Birdsell, who lived in the same apartment complex. Together the two headed off on the double down the road that led to Pearl Harbor. Stopped in traffic right at the end of the road was a Chevrolet hardtop coupe, stuck in the chaotic rush. Byard noticed the driver was a machinist's mate he knew from the *Arizona*.

"So the two of us jumped in this coupe and we started for Pearl Harbor," he said. "When we got right down opposite Hickam Field, there was a sort of a causeway that went over a swampy area, and the traffic was tied up, and absolutely not moving. The Japs were strafing the causeway. The driver was able to back out and go the other way, and he went up over Red Hill and came down at the submarine gate. I remember we came to there and then followed the road around that would take us to the main gate, the main Navy landing. He left Birdsell and me off there."

Hoping to catch a launch out to his ship, Byard and his friend Birdsell raced around the bend to the landing. So many planes filled the sky that the sun was intermittently blocked out. Explosions roared all around. He looked out to Fox 8.

The Arizona's big explosion had already occurred, and the ship had sunk into the harbor. Vast clouds of billowing smoke and flames emanated from the vessel.

"The moment that will never leave my mind is when I walked up on the Navy landing and saw the *Arizona*," Byard said. "The Japanese were overhead, the *Arizona* was down and burning, the *Nevada* was under way and I stood there and watched her go aground. The *Oklahoma* was upside down. I still see it."

When the attack finally ended, eight battleships, three light cruisers, three destroyers, and four auxiliary craft were either sunk, capsized, or damaged. The Navy, Marine Corps, and Army lost 188 aircraft. Another 159 planes were damaged, and 2,403 people were killed or missing. Another 1,178 were wounded.

Survivors and observers on other ships offer a confusing array of accounts of the USS *Arizona*'s end. The stories of the survivors, in the fog of battle, evocatively convey their individual experiences. Piecing them together, along with the evidence of the battered, sunken ship itself, a picture emerges of the *Arizona*'s crew rallying after the surprise of the attack, taking their stations and engaging the enemy, fighting the ship's fires, and then, in an instant, either dropping in their tracks or fighting for survival after the fatal blast.

Moored at Quay F-7 on the east side of Ford Island, the *Arizona* lay starboard side to the island, two hundred yards separating it from the nearby battleships *West Virginia* and *Tennessee* ahead, and *Nevada* to the rear. The repair ship USS *Vestal* was anchored off the *Arizona*'s port side. At 8:00, as the *Arizona*'s color guard stood by to raise the flag at the stern, a Japanese plane had passed overhead, strafing, as the men ran for battle stations. Reconstructing the attack and the battle damage in the immediate aftermath, Commander Ellis Geiselman, the *Arizona*'s executive officer, reported that eight bombs and at least one torpedo had struck the ship. The reported blows included the first hit, a 500-pound bomb that bounced off No. 4 turret, punched through the deck, and exploded below. Geiselman, working from survivor reports, reported that a bomb had gone down the ship's stack. Many analysts later concluded the bomb down the stack was the fatal hit that destroyed the *Arizona*.

Historians John F. De Virgilio and David Aiken disagree. Working from the available evidence, they believe that four 1,760-lb. bombs hit *Arizona* and three splashed into the water nearby. Another two bombs hit the *Vestal*, with another near miss off its starboard side. The *Arizona* took a hit near No. 4 turret, two hits on the port side aft of the bridge, a near-miss that exploded near the port bow, and then a hit that punched through the deck on the starboard side of No. 2 turret. The explosion in the water alongside the bow, in between the *Arizona* and the *Vestal*, may have been mistaken for a torpedo hit. But the fatal hit was the last, near the No. 2 turret. Tearing through the upper teakwood deck, the main deck, and the second deck, the shell finally detonated in the vicinity of the forward magazines. In this area, protected by a five-inch-thick armored steel deck, lay 1,075 pounds of highly explosive black powder, as well as the 14-inch magazines and the 5-inch magazines, all full of shells. The explosion of the Japanese shell somehow set off the magazines. The Navy's Bureau of Ships, analyzing the destruction, surmised that a fuel-oil fire set off the black powder and then the stored shells, probably through an open hatch that led into the black powder magazine. Aiken and De Virgilio believe that the shell

Launching of the USS *Arizona* at the New York Navy Yard, Brooklyn, New York, 1915. (Photo: USS *Arizona* Memorial/National Park Service, Photo Collection)

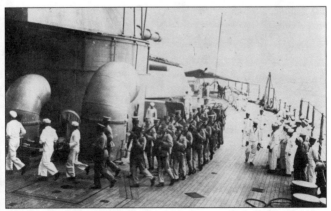

USS *Arizona*: Ship's divisions and Marines on deck during morning drill, 1916. (Photographer: U.S. Navy, Photo: USS Arizona/NPS, Photo Collection)

USS *Arizona* steaming with other Atlantic fleet battleships during gunnery practice, 1917. (Photographer: U.S. Navy, Photo: USS *Arizona*/NPS, Photo Collection)

USS *Arizona* heading down the East River from New York City on its way to sea trials, 1918. (Photo: USS *Arizona* Memorial/NPS, Photo Collection)

USS *Arizona* gun crew goes through practice drill for one of the ship's 5-inch secondary guns, 1920. (Photographer: U.S. Navy, Photo: USS *Arizona* Memorial/NPS, Photo Collection)

USS *Arizona* at anchor in Guantánamo Bay, Cuba, 1920. (Photo: USS *Arizona* Memorial/NPS, Photo Collection)

Sailors relaxing on deck of the USS *Arizona*. (Photo: USS *Arizona* Memorial/NPS, Photo Collection)

Hammocks laid out for inspection aboard the USS *Arizona*, 1920s. (Photo: USS *Arizona* Memorial/NPS, Photo Collection)

USS *Arizona* anchored off Brooklyn, 1927. (Photo: USS *Arizona* Memorial/NPS, Photo Collection)

USS *Arizona* crew cleaning the forward section near the gun turrets, late 1920s. (Photo: USS *Arizona* Memorial/NPS, Photo Collection)

Sailors sweeping the deck of the USS *Arizona*. (Photo: USS *Arizona* Memorial/NPS, Photo Collection)

USS *Arizona* returning from a West Indies cruise with President Herbert Hoover on board, 1931. (Photographer: USAAC Plane from Langley Field, Virginia. Photo: USS *Arizona* Memorial/NPS, Photo Collection)

USS *Arizona* at sea just off Virginia, 1931. (Photo: USS *Arizona* Memorial/NPS, Photo Collection)

View of the bow of the USS *Arizona* at sea, 1930s. (Photo: USS *Arizona* Memorial/NPS, Photo Collection)

USS *Arizona* being moored in dry dock, Pearl Harbor Navy Yard, 1932. (Photo: USS *Arizona* Memorial/NPS, Photo Collection)

USS *Arizona* getting her annual scrub-down at Pearl Harbor, 1934. (Photo courtesy of John Charles Roach, Photo: USS *Arizona* Memorial/NPS, Photo Collection)

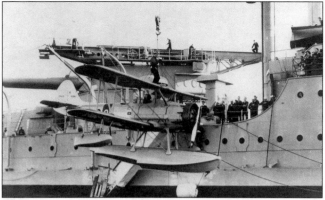

Observation airplane being hoisted aboard the USS *Arizona* in California, mid-1930s. (Photographer: Watson Airfoto Inc., Photo: USS *Arizona* Memorial/NPS, Photo Collection)

USS *Arizona* passing the unfinished Golden Gate Bridge, San Francisco, California, late 1930s. (Photo: USS *Arizona* Memorial/NPS, Photo Collection)

Loaders standing by with shells to feed into the breech of one of the *Arizona*'s 3-inch anti-aircraft guns. (Photographer: Bernard Pawlack Collection, Photo: USS *Arizona* Memorial/NPS, Photo Collection)

Sailors' hammocks hanging out to dry on deck, late 1930s. (Photo: USS *Arizona* Memorial/NPS, Photo Collection)

USS *Arizona* making its way out of the channel of Pearl Harbor, 1940. (Photographer: Tai Sing Loo, Photo: USS *Arizona* Memorial/NPS, Photo Collection)

Japanese torpedo tracks head toward Battleship Row. Oil gushes from the *West Virginia* as torpedo strikes. Smoke billows from Hickam Field in background, December 7, 1941. (Photographer: Japanese Navy, Photo: USS *Arizona* Memorial/NPS, Photo Collection)

View from pier looking towards the Pearl Harbor Navy Yard's dry docks, December 7, 1941. (Photo: USS *Arizona* Memorial/NPS, Photo Collection)

Battleship Row: Smoke barreling from the *Arizona*, the sinking *West Virginia*, and a slightly damaged *Tennessee*, December 7, 1941. (Photo: USS *Arizona* Memorial/NPS, Photo Collection)

USS *Arizona* burning furiously after the explosion of its forward magazines, December 7, 1941. (Photo: USS *Arizona* Memorial/NPS, Photo Collection)

USS *Arizona* sinking and on fire, December 7, 1941. (Photo: USS *Arizona* Memorial/NPS, Photo Collection)

USS *Arizona* sunk and burning with the tug *Hoga* alongside fighting fires on board the wrecked battleship, December 7, 1941. (Photo: USS *Arizona* Memorial/NPS, Photo Collection)

The wrecked USS *Cassin* capsized against USS *Downes* in dry dock with the *Pennsylvania* behind. The smoke comes from the burning, mortally wounded *Arizona*, out of view behind the *Pennsylvania*, December 7, 1941. (Photo: USS *Arizona* Memorial/NPS, Photo Collection)

The USS *Bennington* passing the sunken *Arizona*, 1958. (Photo: USS *Arizona* Memorial/NPS, Photo Collection)

Captain Franklin Van Valkenburgh, U.S. Navy, Commanding Officer of the USS *Arizona*. (Photo: Naval Historical Foundation)

Rear Admiral Isaac C. Kidd, U.S. Navy, on the USS *Arizona*. (Photo: Naval Historical Foundation)

John Rampley, USS *Arizona* survivor of the Pearl Harbor attack. (Photo courtesy of John Rampley)

James Foster, USS *Arizona* survivor of the Pearl Harbor attack. (Photo courtesy of James Foster)

The USS *Arizona* Memorial, Honolulu, Hawaii. (Photo: USS *Arizona* Memorial/NPS, Photo Collection)

pierced the armored deck and exploded inside the 14-inch magazine.

Regardless of where the shell exploded, what is clear is that within the seven seconds captured on film, a hundred tons of explosive detonated inside the Arizona less than a minute after the high-altitude bomber's shell hit the ship. With a huge blast and searing heat, the *Arizona* heaved and bucked, the bow twisted up out of the water and the sides of the hull near the bow blasted out as the decks collapsed into an almost volcanic crater of twisted, melting steel. By some reports it was 8:05, and the Japanese attack was only ten minutes old, although other reports place it closer to 8:20. But in a minute fragment of time, the U.S. Navy suffered the most devastating loss in its entire history. Only a few hundred men remained alive on the *Arizona*. Sailors on nearby ships watched in horror as men walked out of the flames, themselves on fire, and fell to the deck. Out of about 1,500 men comprising the ship's crew, 1,177 were lost that morning along with the *Arizona*. The fires aboard continued to burn until Wednesday, December 10. The efforts of firefighting ships, including the yard tug *Hoga,* finally won out as a lack of anything left to burn left the battleship a smoking, abandoned hulk. The battleship was slowly settling into the mud as the water closed over the decks.

On December 8, less than twenty-four hours after the attack, as the fires still burned out of control in Pearl Harbor, President Franklin Delano Roosevelt stood before Congress. "Yesterday, December 7, 1941—a date which will live in infamy—the United States of America was suddenly and deliberately attacked by naval and air forces of the Empire of Japan." Denouncing the Japanese, who were still negotiating with the United States government, Roosevelt reported that Japanese forces had launched other offensives against Malaya, Hong Kong, and American possessions in the Pacific, namely the Philippines, Guam, Midway, and Wake islands. A state of war existed, and the President, in asking that Congress formally declare war, promised the nation that no matter how long it took, "the American people in their righteous might will win through to absolute victory."

The men who carried the title *Arizona* sailors were homeless on the night of December 7. The ship that had been their home, their family, and their life had been lost in the blink of an eye. Most of the senior officers were dead. Everyone had lost good friends. John Anderson of turret No. 4 had lost his twin brother, Delbert. To be sure, every man from every battleship and Hickam Field was mightily traumatized, but the *Arizona* men fared worse than most. By evening time they were lucky to find a pair of shoes to wear and a bunk to sleep.

Strange things happened in the chaos following the attack. Officers were dead or missing, men wandered half-naked and wounded across Ford Island and Hickam Field. That afternoon and evening antiaircraft guns were fired at planes in the sky, planes that turned out to be American. None were struck, as luck would have it. Sailors whose berth had been the *Arizona* were homeless. Men of every battleship were in shock. Anger was yet to come, but it was building. On the evening of December 7 the survivors of Pearl Harbor Day were still fearful of another attack, but by December 10 they were making ready to go to sea and punish Japan.

Ralph Byard and his friend Birdsell had rushed to the harbor, too late to help the *Arizona*. A smoking pile of metal signaled the demise of their ship. Byard, who years later would retire as a lieutenant commander, fought to stay composed. "Birdsell said that I behaved as if things were normal. He said he took strength from that, and felt if I could be so undisturbed that he would try to do likewise. He said that I set an example for him. And it was three days before I got emotional about it."

That afternoon the two young men joined the dramatic rescue mission to the USS *California*, which was listing dangerously. Small boats took off men from the decks, and engineers cut into several compartments to remove sailors alive inside. Crew members fought madly to plug leaking holes with mattresses, but the fight to keep the ship afloat was lost. Slowly and gently the *California* sank to the bottom.

With the *Arizona* gone, Byard had no captain to report to, no duty, and no home. Like the other survivors of the *Arizona, Oklahoma,* and *West Virginia,* he went to the officers' club for a meal, and then on to the receiving station, the clearinghouse for assignments. Until he got a new post—perhaps a new ship—he didn't know where he'd be sleeping that night.

A couple of days later, Byard heard the chief gunner's mate Hendon was going to dive on the *Arizona* to open the paymaster's safe. "He got all the money and all the pay receipts for the quarter, and I took them down in to the furnace room of the receiving station and spread the pay receipts out on the deck. They were so hot there that they'd dry in just about the length of time it took you to lay them out. Then I would pick them up in the same order I laid them down, because they were in numerical order. And then I took them up and we reconstructed the payroll for the quarter, and figured out what each man had still coming to him. We transferred that to wherever they had gone if they survived, and we transferred the information to Washington for those who were dead or missing."

The furnace room was in the basement of the receiving station. It was so hot down there that Byard had shed all his clothes except for his shorts. "Then I'd squat down there and lay those pay receipts out there on the deck to dry and put them back together. Fortunately I didn't lose any. The disbursing officer, who just died recently (1980s) in Norfolk, Ensign Homan Walsh, was bound and determined that anybody, all the people dead or alive, should have their pay computed as accurately as possible.

"Now remember, they had recently passed the Act of 8-18-41, which allowed sea pay to people on sea duty. Before that you got the same pay on sea duty as you got on shore. But that sea pay had never been credited to the payroll, so we had to recalculate and credit everybody's pay record with that allowance.

"Where I went after Pearl . . . even though I was a chief warrant officer and could have sat with my hands undirtied, I went to the commissary officer of the receiving station and asked him if there was anything I could do to help him, because I knew they were desperate for hands. They had a chow line. Everybody that survived any of the ships had nowhere to sleep—they were unlivable—so the survivors of the *West Virginia,* the *California,* the *Arizona,* the *Oglala* reported to the receiving station. We were only partially outfitted. I was fully clothed, but not everybody was.

They opened up the clothing and small stores and issued whatever anybody asked for, and figured they'd account for it later. I saw the documents—see, I was later supply officer at the receiving station—and I saw the document that they used to account for it, giving away all the clothes, thousands of dollars of them. I admired the guts of the then supply officer, who became a good friend of mine."

He recalled that the chow line was continuous. "There was some fellow that got in line about noon one day and I forget how the conversation went, but it developed that the guy in front of him was waiting for breakfast, and he was following in line wanting what we call noon meal— dinner. He thought he was in there for the noon meal. So you can imagine the burden on the supply department of the receiving station.

"So I went to the supply officer, who I saw around the place. I realized who he was, but he didn't know who I was. Once you're a chief commissary steward, you have a different rating than I had as a ship's cook. I told him I was a former ship's cook and that I had been a qualified butcher. God, he practically fell on my neck and wept. He desperately needed somebody to butcher. So I went down to the small stores and drew out a pair of shoes and a suit of dungarees, and a blue shirt. I only had the shoes on my feet. I went to that butcher's shop and it was dark and no lights. I worked from daylight to dark. And at night I laid five or six orange crates in a row and laid down on the orange crates, and slept all night and got up at daylight and started butchering again.

"I kept that up for a couple of weeks, until Ensign Walsh came down and asked me if I'd be interested in getting in on the settling of the pay records because there were no storekeeper survivors. He knew that I'd been considered eligible for a warrant and knew quite a bit about the store-keeping end of supply, and the pay records, and so on. So when he was ready I left the butcher shop and went up to the *Arizona* pay office and stayed there. I was one of the last five people to be transferred."

Byard spent a year at Midway, then was ordered back and promoted to junior grade lieutenant. He was sent to Aiea barracks, the receiving barracks, to set up a supply department, where he stayed for a couple of years. Next he was ordered to the USS *Tucson* as supply officer, where there were five former *Arizona* men.

His memories of the *Arizona* are stark and painful. "I've never dared go near the *Arizona* Memorial. I was in and out of Pearl Harbor for years after the *Arizona* was out there, but the memorial was built after I retired from the Navy. I don't think I could go aboard it. But I have the layout of that ship indelibly in my mind. I'll never forget it."

Unlike Ralph Byard, who was able to keep some compo-sure, Jim Foster was so traumatized by his flight through flames and smoke that he felt under attack all day. He had made it to Ford Island, but the scene there was pure chaos. "They were still strafing then," he recalled, "the second wave, rolling and dying and high flying on the beach over there. Crazy. We didn't know what was going on. They took us up to a little bitty private hospital. The doctor—when we got up there he like to go crazy. It was a private Japanese hospital, for rich Japanese or something. He was going round with a six-shooter in his hand, saying "They'd better get out or I'll blow their heads off." He wanted the beds so the sailors could use them.

He couldn't recall how many days he stayed there. "And then we were coming down to the main hospital. There were a lot of guys just lying there. I was burnt. I'd go round with cigarettes and a jar of Vaseline. They'd raise their lips up and I'd put a cigarette in their mouth.

"The *Arizona* men got burned . . . from the stuff burning on the decks, and from flash burns. I was burned on the legs, burned all over pretty good, before I got in the water. I remember how cool that water felt. It was a good feeling. McCarron was the gun captain, and Stratton, well, I didn't see him. He got burnt real bad. He was somewhere on the bridge. He slid across that line to the ship that was tied to the side of us, the *Vestal*. He was saved. But that was about all.

"At night they were shooting at planes in the sky. I was sitting way up on the mountain. Man, every gun opened up there. I thought they was invading us that night. That was just Americans firing. They sure opened up that night.

"Anyway, one day the *Chokto* [Marine] came and got the three of us—it was like we were in prison—and took us down and put us aboard the *Salt Lake City*, a heavy cruiser. I don't know if it was two weeks or longer. And then we went to war."

Foster spent two years on the *Salt Lake*, going to Guadalcanal, the Solomons, even over to Brisbane, Australia, once after a battle. The Pacific theater melted together into a series of battles, "I don't know if it's the Coral Sea battle or some other battle, but we wound up with a lot of ships battling. We got into a battle, a real big battle, and the next morning when the smoke cleared and everything, there's two of us left. I don't know if the rest of the ships got sunk or what happened to them, but we went up to Brisbane and lay about a couple days." After two years he came back into Pearl and was transferred to the *West Virginia*. He got on that ship and headed back home.

Nothing equaled that day on the *Arizona*. "I saw the *Arizona* that day in Pearl. Wasn't nothing. Just a little pile of junk sticking up there. I had nothing very valuable. I can't remember those things. I can't remember it all. But that swim over to Ford Island was a struggle, I remember that. It took months for my nose to heal. And my feet—I couldn't wear shoes on the *Salt Lake City*. I was in a battle before I could wear shoes. I went barefooted.

"There's a lot of good old boys down there on the *Arizona*. It just broke in two, or something. It did jar us, I know that. That was quite a wake-up drill. That submarine out there . . . coming in. They didn't have any opposition. I always expected the same thing to happen when I was on the next ship, the *Salt Lake*. I expected it to blow sky-high with the powder. That's why I got off it at Pearl. I brought the *West Virginia* back. I could have gone to Japan, but instead I just got out of the Navy. I just had more than I could take. They offered me anywhere I wanted to go, but I said no. So I got out, and that was it.

"Losing the *Arizona*, that was a rough way to start the war. I just feel sad about it. I think most of them on the beach survived. I think less than a hundred got off the ship itself. After that I was scared every time we got in a battle. I thought we'd get it again, but we always got the best of them after that.

"I often wondered what would have happened if we'd

have been sitting there waiting on them. We'd have shot them all. They were coming in there all nice and slow. We'd have probably tore Pearl Harbor up, though, but we'd have shot a lot of them down. They wouldn't have sunk all those ships, because they'd have the watertight doors closed—they were sitting there open. They just caught us by surprise. If we'd been waiting, they might have sunk one or two of us, but it wouldn't have been so bad. But the way it happened, they just laid us open. I guess them kind of wars is over."

Clint Westbrook had an easier time than Jim Foster, thanks to his chance encounter with the two admirals that netted him a new—and immediate—assignment. When the inquiring admiral discovered that Westbrook was off the *Arizona,* smoking and sunken in the harbor, he instantly took stock, and said to Westbrook, "Then you're not assigned to anything, are you, son? Well, you are now. You're going to go off in the boat with this admiral, and you're going to be his guard."

At first Westbrook had no idea what his duty would be with the new boss, but he found out later on that it was something to do with salvage or planning of salvage. "He evidently had stuff with him so important that they wanted him guarded," he said later. "I don't know what it was, but I was in that boat with him. If we saw a mess line we'd stop, get something to eat. He was all over the harbor, day and night. I think I had maybe four or five hours of sleep in the next two days, but it didn't seem to bother me at that particular moment."

Westbrook accompanied his new boss, the admiral, wherever he wanted to go. "He had a boat crew and a boat, and so we just putt-putted all over. Finally they relieved all of us after about three days, on the afternoon of the tenth. Then I'm standing on the dock when we got relieved and switched crews. I gave up my guns. I guess they probably figured I was too dangerous. But I had a khaki officer's coat on and a Marine pith helmet, that was my uniform, plus the white ducks that were no longer white. I don't remember where I got the helmet. No idea. Probably, rambling around on the beach, I was cold and just picked them up."

He kept looking over at his old ship. "I knew how bad it was for the *Arizona,* oh yes. I could see the ships during the day. It was unbelievable. Everything was turning black now, because the water tide would rise and fall so it was coating everything that was against it with this tar, this oil. You look at the ships and there's the *Oklahoma* capsized, the *West Virginia* sitting on the bottom, the *Arizona*'s a mess, the *Nevada's* beached, the *California*'s down by the bow. In fact I think they finally settled her just to even it out so they could work on her."

Westbrook pitied any incoming American fliers, who took the heat from scared soldiers and sailors. "The poor guys," he said. "The Air Force flew in a bunch of bombers, they got shot at. They had a bunch of fighter planes come in up the channel. That was later on, at night after such a terrible day. They had their lights on and everything else. They're screaming in the radio. All the ships were shooting at them. They shot one of them down, if I remember correctly."

Westbrook was in a gig up at West Loch, which led to the ammunitions depot. "We were mad. Mad. I think if any of those Japs on that island had dared to walk into sight of a military man he have gotten killed piece by piece. It took me a long time to get over hating them. I was spoiling for battle. So I said to an officer on the pier, I've just been relieved from guard duty. Where do I go?"

The officer told him to report in to the center, and pointed out the building, apparently a former warehouse or a mess hall, because it was open inside, with rows of tables set up. Every table was marked with names, ships' names, and they were taking roll. Westbrook stepped inside that door and asked a Marine: "Anybody here from the *Arizona*?" Sixth table down, he was told.

"There was a chief sitting there," Westbrook said, "and I walked up, told him who I was, and he looked down the list and said, 'Holy smoke!' Instantly he's up, runs out the door and comes back with a Marine who's got a briefcase. He takes out a sheaf of papers and changes one—'We had you missing in action.' Westbrook's wife didn't hear that he was alive until New Year's Day when the postman delivered a letter.

"The chief brought the roll call up to date and said, go to the other side of the building, they've got an assignment desk over there. So they assigned me to the USS *Cunningham 371,* a destroyer, and they gave me a chit and sent me down to the dock. A boat was just coming and going. They'd fill a boat up and take them off, they were bringing 'em up to wartime strength, whoever was unassigned. There was no gangway down or anything on the ships. They was all on close anchor, close stay, short stay as they call it, so they could get under way right away if they had to, and if they were nested, they were only single-lined."

Westbrook was still wearing the borrowed officer's jacket. "An officer came alongside and I'm going up the ladder, the pith helmet comes level with the deck, and right behind that is the gold bar on the jacket, and suddenly the whole quarterdeck comes to attention. That's when I realized exactly how serious it was and how everything had changed . . . I hadn't given it a thought. Nobody had saluted me before. They weren't doing much saluting anyway. But I said, no no no, I'm not an officer."

He checked in with the quarterdeck, who then called the boatswain's mate, saying, "Take this man over and get him some clothes." So they dashed across the other destroyers to the tender down below to the provisioning room—small stores. "Big long line," Westbrook remembered. "The guy said to stay here, and he went on ahead. Then he comes back and says come on. He takes me up to the head of the line, and I get two of everything, except the shoes. He just asked me sizes, whatnot, and he's stacking them in a stack, and the boatswain says, come on, come on let's go.' I say what's the rush? They say, we're getting under way. So I walked back aboard and they pulled the gangway up behind me and we got under way. We were going out looking for Japs, it seems. They just took whatever ships could get under way and just fanned them out all around the island."

He never set foot aboard the *Arizona* again. "That was the tenth. I guess they didn't assign me to anything the first day. You just go shower, find your bunk, learn the ship. The guys opened the ship store and gave me a toothbrush and razor, 'cause I didn't have anything. I soaked in the shower, took my white pants off, so-called white. And to get them off, I had to sit down and a guy helped me. They were so stiff I couldn't really get 'em off. We stood them up in the corner.

"I didn't realize I was wounded until probably the fourth

day at sea. One morning I opened my eyes and it was like somebody had stabbed me with a knife in the eye. The next thing I know the captain's down there and the exec, and they both helped me up to sick bay, and then he packed the eye in grease and bandaged it. The doc got a magnet on the end of a little shaft. He stuck it right up close to my eye, held it up and says, well you ought to get a Purple Heart. You're lucky—that was a sixty-fourth of an inch from your pupil."

He also had sustained a shoulder wound that wasn't discovered till January. "The doctor's diagramming and he says, oh, what's this? He tells the nurse he needs forceps and he pulls a slug out. It wasn't much deformed, so maybe it had hit water and bounced, and when it hit me it was almost spent. It was probably from one of the strafing runs on that boat with all the shrapnel falling out of the sky."

Westbrook went through the war on the *Taylor,* a destroyer. "I went through twenty-three campaigns, all told. I was in the war on the first day, and I was in on the signing of the peace treaty in Tokyo Bay. The *Taylor* was the first ship in Japanese imperial water. We led the *Missouri.* And it was the *Prince of Wales,* the British, and the *Canberra* was the Australian, and they each had their own escort and destroyer. We steamed up the channel into Tokyo bay with 18-inch gun turrets staring down at us from the beach above us. It was like a gorge, a real steep one, so the guns were above us, on the destroyers especially. We were general quarters, and we had every other gun turned in the opposite direction. The agreement was that as we approached, each turret, each gun mount, would surrender and run up a white flag. Well, the first one run up the white flag right away. The second one was a delay, and everybody got very tense. With 18-inch guns they'd have gone straight through us. Probably never would have even exploded. So we proceeded from fort to fort till we got to Tokyo Bay. Our assignment was to go to a small city on the west side of Tokyo Bay, opposite from where the *Missouri* was anchored, and we picked up all the correspondents from around the world, took 'em out to the *Missouri*, unloaded 'em, and just drifted alongside. They wouldn't let us stay tied—it was too historical a moment for another ship to be in on it.

"So everyone was on the port side of the *Taylor*, and we're leaning. It was like a silent movie—you could see everything but you couldn't hear anything. We were a member of a fleet unit that had the last kamikaze attack off Japan. After the truce had been signed, the last diehard aviator came out—our cat got most of them but we got a chance to shoot at a couple of them. And then that was the last fighting, and we proceeded into imperial waters."

After the attack, Jim Lawson wasn't composed and he wasn't frightened either—he was mad as a hornet and seeking revenge. "Once the initial shock wore off we were mad, so ultimately after the raid was finally decided it was over and the planes left, they started taking us into the naval air station, and we survivors who'd come through the water were all just covered with oil. Then we found out there was no water on the island, because a battleship had gone down on the water line. I think it was the *California* but I'm not sure. It settled down on the main water main to Ford Island, and the only water there was in the swimming pool. The Airedales—the air crew guys from the Naval Air Station— were real good, they treated us like royalty. They cleaned out their lockers, gave us dungarees, towels, and whatever else.

"My clothes looked fine on the outside, but take them off and they were oil on the inside. because once you put them on, that oil was going from skin to the inside of the fabric. And from the outside you looked clean as a whistle. It was all clean clothes right out of those guys' lockers. You wiped off as much as you could with towels and whatever rags you could find, but there was no way in the world to get it all off. There was nothing to eat and nothing to cook it with. They used the water from the swimming pool to do whatever they could. But for the rest of that day and on into Monday we were out of our minds with fright. We all got scared out of our wits that night because the planes were coming in that were supposed to be coming in but nobody knew about, or had forgotten about, and here we were laying up in strange barracks, wearing other people's clothes and getting over the trauma of being washed off your ship like that. And all of a sudden the antiaircraft guns were going *ch-ch-ch-ch* and they were shooting at the Navy planes coming in." None were hit, he said, adding that the shooting was stopped.

"It hit me the next day how bad it had been for the *Arizona*. I think I stayed on Ford Island all day Monday. Nothing to eat, no coffee, no nothing, so a couple of guys and myself decided we were not going to stay here, we were just going to find a ride over to Merry Point, get us another ship or something, get the hell off there. So we went from the barracks we were in to the administration building and there was a Marine there, fully armed, guarding the front door of the administration building. We walked up to him and said, 'We're leaving.' He said, 'No, you're not.' 'Yes we are.' And he said, 'I'll shoot you if I have to.' And we said, 'Go ahead. We're leaving.' And we left. He sat there and said ''bye.'

"So we caught a ride somehow. Whoever else left and stayed I didn't know or care. And of course, being a battleship sailor, I fully expected to be reassigned to another battleship. When we got over to Merry Point and checked in with somebody, there was mass confusion. It was like an anthill. We finally found somebody to check in with and identify ourselves. Whoever I was with, I never saw them again—whether they were people off the *Arizona* or not I still to this day don't know. But when it finally was established that I was a 1st class gunner's mate, they got me cleaned up as best they could, because I was still covered with oil from head to foot. Actually it took a couple of months to get it all off, before I could tell I had white skin, but they put me to running working parties out to the ammunition depot, and out into the bunkers to load up, particularly the 5-inchers for the destroyers. I guess I was there the better part of a week, doing that almost daily, every day looking at the bulletin board to see if my name was up there to go somewhere. The bulletin board was at the end of the admin building somewhere. It was mass confusion."

Lawson finally saw his name on the list for the USS *Mugford,* a destroyer. "There was one book left aboard the *Mugford,* it was God's Little Acre. Why that didn't get into the harbor I don't know. Anyway, it wasn't too long after that we went to sea."

During the attack, while Lawson sat in the gun turret waiting to be released, William Goshen was off the ship and gone by twenty minutes after eight. "It was all over for me in twenty-five minutes. I'd say fifteen minutes after I got to my battle station is when the ammunition blew up or the bomb hit the inside, I don't know which. They said it was approximately 4,500 Fahrenheit, so they think it was probably a thousand-pounder that hit the barbettes of the turret. We had four or five torpedo hits. I had read reports on it, but I didn't feel nothing. I didn't feel the bomb hit."

A couple hours later when he was in the hospital, somebody came by and asked him if he'd like to have a drink of water. Yes, he said, and drank it, but right back it came. "They gave me another and another and it all come back. I'd swallowed a lot of salt water. Then someone offered me some brandy, but I couldn't hold that down either. Finally they gave me a glass of water and told him to sip on it. For the first time I was able to drink."

About one o'clock in the afternoon a couple of Marines came in with a stretcher and told him he was being transferred to the main hospital. "Oh, no problem, I said. I'll get up and walk. They said, OK, if you can. I started to raise up and I got only so far and I fell back. I said, I'm sorry, fellows, but that's it. So they put me on the stretcher and took me down to a boat and took me to the main hospital in Pearl Harbor. I was conscious up until about eight or nine o'clock that evening. About nine o'clock that was the end of me. I was gone, and I didn't know anything until the seventeenth day of December. That day my division officer, Mr. Lennox, came in and came up to my bed, kind of laid his hand on my shoulder and said, 'Goshen, how'd you like to go back to the States?' I opened my eyes and looked at him and said, it'd be wonderful. And he said, 'We're going to move you out today.' I said OK, so sometime that day they put me in an ambulance, took me to Honolulu and put me aboard the *President Coolidge* yacht—about six hundred of us went aboard the *Coolidge*.

"They treated us like kings. Anytime anybody in the sick bay wanted anything, they got it right away. There was twenty-four of us in the sick bay; and the rest of them were wounded but could walk around, they had state rooms, anything, wherever they could put them. But if somebody wanted a candy bar, here'd come a whole box of candy. Anybody needed cigarettes, there'd be a whole carton of cigarettes come down. Whatever we wanted we got, and we got fed like kings."

He caught the first ship out to the States and was accompanied by the entire Oregon State football team, who had played in Oahu December 6. The yacht pulled into San Francisco's Christmas Island and took him to Mare Island Naval Hospital. His burns kept him there until the first week of April. Later he was reassigned to ship 445— *Fletcher*, the first 2100-type destroyer in service. He saw duty at Guadalcanal.

He got to Guadalcanal just after the invasion. "We left with the task force to go back to Espiritu. We got two hundred fifty, three hundred miles from Guadalcanal. About five o'clock in the evening, they turned around. It was ten, eleven, twelve when the planes attacked us. On the evening of the twelfth we turned around and headed back for Guadalcanal. They passed the word that the Tokyo Express was running. We were with the *O'Bannon*, another *Fletcher*-type ship. We got through there and got orders to lay a smoke screen, and we went to the right and the *O'Bannon* to the left and laid smoke screens. We come back out and starting throwing torpedoes in. They gave us credit for a battleship and a heavy cruiser, a light cruiser and two destroyers. We burnt the engines up in the main engine room and went to Mare Island for overhauling."

Just like Westbrook and Goshen, Jimmie Burcham had no place to sleep on the night of December 7. In the rubble of the Pearl Harbor attack, all the able-bodied survivors of lost ships were asked to help fill the diminished ranks of ships that still were seaworthy. Burcham was immediately taken aboard the battleship *Tennessee,* and for the next few days he helped dredge up bodies from the bloody waters.

"Then the *Lexington* wanted two hundred volunteers, so I joined up," Burcham said. But his decision to cast his lot with that aircraft carrier opened the door to similar horrors, for five months later the *Lexington* was blown up in the Battle of the Coral Sea. Burcham lived to tell that story, too.

"I've never been back to Pearl Harbor in the years since the USS *Arizona* Memorial was constructed over the ship's partially visible hull," he said years after. "It's a trip I intend to make someday. I want to get back sometime and read that roster of names of men who died there. I lost some of my best friends."

Every *Arizona* sailor lost some of his best friends. Vern Olsen had saved a photograph taken in October 1941 of a group of saluting sailors on the *Arizona.* He held bitter memories of all that was lost, and he spoke angrily of his last look at the Arizona on December 8 or 9. "It was just a total disaster. It was burning. It burned for a long time.

The men who were gone, that idea settled in afterward. At the time everything happened so fast. You were so confused, and just preparing for the next event."

The night after the attack Olsen and some shipmates slept at Aiea. They'd put up cots, tried to get everybody safe, then they set the men up with rifles in case of further attacks. Olsen says there probably wouldn't have been able to do much anyway, but at least they had firepower. The next day officers were asking who wanted to volunteer. The *Lexington* was out at sea and had just come in after the attack. It picked up a bunch of survivors and went out to sea again.

If Olsen had complained of his trauma, he probably would have gotten a medical discharge, but he volunteered to go on the *Lexington*. All told, he'd only been onshore about two days, because he went right back out to sea again, probably the following Monday or Tuesday. "I was pretty shook up. Shook up for two years. I lost a lot of weight. I was a bundle of nerves. Then I got sunk again in the Coral Sea. Then I lost everything all over again on the *Lexington*—money, billfold, all down below in the lockers."

Despite the loss of the *Lexington*, the *Arizona* was the worst, he said, "because it was a complete shock and it happened so fast. At least with the *Lexington* we were out at sea, but the *Arizona* was in the harbor. When I went out there to the Memorial, the Navy gave me a bunch of official photos. After the ship was sunk, they cut all the superstructure away. Our living quarters were right by the big gun, No. 1. When they attacked, that's where I was, and I ran to my battle station on the after mast."

Olsen had some old photographs he still treasured. "That

picture is some more of Ford Island. It was just a complete and total disaster. Here's another picture of the *Arizona*—it burned for quite some time."

The second-to-last picture he showed was the group of *Arizona* survivors that had flown in from Chicago for the reunion in 1971. The last image he fingered was the oldest, taken in October 1941, a line of men on the decks. "This is a picture," he said with tears, "of all the men that got killed on the *Arizona*."

CHAPTER 9

SYMBOL OF WAR

The first step to victory was an unprecedented salvage effort that began even as the last wave of the attack ended. By January 9, the Navy had assigned Captain Homer N. Wallin to lead the Pearl Harbor salvage. In those early days after the attack, divers began recovering bodies from the *Arizona,* but after two hundred were taken off, the effort was stopped. The difficulty of removing them and the priorities elsewhere in the South Pacific left commanders feeling that the *Arizona* should be left as a shrine, a fitting memorial itself to the men who died there. The *Arizona*'s superstructure, though, was a shipping hazard to other large vessels, so it was cut down and removed in the months after the Pearl Harbor attack.

Throughout 1942 Wallin's divers and engineers raised the sunken battleships *Nevada, West Virginia,* and *California* and returned them to action. The damaged battleships *Maryland, Tennessee,* and *Pennsylvania* were also repaired, along with the cruisers *Helena* and *Raleigh,* and the badly damaged destroyers *Cassin, Downes,* and *Shaw.* All fought in the war. But three ships remained behind, too badly damaged to either raise or fight: the capsized *Oklahoma* and *Utah,* and the broken *Arizona.*

Assessing the damage to the nearly sunken ship, the *Arizona*'s senior surviving officer reported, "The USS *Arizona* is a total loss except the following is believed salvageable: 50-caliber machine guns in maintop, searchlights on after searchlight platform, the low catapult on quarterdeck and the guns of numbers 3 and 4 turrets."

Navy salvage diver Edward Raymer reported for duty at Pearl Harbor on December 9, flying in from California with other divers to start the long and difficult job of repairing and raising the battle-damaged fleet. Smoke still rose into the sky, and a thick sea of oil covered the harbor.

"The hulls of ships and the pilings on docks were coated with it, and the entire shoreline was blackened," he reported. After weeks of salvage dives on other ships, Raymer and his mates began work on the *Arizona* on January 12, 1942. In his memoirs, *Descent into Darkness,* Raymer writes of being the first diver to walk the debris-littered decks and go inside the battleship.

"My helmet was barely awash as I walked aft on the battleship's main deck, skirting wreckage," he said. Thick masses of oil swirled up against Raymer's helmet, leaving him in darkness. Opening an access trunk hatch, Raymer dropped down to the third deck, searching for an unexploded bomb somewhere in the area of the general workshop.

Even in the darkness Raymer felt he was not alone, and as he reached over his head, his fingers touched "what seemed to be a large inflated bag floating on the overhead." It was a body, bloated and trapped inside the ship. As he continued his walk, Raymer found many of the dead men. "My movement through the water created a suction effect that drew the floating masses to me. Their skeletal fingers brushed against my copper helmet. The sound reminded me of the tinkle of oriental wind chimes."

Raymer also found a bomb, a "large-caliber shell" with "metal fins welded to its base" but "shaped much like a shell," possibly one of the modified 1,760-lb. shells dropped by the high-altitude bombers. The bomb was wedged beneath a lathe in the workshop, so Raymer left it there. But the divers working on the decks did remove the ship's 5-inch antiaircraft guns. They also cut holes into the decks and removed 5-inch projectiles from the aft magazines, battling both the darkness and occasional explosions as their cutting torches set off pockets of trapped oil fumes and oxygen.

The "minor explosions," explained Raymer, rattled the divers, who nonetheless pressed on, but only after they lined the lower portions of their helmets with foam rubber to keep from getting their chins and lips cut when the blasts slammed their heads into the unyielding metal.

One of the divers, Ben Apple, discovered another 1,760-lb. shell after his leg fell into the hole it made in the deck. Tracing the hole, Apple discovered the bomb in a walk-in meat freezer and managed to get it out and onto a salvage barge. The divers also recovered a number of bodies, and Raymer's description of rotting, headless corpses, bloated and disintegrating, makes it clear why the Navy ultimately decided not to continue the horrible task. With their heads gone, the dead sailors' dog tags had fallen free, and in an age before DNA testing, there was no way to identify the dead. Other work included removing classified material, the ship's money and pay records, and sailors' and officers' personal effects.

The divers' last job was to dig tunnels, using hoses and

high-pressure water to jet through the soft mud and pulverized coral, in order to determine if the *Arizona*'s back was broken, which would make it nearly impossible to raise it. Digging through the mud, they finally discovered a large crack, about 120 feet aft of the bow. About "a foot across, jagged as hell," it descended past a "wrinkled and warped" hull at an angle toward the keel. This discovery, said Raymer, left the Navy with three options—to blast off the badly damaged bow and refloat the intact stern section for salvage or scrap, to blast and flatten the wreck to open up its berth for other ships, or to cut off the superstructure and leave the ship in place because otherwise "the graves of the crew would be desecrated."

Salvage of the *Arizona* began in earnest in May 1942. On May 5, the toppled foremast was cut free. The mainmast followed on August 23, and the stern aircraft crane and conning tower were removed by December. The major job began in April 1943, as pumps cleared water from the less damaged stern section, and workers struggled to remove shells from the aft magazines, inside the dark, oil-smeared, and decaying hulk. When the job was completed, the 14-inch guns in the Nos. 2, 3, and 4 turrets, as well as the armored turrets themselves, were salvaged. The salvage crews also removed the rotating parts and hoisting mechanisms from the turrets, and all of the remaining 5-inch guns.

As part of a plan that envisioned ringing Oahu with battleship turrets to fend off a Japanese invasion, the guns from the *Arizona* and the guns of the badly damaged *Oklahoma* were raised for reconditioning and installation ashore. The *Oklahoma*'s guns were too badly damaged, but work to clean, repair, and reassemble the *Arizona*'s turrets proceeded. This work included building nine-to-fifteen-foot-thick concrete barbettes and mounting the turrets on them at coastal defense batteries, one at Mokapu Head and the other up the slopes of the Wianae Mountains on Oahu's western shore. The work was for naught because it took so long: It was only mid-August 1944 that the first battery was completed and the guns tested, just days before the Japanese surrender.

Since 1980 the U.S. Navy and the National Park Service have worked together to preserve the wreck of the *Arizona* and to tell its story. That year, after decades of Navy management of the site, Congress authorized the National Park Service to operate the *Arizona* Memorial and the nearby onshore visitor center. The stated mission was to interpret not only the sunken battleship but also the Pearl Harbor attack in its entirety, the U.S. reaction, and military actions in the Pacific through the Battle of Midway in June 1942. The visitor center houses exhibits models, artifacts, and images from the attack, and a theater with an orientation film that sets the stage for the ride across the harbor to the Memorial.

In 1983 the first National Park Service superintendent of the Memorial, Gary Cummins, asked archaeologists from the Service's Submerged Cultural Resources Unit to survey the remains of the *Arizona*. The project that began then has continued, off and on, for over seventeen years, and involved a wide variety of people ranging from Navy and Park Service divers and scientists to civilians and student archaeologists, all of them drawn back into time and to a special wreck that very few have been privileged to see and touch in its underwater tomb. In time, the project expanded to a survey of all of Pearl Harbor, including a search for remains of crashed Japanese aircraft, the midget submarine lost in the early stage of the attack, and a survey of the wreck of the USS *Utah*, also sunk on December 7, 1941. But the focus of the effort has always been the *Arizona*.

When the National Park Service archaeologists first planned their survey of the *Arizona*, their goal was to assess its condition, appearance, and status of preservation. A number of questions had remained after the last Navy divers had departed in 1942. One Navy account reported that all the guns had been salvaged except those in No. 2 turret. The passing of the years had also allowed a considerable amount of rumor and myth to grow up around the sunken battleship, with tales of exploding ammunition and divers killed. There was also the theory of the bomb down the stack, and torpedo hits.

What the dives revealed is a ship listing slightly to port and buried in mud that covers the lower hull. Silt on the decks partially hides intact teak decking, holes, and small debris. Thick marine growth and corrosion have obscured details. With visibility limited to just a few feet ahead, the *Arizona* is a confusing jumble of rusting steel for the uninitiated. Portions of the ship rise up out of the water, and some decks lie within a few feet of the surface. The armored barbette of the No. 3 turret, and the sloping armored sides of the No. 2 turret, are reminders of the battleship's main weapons—never fired in war—while bulkheads and white tile decks nearly beneath the Memorial are left from the cut-away superstructure and the ship's galley. Divers investigating these shallows in the 1980s found bowls, forks, and spoons, and surprisingly, a number of live 5-inch shells that the Navy quickly removed.

The survey clearly showed the extent of the battle damage left after the salvage work cleared away the upper works. Just as Raymer and his fellow divers reported in 1942, the bow is cracked free of the rest of the hull, though still attached, probably at the keel. The distorted hull plates and the crack run from gunwale to keel on the port side, and nearly to the keel on the starboard side. The armored casemates at the bow blasted outward by the explosion, were partially destroyed and then cut away by divers, leaving a gaping death wound lined by up-thrust armored decks at the bow and battleship's armor belt at the waterline. Inside the crater left by the blast, the No. 1 turret sits with its guns broken inside and resting at an unnatural angle, nearly thirty feet deeper than it once did on deck.

Diving the *Arizona* for many years consisted only of work on the exterior of the ship, out of deference to the survivors and families of the dead, and because no need existed at that time to enter the ship. It was only in the late 1990s, with evidence of internal collapse and trapped fuel oil that might be released if the decks broke open, that divers would venture inside the *Arizona* for the first time since 1943.

During the years 1983 to 1988, the Park Service conducted a series of projects to assess the condition of the shipwreck and to map it. Researchers began a biofouling/corrosion study and also established a program for long-term monitoring of the *Arizona*'s condition and processes of corrosion. Jim Adams initially volunteered to assist with the monitoring program, then became the park's cultural resource manager whose job it was to direct and expand it.

"As the park's dive officer and cultural resource manager I tried to be very strict and selective in whom I would accept to work on the park's dive team and projects. I felt this to be my duty as part of the respect due to the crew who was buried within the wreck and to the survivors who 'monitored' our stewardship of 'their' site. We never wanted to show any disrespect to the living or the dead as we carried on with our work. I always wanted the survivors, especially those volunteers that worked at the Memorial, to be aware of what we were doing and why so that they would understand and hopefully I would receive their support. In my case, I felt it was easy for me to understand why the *Arizona* was sacred. I had been a career Marine Corps Officer, coming from an organization built on sacred traditions and customs. And as the son of a Pearl Harbor survivor, I felt an indirect connection. I grew up seeing what the Pearl Harbor attack meant to those that had survived."

Everyone wanted to be a volunteer, but Adams had two requirements: a special skill and an attitude. A diver had to have some skill to offer that would assist the research and management of the site; and any participant had to share the belief that the *Arizona* was sacred.

The park continues a monitoring and evaluation project that has been ongoing in recent several years, designed to evaluate the preservation conditions and structural integrity of the shipwreck. Of particular concern is the amount of fuel oil that is contained within the ship's tanks and whether there is a potential for a major leak and environmental hazard within the harbor.

It is ironic that the natural growth of biofouling marine organisms on the exterior of the *Arizona*'s hull may be forming a protective layer that prevents oxidation and deterioration of the metal structure. However, at the same time, the leaking oil and potential for a major oil spill are detrimental to the natural environment.

In September 2000, a research project managed by the

NPS Submerged Resources Center was designed to cover a myriad of monitoring needs. The project would gather images of the interior spaces in order to determine structural integrity and presence of oil. It would also document exposed portable artifacts on the maindeck. In order to develop a cumulative GIS database of the site, the project aims to survey key points on the wreck for georectification of maps, blueprints, historical data, and scientific data, and will produce an orthographic projection of the main deck with video. To measure corrosion, the researchers will collect metallurgical and microbiological samples for laboratory analysis to aid in establishing the nature and rate of corrosion processes. Cathodic protection for portions of the *Arizona* will be evaluated.

The *Arizona* site is still restricted, for two major reasons: because it is a sacred war grave for approximately one thousand heroes, and because the waters surrounding the *Arizona* are still hazardous from ordnance and obstacles in the water. Diving on the *Arizona* is restricted only to U.S. Navy, National Park Service, or research divers associated with NPS on approved projects. The *Arizona* is not a public dive site, and sport diving is never permitted. NPS and Navy diving focuses on safety issues as well as monitoring the ship's physical condition and rate of deterioration.

Recognizing that the *Arizona* is a sacred place to Americans, the National Park Service takes its stewardship of the site very seriously, and demonstrates as part of its caretaker responsibilities the need to be knowledgeable and concerned with the *Arizona*'s condition.

Time has not lessened the bond *Arizona* sailors feel with their ship. For the many surviving *Arizona* crew members who have elected to have their cremains interred inside the

Arizona, to be buried back on their ship, it is as if they are returning to their home, to their *Arizona* family, to rest for eternity with their shipmates. Choosing this final resting place and not the "traditional" family plot says something about the special bonding these individuals have with their ship and shipmates.

There is a protocol to interments and ash-scatterings: Only USS *Arizona* survivors who were stationed on the ship at the time of Pearl Harbor Day may be interred on the wreck itself, and their cremains are interred in gun turret No. 4. The ashes of *Arizona* crew members who left the ship before December 7, 1941, are spread in Pearl Harbor over the *Arizona*.

Current records as of December 7, 2000, show that seventeen *Arizona* survivors have either been interred or had their ashes scattered at the Memorial. The first-known *Arizona* survivor to be buried there was in 1982.

In addition to the seventeen crew, two non-*Arizona* crew have been honored with ash scatterings on the *Arizona*: Joe James Custer in 1965, the former executive secretary of the Pacific War Memorial Commission, and Alfred Preis, the Memorial's architect, in 1994.

Not quite every survivor wanted the same fate. Jim Adams met one *Arizona* survivor who had no desire to be cremated and placed in the ship. He explained that he had witnessed too many of his shipmates burned to death when the *Arizona* sank, and he didn't want to join them now.

Funeral services conducted around the *Arizona* consist of a full military funeral held on the Memorial. The funeral, whether for an interment or scattering of ashes, is a private event reserved only for family, guests, Park Service rangers, and Pearl Harbor survivors. In recent years a retired U.S.

Navy chaplain who is also a Pearl Harbor survivor has offi-ciated at the service. The Navy or Marine Corps provides a rifle honor guard and bugler. An American flag is flown over the Memorial during the service, then lowered, folded, and given to the next of kin. The service is usually held at day's end, when the Memorial is closed to the public, so that mourners can linger as long as they desire.

As a Marine, Jim Adams had been conversant with death. His duty during one Marine Corps assignment was to notify next of kin when a Marine was hurt or killed. He also conducted military funeral services and handled burial de-tails. Still, he claimed the emotion he felt at an *Arizona* survivor funeral outweighed any feeling he'd ever experi-enced at the others, saying that the *Arizona* interments ranked as some of the most emotionally intense moments of his life. Of all the duty he'd ever pulled, Adams called it a "distinct honor" to have been involved with the burial of seven *Arizona* survivors.

The first such burial was on January 12, 1993. On that day Adams served as an observer in the water while a U.S Navy dive team placed the urn containing the ashes of Paul Egan, FC3c.

The second interment took place on December 7, 1993, when former seaman 2nd class Grady Nelson Jr. was reu-nited with his shipmates. His widow carried an urn con-taining his ashes to the edge of the dock at the Memorial. The park superintendent assisted her as she leaned over the edge to hand the urn to Jim Adams, who was waiting in the water.

"It was obvious that Mrs. Nelson did not want to let go of the urn," Adams said, referring to her emotional de-meanor. "After she finally released it into my hands, another diver and I swam on the harbor's surface till we were over the top of the shipwreck *Arizona*."

Marine Master Sergeant Todd Hall, also a park volunteer, assisted Adams. While the two Marines were carrying the remains of the former *Arizona* sailor to his final home, a rifle honor guard fired volleys in salute. As the widow and family watched, the two divers slipped under the water and swam down inside the remains of turret 4. Once on the bottom they placed the urn deep into the silt, its resting place for eternity. After placing the urn on the bottom, Adams and Hall each rendered a hand salute and returned to the surface.

After the interment, the two Marines floated quietly on the surface as they listened to the Navy bugler playing taps and watched those on the Memorial. They watched the flag being lowered, folded, and handed to Mrs. Nelson. They were filled with intense pride and honor as they swam back to the dock. They looked across the water and up at the Memorial as the bugle's notes played out over the harbor at the end of the day.

The next occasion was on June 5, 1995, when LCDR Kenneth R. Norton, USN (retired) had his ashes scattered from the Memorial over the water above the *Arizona*. At the time of the attack, then Seaman Norton had been temporarily detached from the *Arizona* and was on the island of Maui conducting gunnery-training exercise.

On Friday, June 9, 1995, the cremated remains of BM1 Harold Woodson Gaut, USN (ret.) were interred inside the *Arizona*. He had been aboard the *Arizona* on December 7, and his battle station was inside turret 4. After the ship sank, he made his way to gun turret No. 3 and escaped. All these years later, an urn containing his ashes was tenderly carried by one of his granddaughters over to the water's edge at the Memorial's landing dock. She lowered the urn down to Adams.

He and his dive buddy, Master Sergeant Hall, swam on the surface of the water till they were over the top of the sunken *Arizona*. Reaching gun turret No. 4, together Adams and Hall placed the urn inside the turret remains, returning BM1 Gaut to his battle station after so many years.

While the two Marines were carrying the remains of the former *Arizona* sailor to his final home, three rifle volleys were being fired on the Memorial. After burying the urn deep into the silt at the bottom of the turret, the divers presented a final hand salute to the dead sailor and returned to the surface, where they heard the poignant notes of taps being played by a Navy bugler.

"There is no easy way to describe the feeling of pride and honor that both the 'Top' (the Master Sergeant) and I felt as we swam back to the dock," Adams recalled. "But we both could see it in each other's eyes as we looked across the water and up at the Memorial, and watched the survivors, sailors, and park rangers salute as the notes from taps gently floated over the waters of Pearl Harbor as the late-afternoon sun began to fade."

On a later reconnaissance dive inside the *Arizona*, Adams thought again of Gaut and the others who'd been interred on board. At that time Adams had dived into barbette 3 and had gone down the passageway that connected turrets 3 and 4. In the blackness illuminated only by dive lights, he thought of the various Arizona crew members he had interred whose battle station on December 7 had been turret 4. Gaut had escaped by exiting through this same passageway between Nos. 3 and 4.

Adams left the Arizona Memorial in June of 1996 to work in Florida, but six months later he returned to Pearl Harbor for the fifty-fifth anniversary of Pearl Harbor Day. It would be his job during the ceremonies to lead a dive team to inter three *Arizona* survivors, the first time a multiple interment occurred. To date it was the last occasion for Adams to partake of an interment ceremony.

"I wanted to return to Pearl Harbor for December seventh," he explained. "I had to. Once you leave the *Arizona,* you never really leave it, at least for me. I just had to be a part of it even though I had left. You never leave the *Arizona* once you feel her spirit."

That burial day in 1996 was the first time that multiple interments were conducted on the *Arizona.*

On that day, urns containing ashes of former *Arizona* shipmates Ensign Frank Campbell, Gunners Mate 3rd Class James Green, and Seaman 1st Class Norman Coplin were placed inside gun turret 4. Carrying the urns were Jim Adams, Marine Corps Master Sergeant Todd Hall, and Robert Venema, Marine Corps Captain. Both Hall and Venema were serving as park volunteers. Also assisting was the *Arizona* Memorial's Chief Ranger Randy Wester, a former U.S. Navy sailor. After receiving the three urns from family members on the dock, the divers swam on the surface in a line of four across until they could slip under the surface.

Each was alone with his thoughts as he placed—one by one—the urns into the bottom of turret 4. Somberly each saluted. When all had finished, all four men returned to the surface. They were voiceless as they slowly swam back to the dock and reflected on the day. The sound of taps echoed its ending.

For Adams, all the funeral services at the *Arizona* were

profound. "Each of these dives were very intense and emotional," he said. "They've been some of the scariest and most dangerous dives I've ever done.

"The military pays great homage to its deceased members. You never treat this duty lightly. Having an active role in the funeral service of an *Arizona* survivor ranks as some of the most intense experiences of my life. I'm forever grateful that I had the honor."

Of the seventeen burials, including ash scatterings, that had taken place for *Arizona* crew members, Adams had carried three of the urns, assisted in the water with three others, and took part in one ash scattering on the Memorial itself. He was also present to assist at the funeral service of Memorial architect Alfred Preis. When Preis's ashes were dumped by the Navy public affairs officer, it was windy and some of the ash blew back in Adams's face. He took it as a message from the gods.

"The *Arizona* has come to represent all the events of December 7," he summed up. "It guides me in a mission to help preserve the heritage. We can give meaning to those lives that were tragically lost so young by remembering the heroism on the *Arizona*, and we can try to find a better way. They did not die to allow the world to continue to hate. If we can prevent the horrors that the *Arizona*'s crew felt—and all of those who have experienced war—then they will not have died in vain."

CHAPTER 10

THE *ARIZONA* UNDERWATER

The moment of the *Arizona*'s death exists as a series of smoky images flashing across a movie screen. Filmed from a distance, the footage is unforgettable. There is a bright flash, shocking red fireball, and then a thick black cloud that climbs into the sky just as the jolt of the blast hits the camera. It is the last fiery gasp of a battleship, caught on film the instant the *Arizona* was destroyed. With most of its crew dead, the hull shattered and opened to the sea, the *Arizona* sank at its shallow anchorage on Fox 8.

The oil-fed flames burned for the next forty-eight hours. The image of that broken hulk, and the smoke rising from the wreckage, is one of the most famous photographs of World War II. It rallied a nation to remember Pearl Harbor. It remains a powerful image of the face of war, even now, sixty years after the destruction of the USS *Arizona*.

Shattered by explosion and fire, the *Arizona*'s hulk was never raised from the muddy waters of Pearl Harbor. Navy hardhat divers explored the wreck, raising guns, ammunition and some of the dead before the Navy abandoned its efforts at recovery in 1942. Salvage cranes plucked off *Arizona*'s blasted, burned superstructure, and the battleship settled deeper into the mud of Pearl Harbor as the Pacific

Fleet's other warships sortied from Hawaii to strike back at the Imperial Japanese Navy.

But amid the hurried pace of war, the *Arizona* was not forgotten. Ships passing the wreck always rendered honors to the lost battleship and its crew. Admiral Isaac Kidd Jr., whose father died aboard the *Arizona* on December 7, 1941, recalls that during the war, the wreck was a "monument to valor" as well as a grim reminder to the active units of the fleet as they sailed from Pearl that their mission was always to "seek out and destroy the enemy."

Six decades after the attack on Pearl Harbor, the United States still remembers the *Arizona*. The gallant battleship's sunken hulk, now spanned by the *Arizona* Memorial, is visited each year by millions of visitors. They stand at the railings, gazing into the murky waters at rusting bits of the lost battleship that rise from her grave. They watch the iridescent sheen of oil leaking from *Arizona*'s fuel bunkers, and they quietly approach the white marble Memorial wall to read the names of *Arizona*'s 1,177 dead.

The *Arizona* is unique, the United States' only major naval memorial to disaster and defeat. Dozens of World War II warships are displayed throughout the country, and this fleet of carriers, battleships, a cruiser, destroyers, submarines, and auxiliaries is practically a navy unto itself. Plentiful, too, are those U.S. fighting ships that rest beneath the waves—during World War II, 167 American warships were lost in action. Many of them lie deep, their graves unmarked save for plaques ashore that commemorate them and their crews. But the *Arizona* remains, a visible reminder of December 7, 1941, a terrible statement of the cost and the finality of battle.

It is "sacred ground," this lost battleship and its memorial. The tragic loss of the massive, seemingly impregnable ship and so many of its crew transformed the ship into something larger than life, into an icon. Like the relics of a medieval saint, pieces of the *Arizona*—anchors, the ship's bells, a section of mast, and many smaller items—made their way into patriotic displays, war bond drives, and finally museums. These pieces, like the broken ship itself, are powerful reminders and a physical link to the "Day of Infamy" and to the ship whose loss both devastated a nation and rallied it as we went to war. The *Arizona* shares the role of inspiration with the USS *Maine,* whose destruction in Havana Harbor on February 15, 1898, propelled the United States into war with Spain.

Just as it did with the *Arizona* more than forty years later, the Navy sent bits and pieces of the *Maine* around the country for memorials and exhibits, including deck guns and bitts. The mainmast ended up at the Naval Academy in Annapolis, Maryland, and the foremast marks the grave of the *Maine*'s crew at the National Cemetery at Arlington. When some cities and groups complained that they did not receive a relic of the *Maine,* the Navy even melted down tons of scrap from the wrecked battleship and cast memorial plaques that to this day are found throughout the country.

But in sharp contrast to the *Arizona,* the *Maine* itself never became a memorial. The badly damaged ship lay on the bottom of Havana Harbor in a shallow grave until 1911, when salvage workers built a cofferdam around it and pumped out the water to both inspect and raise the hulk. Covered with barnacles and with human bones scattered on the decks, the *Maine* could not be raised intact. Workers cut free the mangled bow, scrapped the topsides of the wreck, and finally refloated the less damaged stern section. With the flag flying from a temporary rig, the shattered wreck of the *Maine* sank yet again off Cuba on March 16, 1912, when the Navy scuttled it to a deep water grave, the only memorial being its relics scattered across the country and the crew's graves at Arlington.

It took time for the *Arizona* to be viewed as more than a savage casualty. In early 1942 the ship and its dead were left at the site of the attack mostly because the exigencies of war left little time to raise the ship. Other practical concerns intervened, such as the difficulty of salvage. Immediately after the attack, some of the *Arizona*'s dead were recovered, including parts of bodies blown across the harbor by the force of the explosion. Other dead floated free of the sunken ship or were recovered by divers. Perhaps 105 of the battleship's crew were removed from the *Arizona* early in 1942 and buried ashore. Ultimately, about 274 bodies were recovered. Many others, perhaps as many as 900 resting deep inside the ship or sealed behind collapsed bulkheads and decks, were left to the sea. The pragmatic reasons for their continued interment in their ship, enunciated by the Navy in 1947, were simple: the costs of salvage were too high, and bodies, if recovered, were "medically unrecognizable" and would offer little consolation for families seeking to reclaim their lost sons, brothers, and husbands. And so the *Arizona* remained a tomb.

But the hulk was not universally viewed as an appropriate resting place or memorial. In 1955 the commander of the 14th Naval District, at Pearl Harbor, wrote to the Secretary of the Navy to ask that the Navy do something, because "this burial place . . . is a rusted mass of junk." Proposals to scrap the wreck and bury its dead in the National Memorial Cemetery of the Pacific, or to bury it beneath landfill and build a landscaped memorial park over it, came to naught. Instead, it was decided to honor the battleship and its men in the tomb where they lay.

Thus the USS *Arizona* Memorial, with its clean, white concrete arch, rose over the wreck in 1962. Architect Alfred Preis's final design, as built, is said to dip in the middle to symbolize the initial low point of U.S. fortunes after the Pearl Harbor attack, and then to rise at either end to represent the nation's rise to victory.

All the world seems to understand that the Memorial is not only for the lost ship, despite the names of the *Arizona*'s dead listed inside, and its formal designation. The *Arizona* Memorial is a war memorial, a reminder of the Pearl Harbor attack, and a symbol of the costs of war, with the lost battleship beneath it serving as a metaphor.

The Navy was not eager for the public to confront the rusty and fouled remains of the *Arizona*, preferring the clean, white concrete and marble of the Memorial. Portions of the wreck were actually cut away and hauled ashore to a storage yard on the Waipio Peninsula to "clear" the way for the Memorial. Architect Preis's original design, first envisioned in 1950, called for a floating "eternal flame," with a memorial similar to the Imperial European crypts he had visited as a youth. A submerged viewing chamber, open to the sky, would have included portholes so that visitors could see the wreck's rusted hulk. But that design, with its stark confrontation with death, met with a decided lack of enthusiasm from the Navy and other backers.

And so in 1962 the *Arizona* Memorial that was built offered a sanitized view of death and disaster. But it also offered glimpses of the destruction, visible to any visitor standing on the Memorial and gazing into the water. Dimly viewed decks and fittings, and openings in the decks that lead into darkness, show torn and ragged edges of metal. Into those waters and onto those decks, visitors have tossed flower leis, coins, and some of their own cherished personal effects as offerings to the ship and its dead. Divers cleaning the decks routinely find photographs of widows, of brothers and sisters gone gray, of children grown up, of life as it went on, all dropped into the water to share with those for whom time stopped on the morning of December 7, 1941. Although the Memorial does not physically touch the wreck, the wreck still beckons and calls to its visitors. That is why some *Arizona* survivors, as their lives draw to a close, ask that their ashes be interred inside the hulk, so that they can rest with their shipmates.

Sixty years after the attack on Pearl Harbor, the *Arizona* Memorial is the focal point for visitors to Pearl Harbor, and millions of Americans and foreign tourists ride the Navy tour boat out to the Memorial to pay their respects. It means different things to many people as they gaze at the marble wall or the rusted pieces of the battleship, not only to foreign visitors, particularly the Japanese, but for Americans as well.

Over time, as the nation's shock and anger over December 7 diminished, the *Arizona* transmuted into a symbol whose meaning continues to alter with each passing year and generation. By the 1960s, when the Memorial was built, it was a vehicle for personal reflection on war's causes, conduct, and results. It was also seen as a reminder of what could happen if an enemy again caught the nation unaware. The wreck itself stood as a symbol of the need for military preparedness and alertness. To some it is a reminder of the price of peace. For others it is a symbol of a particular enemy, a reminder of a surprise attack, a "sucker punch" from a stealthy opponent.

And for a dwindling number of people personally and intimately connected to those events on that fateful day, it is a reminder of lives and innocence lost, of lives forever changed. Through the long slanting windows of the Memorial, a shrine to the American dead, those visitors from many lands drop orchids onto the oil-stained waters where so many sailors and Marines perished.

Those flowers float on a gentle taffeta slick, still fed by bubbles of oil oozing up from the *Arizona*'s fuel tanks. Beneath the waves, the heroes of the attack rest in perpetual slumber.

Underwater on the *Arizona* it also feels like a shrine. The working divers who come to study the ship's condition or inter survivors say they always feel the presence of the dead. Never a day goes by that the men entombed on board are forgotten. Divers emerging from the water talk of the intense field of energy they experience in the environs of the battleship.

Such a day happened in July 1983, when a group of reconnaissance divers visited the gallant battleship on a photographic assignment. They arched upward in the water column and fin-kicked along the rounded stern to the upper deck. The only sound was the hiss of bubbles escaping through the regulator held between clenched teeth. They turned up and breasted the railing to swim along the deck. Standing vertically in place for a moment, the divers slowly moved their fins up and down to prevent sinking, all the while looking over some scrap metal and chains that lay scattered around a gaping hole in the deck.

The resident Moorish idols—those exuberant racing fish—raced by again, fled over the deck and out through a rusted railing past a mooring bitt. Pink roselike corals dotted the flat endless plain of the reddish-brown hulk. Silt dusted everything.

Fifty feet along the ship's topside the divers came to an enormous metal wheel bolted flat on the deck. It was the catapult base for the No. 2 catapult manned by Jim Lawson. The planes were gone, of course, and the catapult itself long ago had been salvaged, but the wheel still showed its arc where the mount could swivel and send a plane off into the wind. They stared at the catapult tracks and thought of the *Arizona* on maneuvers.

The diver-archaeologists were nearly finished with their task at the catapult and were ready to move on. They had laid their baseline to the right of the catapult, in order to mark off the centermost point of the ship.

They moved silently forward, passing round ventilators protruding like mushrooms above the deck. Hatches lay exposed, the hatch covers blown off in the chaos. The base of a gun turret appeared in the twilight haze. It was gun turret No. 4, the farthest back of the *Arizona*'s four turrets. Its three 50-foot-long guns had been salvaged after the attack, but the base of the gunhouse remained. Turret No. 4 had been the battle station of Jim Lawson of Pasadena, Texas, and John Anderson of Roswell, New Mexico, who remembered when a bomb hit the turret with "a big mound of molten steel." The divers slowed to stare at the turret's remains, a gaping maw of death.

They kicked on and reached turret No. 3, the duty station of gunner's mate Jimmie Burcham of Portales, New Mexico. More than forty years later he could still recall the instant when the main explosion went off. "I don't know how many thousands of pounds that gun turret weighed," he told me, "but the blast just lifted it up—and set it down." His turret mate, John Rampley of Chino Valley, Arizona, had been the telephone talker who took orders from the bridge and relayed them to the turret commander. Only that day no one was at the bridge when the telephone rang.

The other airplane catapult had been located on top of turret 3, but it was gone now. So were the gunhouse and the guns.

The ship had carried two tripod masts, and the second of the two had stood in a triangle over the galley area. All that remained now were the round metal shoes for the steel tripod legs. Vern Olsen had been a machine gunner in the crow's nest, way up on the tripod mast.

Farther on they reached an area that was close to another antiaircraft gun battle station, where Jim Foster of Cold Spring, Texas, and two other men tried to load and fire one of the 5-inch/50-caliber guns. The gun had jammed, right after they tried to fire . . . It was the same spot where Admiral Isaac Kidd clapped Foster on the shoulder and said, "Man your battle station, son," in what were probably his last words to an enlisted man.

They inched forward. Odd bits of ladders, chains, and twisted strips of metal lay in jagged paths across the deck. Turning toward the galley area, they saw dishes and silverware lying everywhere, flung by the tremendous explosion. One lone cup sat upright, as if placed for a moment by a sailor intending to return. A diver brushed a gloved hand over the galley floor, revealing bluish-white octagonal tiles. Covered for years by slime and sediment, they now sparkled in the light. Of course the galley, where so many enlisted men had worked their way through messcooking, had its own tragedy: the *Arizona*'s cook found floating in the water, impaled by one of his own cooking knives.

With visibility so low, the massive hull seemed endless, its enormous sides dropping off from sight. Ahead the deck area faded into the gloom. On through the dusky light they went, breathing out silver bubbles in a whisper. The surge crackled in low smacks and grunts, the subliminal chatterings of undersea creatures. A whitespot goatfish trailed along, its barbels drooping in a sad mustache.

Stopping for a moment, one diver signaled the scientific illustrator that she wanted to change direction and go to the ship's rail. Borrowing his mylar clipboard, she wrote, "Show me the torpedo blister" and handed it back. He nodded and they went over the railing. Below it lay the torpedo blister, a black layer that engirdled a section of the ship's hull to prevent a torpedo from penetrating at that level. The blister protruded out several feet, creating a ledge they could walk on.

She was hoping to find the particular spot marking the damage of the *Arizona*'s second-to-last voyage. Jim Lawson's memory of the mishap during maneuvers on the *Arizona*'s last voyage came back to me, when the *Oklahoma* missed a cut in formation and crashed into the *Arizona*'s port side. The blow had torn off the torpedo blister somewhere aft of the bridge and destroyed several hull plates. She poked and prodded the plates, but couldn't find the spot now, because of course the ship had been repaired in drydock and repainted. Somewhere in the dark water was the ghostly echo of the October crash on maneuvers that threw men to the decks, followed by a grinding screech as the *Oklahoma* scraped along the *Arizona*'s bow.

The paint color no longer registered, yet just weeks before the big bang the *Arizona* had had a final touchup, after a year of high maintenance and three different paint jobs. Now the paint was gone. Forty years of corrosive seawater had separated the flakes from the giant metal sheets. They swam back up to the deck to continue the journey.

Caught by a glint of brightness, the illustrator paused and raked a hand over the slimy deck. Polished teak stared back. The words of sailor John Rampley echoed somewhere: "You'd get up at five in the morning and swab decks with a holystone. It was a form of slavery, but it made those teakwood decks gleam."

They came upon something that first looked like a strange black fish, turning over and over in a circular pattern of breaking light, but climbing upward to the surface. Another one belched out of the hull in front of them and they realized what it was: A bubble of oil had squeezed out through a break in the structure and was making its way up to the surface. Deep in the ship's hold, the oil bunkers were leaking from the last fueling on December 6, 1941. Oil still oozes up at the rate of one to two gallons a day, smudging the waters of Pearl Harbor with a rainbow shine.

They fishtailed on toward the bow, passing the hulk of gun turret No. 2 that, like the third and fourth, had been salvaged during the war to become a shore battery. Below were the quarters where still slept the members of the *Ar-*

izona's band, who'd played their music for the last time on Saturday night and won second place in the Battle of the Bands. For a reward, they were allowed to sleep late.

The dive team had been so preoccupied they hadn't realized how the light had fallen. As the late-afternoon light dropped they found themselves swimming almost in shadows, the underwater world a gray blur. Something flickered above. Craning their necks to look upward, they saw large circles pockmarking the water's surface. In the world above it was raining.

They moved forward and looked up. The first gun turret loomed, an angry monolith of war. The only armed turret left on board, its three guns stretched fifty feet long out of the turret's opening. They swam, forever it seemed, along the length of the guns. By the time they reached the end, the embrasure that held them was nowhere in sight, lost in the shadowy twilight.

The *Arizona* had never fired a gun from its batteries in battle. On the day of the attack, the four turrets' big guns were silent, their range too far to be useful. Only small antiaircraft guns tried to stop the relentless Japanese planes.

Moving fins softly up and down, they slowly approached their goal: the forward magazine, the critical area past the first gun turret at the nose of the ship, where long ago the stored munitions had been hit, rendering a mortal wound to the *Arizona*. Forever after, survivors spoke of where they were standing at the moment of the big bang.

Glancing ahead, the divers saw the ship's bow narrowing. In a moment they had passed through the cloudy water to a crystal-clear vision of hell. Where the deck should have been flat, it twisted upward in a hideous crater of metal.

It was quiet under the waves. For some minutes the divers just took in the scene, some hanging in the water, some clinging to a rusted metal bar on the edge of the deck. Time and distance narrowed the gap between today and that December day so long ago. They were all lost in reverie, picturing the *Arizona*'s deck that last morning, listening to sailors whistle as they prepared for colors. Dark specks appeared in the sky, growing larger and louder, until they became a flock of Japanese planes with the Rising Sun insignia on their wings fly over Battleship Row. Down there in the dusky water, one still hears the shriek of bombs falling, the whine of bullets slicing the *Arizona*'s decks.

As they approached the gaping crater where the bomb had torn through the munitions compartment in the forward portion of the ship, the devastation was horribly apparent. In ragged, searing pieces the inside of the ship lay exposed, torn open to the sea. In the underwater silence the divers could hear their hearts pounding. The enormous battleship had been ripped apart, and they were witness to the death spot. The silence couldn't mask the cries of the dead. In the kaleidoscopic shift of the greenish-silver waters, their ghosts were everywhere.

Anyone who dives on the battleship understands why sailors and officers talked of the ship with tears on their cheeks. The USS *Arizona* is even now a powerful being. Although it lies cracked and corroding on the harbor floor, the ship radiates a feeling one can only describe as presence. It has an identity greater than the sum of its metal sheeting, nuts, bolts, and guns. It is a thing alive, a traveling city, another life, another time. It symbolizes a place where men passed from boyhood to manhood, from peace to war.

Down there in the shadow of the *Arizona,* the silence of

the battleship's grave is choking. The sounds of 1941 are in every undulation of the water, not just the sounds of the last day, but the daily lilt and cadence of life at sea. There are the shouts of the men practicing football plays on the boat deck, and the lyrical piping to announce the admiral's coming aboard, the click of heels and slamming of metal doors. Life on the *Arizona* was a world unto itself.

Of the sailors on board, most had been just eighteen or twenty years old. They'd joined the Navy to "see the world" and ended up on the harbor bottom. No one could give them back those lost lives, those unfulfilled dreams. They didn't even know that the United States went to war, for time stopped forever that morning.

Politicians portray war as a noble thing, a cause to save and protect helpless victims, or property. For the soldiers, sailors, Marines and fliers, war isn't a cause—it's dodging bullets, eluding missiles, fearing the shock of a bullet, waiting out the night for a rescue patrol. On the *Arizona*, war was burning oil, fear in the turrets, and strafing planes chasing down desperate swimmers.

Eluding the savagely twisted metal of the ship's broken bow, the divers slipped away, heading for the mooring chain. The survivors' words followed them through the changing light and the rise and fall of the waves.

"I think about the *Arizona* and the guys aboard," survivor William Goshen said many years later. "But there's nothing I can do about it. It's all over and done, although sometimes I'll get a little tear running down my cheek. I lost a lot of friends—all my friends. They're gone."

For John Rampley it was the watershed of his life. "It changed my whole life," he said softly, a knife-edge of grimness shaking his voice. "I don't think you ever get over something like that. It took me years to get over the stench of oil."

In the water column the divers stood on their fins and trod in place, waiting for the scientific illustrator and three other divers. They appeared out of the green gloom, all holding reels of string and mylar clipboards. Like a school of fish they clustered, turned and headed toward the dock. But as they went on, one diver stopped and looked back, not yet ready to say goodbye to the *Arizona*.

The ship still loomed like a behemoth in the dusky twilight. Just at that moment, the blacks grew blacker and the water was suddenly a brighter green. In the sky above, the sun had come out.

The divers met topside, and as nearly everyone does after a dive, they went in and scrutinized the marble wall of *Arizona* sailors' names. Just as thousands of *Arizona* visitors have done over the years, they told the dead, in voiceless prayers, that they weren't forgotten. Sending a last farewell, they turned and looked down through the memorial floor at the wondrous old battleship. The *Arizona* sleeps on, its blind portholes looking inward, the sound of bombs muffled.

In a voice that speaks for other sailors, Jim Foster's words hover somewhere in the atmosphere of the memorial, an intense cry filled with ragged pain. "The *Arizona*'s gone. I don't know if it's ever hit me or not. I just can't believe it. It never has seemed real. The *Arizona* was home to me."

POSTSCRIPT: THE BATTLE OF MIDWAY

The story of the *Arizona* and the events of Pearl Harbor would not be complete without mentioning the Battle of Midway, June 4–6, 1942, the pivotal engagement of the war in the Pacific that established American naval dominance. Both Pearl Harbor and Midway turned on the role of the aircraft carriers. At Pearl, six Japanese carriers launched the attacking planes, while the three American carriers were at sea and thus were spared. At Midway six months later, the American carriers commanded the victory, sending four of those Japanese carriers to the bottom of the sea.

Japan had built an impressive armada in preparation for war, whereas the peacetime U.S. Navy did not operate effectively. The Pearl Harbor attack had caused massive destruction to the U.S. Pacific Fleet. The eight American battleships anchored in Pearl that weekend were the focus of the Japanese attack, and five were sunk. Conspicuously absent, however, were the three U.S. aircraft carriers that were at sea many miles away, a most fortuitous event in an otherwise dismal time.

Just before the attack there were conflicting opinions among the Japanese high command on the importance of the American carriers. On December 6, one day before the attack, Japanese senior officers discussed the position of the

U.S. battleships and carriers. They had heard from up-to-date intelligence that the battleships were anchored in the harbor while the carriers were at sea. Commander Minoru Genda noted that the three carriers might possibly return to Pearl Harbor in time to be attacked on December 7. If that happens, he said, "I don't care if all eight of the battleships are away."

"You naturally place much importance on carriers," said Commander Tamotsu Oishi, the senior staff officer. "Of course, it would be good if we could get all three of them, but I think it would be better if we got all eight of the battleships."

And indeed it was the battleships they pummeled. The U.S. carriers remained at sea, their absence critical to the Japanese plan of striking Oahu and causing the total devastation of the U.S. fleet. Those U.S. carriers would figure prominently in the crucial Battle of Midway.

For the next six months, the war was waged by an initially demoralized but increasingly armed and aggressive U.S. Navy. After the surrender of Wake Island to the Japanese, there followed the battles of Corregidor and the Coral Sea, and it seemed to the Japanese that their forces were superior, an attitude later called the victory disease. By May 1942 the Japanese high command was looking toward the West Coast of the United States, realizing that if they could take that long and thinly defended stretch of mainland, they would have a strategic land base to control the Pacific and the Panama Canal. Accordingly, the next Japanese offensive was planned for Midway Island, a more easterly spot in the central reaches of the Pacific to the northwest of Hawaii. After two months of buildup and mock raids, they were ready to attack.

However, bit by bit, the Japanese naval code had been broken, and the resulting intelligence to U.S. forces indicated where the Japanese planned to strike. Midway was ground zero. The United States soon mounted its own force, which included the aircraft carriers USS *Enterprise, Hornet,* and *Yorktown.*

As the rosy skies paled on the morning of June 4, 1942, the Japanese and American fleets met in the battle that changed the course of the war.

The first American planes departed from Midway at 4:00 A.M. on the search for the Japanese fleet. A half hour later, ten American reconnaissance SBD planes launched from the carrier *Yorktown.* The first sighting of enemy aircraft occurred at 5:20, followed by a sighting ten minutes later of a Japanese carrier by Lt. Howard P. Ady. At 5:52 Ady reported two carriers and main body ships.

At 6:10 in the morning the VMSB-241 Marine bombing squadron took off from Midway, and by 6:16 Japanese planes were attacking the island. The battle had been joined. The Americans were possessed of three advantages: superior intelligence, the longer reconnaissance range of the Midway-based aircraft, and the element of surprise.

The initial part of the battle did not go well for American aviators, as antiaircraft fire and planes splashed the attacking force as they went for the Japanese carriers. For an hour or more they were exchanging firefights aloft with enemy planes, all the while keeping the Japanese carriers under duress.

At precisely 7:55 A.M., the exact minute bombs had first fallen at Pearl Harbor six months earlier, the aircraft carrier *Soryu* came under attack. One minute later, the carriers *Akagi* and *Hiryu* were similarly beleaguered.

For the next two hours American airmen hammered the Japanese ships like ducks in a shooting tank, as they sent wave after wave of high-level bombers to attack the Japanese battleships and widely spaced carriers. When U.S. dive-bombers dropped their loads on the enemy carriers, decks crowded with aircraft in the process of refueling erupted in flames leaping hundreds of feet into the sky.

The sixty-minute slice of time on June 4 constitutes one of the most intense periods in modern naval history, second only to the attack on Pearl Harbor. That day at Midway, from ten to eleven o'clock in the morning, three of the four Japanese carriers were mortally wounded. The carrier *Kaga* was under fire at 9:58, by 10:20 it was being dive-bombed, and fires broke out at 10:24. Soryu was hit twice at 10:25; within 30 minutes the officers gave orders to abandon ship. The *Akagi,* first under attack at 7:56 and later at 10:14, succumbed to the torpedo and bomber attacks at 10:43, when its fighter planes caught fire. Orders to transfer *Akagi* personnel came at 11:30.

As American dive-bombers zeroed in on the carriers, they dropped 500-pound bombs that exploded on the decks and ignited the refueling planes like strings of firecrackers. The intense conflagration melted right through the teak and metal flight decks, hitting munitions and igniting gas and oil stored below, and causing enormous fireballs, in much the same way the *Arizona* had met its end.

As Navy Lieutenant Wilmer E. Gallaher turned the nose of his Dauntless dive-bomber down toward the *Akagi*, the memory of the USS *Arizona*'s volcanic eruption in Pearl Harbor flashed across his mind, for he'd witnessed the death blow. As the *Akagi* exploded under his bomb, he looked back at the fireball, keyed up his mike, and called out over his radio to the other pilots in the sky, "*Arizona,* I remember you!"

After the stunning hits from his squadron, the *Akagi,* queen of the sea and heroine of the strike force of Kido Butai, didn't last long. Less than an hour after its planes were on fire, all surviving personnel had been ordered transferred to destroyers, and the evacuation was completed by four o'clock.

By the late afternoon of June 4, the Japanese witnessed an unthinkable sight—three aircraft carriers, *Kaga, Soryu,* and *Akagi,* were burning and crippled. The fourth, *Hiryu,* was still in attack mode, but soon to be hit with bombs from the VS-6 and VB-6 planes from the USS *Enterprise* and VB-3 dive-bomber squadrons from the USS *Saratoga.* By 5:05 the *Hiryu* was on fire from several hits.

For a few hours the fires on the stricken *Soryu* abated, and Japanese firefighters were prepared to go on board and reclaim the ship, but at about seven in the evening, just as the sunset gilded the horizon, a massive explosion sent a brilliant molten ball into the sky, and the flattop sank below the waves. Ten minutes later a tremendous undersea explosion reverberated through the waters, rocking the ships on the surface.

The *Soryu* sank at 7:15, the *Kaga* ten minutes after.

A half hour later an order was given to abandon the *Akagi.* At that point, an emotional discussion was held among the senior Japanese officers at the battle and General Yamamoto back in the home islands as to the best disposition of the carrier. The question was whether to scuttle the ship—abandon it—or rush in and take it under tow in hopes of a retreat across the ocean to a Japanese navy yard.

One officer opposed to scuttling the *Akagi* argued impassionedly, "We cannot sink the Emperor's warships by the Emperor's own torpedoes." Yamamoto paused for endless seconds and finally replied, "I was once the captain of *Akagi,* and it is with heartfelt regret that I must now order that she be sunk. I will apologize to the Emperor for the sinking of *Akagi* by our own torpedoes." At five o'clock the following morning, June 5, the carrier was torpedoed and sunk.

At 9:00 o'clock that same morning *Hiryu,* the fourth and last remaining Japanese aircraft carrier at Midway, slipped beneath the waves.

On June 6, under retaliatory strikes by the Japanese, the United States sustained its one major loss at Midway, the aircraft carrier USS *Yorktown,* which took a torpedo hit at 1:31 P.M. and sank fifteen hours later, just before dawn on June 7.

Midway was a shocking defeat for the Japanese navy. Perhaps as many as 98 percent of the aircraft carrier personnel who had bombed Pearl Harbor were wiped out. Final figures of casualties on Japanese aircraft carriers totaled 2,155. The same commander of the Japanese forces, Admiral Isoroku Yamamoto, who opened the war on December 7, had just lost all four of his Midway carriers, their planes and pilots, from that first dramatic sortie. The very same carriers of the U.S. Pacific Fleet that so fortunately had been out to sea on December 7 came back to engage Yamamoto's forces at Midway and utterly defeat them.

After the Battle of Midway the war was far from over. There were still three years to fight. But the conflict had altered dramatically to a defensive operation for the Japanese. Once the lords of the Pacific, they never again mounted a mighty armada, as they had for both Pearl Harbor and Midway.

The great meaning of Midway, according to Captain Edwin T. Layton, was the shift of strategic naval and air offensive over to the United States. "At Midway the Japanese lost or left behind a naval air force that had been the terror of the Pacific—an elite force, an overwhelming force that would never again come back and spread destruction and concern as it had over the first six months of the war."

Admiral Yamamoto's worst fear had come true: The sleeping giant had indeed awakened.

APPENDIX A

KEY EVENTS IN THE PACIFIC WAR

The Doolittle Raid with sixteen Army B-25 medium bombers, launched from the USS *Hornet* April 18, 1942—bombed Tokyo, Nagoya, Kobe, Yokahama, and Yokusuka Navy Yard, a great psychological blow against Japan.

The Battle of the Coral Sea—May 7–11, 1942, one U.S. carrier (*Lexington*) sunk and the carrier *Yorktown* damaged; one Japanese carrier (*Shoho*) sunk and the aircraft carrier *Shokaku* damaged, which postponed the Japanese assault on Port Moresby, New Guinea.

The United States then goes head to head with Japan at Midway—sinking four of the six carriers used in the Pearl Harbor attack—Japan now on the defensive.

The United States then goes on the offensive, landing in the Solomons (Guadalcanal) and moving against the Japanese, who have landed in New Guinea. Sea battles off Guadalcanal exact a heavy toll on both sides, but ultimately Japanese forces there are cut off and defeated.

Island hopping starts under General Douglas MacArthur to drive toward Japan, while U.S. submarines exact a terrible price, sweeping the seas clear of Japanese shipping. Japanese warships sunk during the war, many by subs, totaled 402. The merchant fleet was hit hard. The war against Japan's merchant fleet sank 8 million tons of shipping by

August 1945, thereby strangling the Japanese war effort and economy.

By November 1943 the push against Japan struck closer to home, first taking the Gilberts (including the bloody battle for Tarawa—November 20–23), then into the Marshalls, taking strategic bases there, including Kwajalein (February 1–4, 1944).

Japanese Navy's sorties in the Philippine Sea were met and defeated in June 1944, then they were pursued into the Marianas, where commenced the retaking of Guam, Tinian, and Saipan. On Saipan, the commander who committed suicide rather than be captured was Admiral Chuichi Nagumo, who had led the strike force against Pearl Harbor.

The Battle of Surigao Strait off the Philippines, on October 24–25, 1944, defeated the Japanese Navy, and its last major sortie at Leyte Gulf (October 23–27, 1944) was also a defeat. In January 1945 General MacArthur "returned" to the Philippines and retook the islands in an eight-month campaign.

Then Iwo Jima (Feb. 19–March 26, 1945) hosted a pitched battle of kamikaze attacks, as Japan was desperate to hold the island. Next came the hard fight for Okinawa (March 26–June 30, 1945), waged while the U.S. Navy started a blockade of Japan (April 1945). Bomber raids commenced from India in June 1944 and progressively mounted as the islands were taken and bombers were based closer to Japan. Incendiary (fire-bombing) raids began in February 1945, and between March and August 1945 American forays destroyed more than 2 million buildings, killed 700,000 people, and left 9 million Japanese homeless. By mid-July ships were shelling Japanese shore installations, and on August 6 and 9 Hiroshima and Nagasaki were devastated by atomic bombs.

Japan surrendered in a formal ceremony on the USS *Missouri* in Tokyo Bay on September 2, 1945.

The war in the Pacific that commenced for the United States at Pearl Harbor on December 7, 1941, ended with:

- U.S. servicemen dead—90,000
- Philippine servicemen dead—40,000
- British and Commonwealth dead, missing and wounded—227,000
- Australian dead—46,000
- Japanese military dead—1,140,000
- Missing in action—240,000
- Wounded—295,000
- Civilian dead—668,000

APPENDIX B

USS *ARIZONA* CASUALTY LIST

A total of 1,177 sailors and marines died on the USS *Arizona*.

NAME	RANK	SERVICE	HOME
AARON, Hubert Charles Titus	F2S1c	USN	Texas
ADAMS, Robert Franklin	S1c	USN	Alabama
ADKISON, James Dillion	S1c	USN	Texas
AGUIRRE, Reyner Aceves	S2c	USN	
AGUON, Gregorio San N.	MATT1c	USN	Guam
AHERN, Richard James	F1c	USN	California
ALBEROVSKY, Francis S.	BMKR1c	USN	California
ALBRIGHT, Galen Winston	S1c	USN	Indiana
ALEXANDER, Elvis Author	S2c	USN	Arkansas
ALLEN, Robert Lee	SF3c	USN	Texas
ALLEN, William Clayborn	EM1c	USN	California
ALLEN, William Lewis	SK2c	USNR	Texas
ALLEY, Jay Edgar	GM1c	USN	
ALLISON, Andrew K.	F1c	USN	Missouri
ALLISON, J. T.	F1c	USN	
ALTEN, Ernest Mathew	S2c	USN	California
AMON, Frederick Purdy	S1c	USN	
AMUNDSON, Leo DeVere	PVT	USMC	
ANDERSON, Charles Titus	CM2c	USN	California
ANDERSON, Delbert Jake	BM2c	USN	Minnesota
ANDERSON, Donald William	SM3c	USN	

ANDERSON, Harry	S1c	USN	California
ANDERSON, Howard Taisey	F1c	USN	Maryland
ANDERSON, James Pickins Jr.	S1c	USN	
ANDERSON, Lawrence Donald	ENS	USNR	
ANDERSON, Robert Adair	GM3c	USN	Missouri
ANDREWS, Brainerd Wells	CCMP	USN	Vermont
ANGLE, Earnest Hersea	F2c	USN	West Virginia
ANTHONY, Glenn Samuel	S1c	USN	California
APLIN, James Raymond	CWTP	USN	California
APPLE, Robert William	F1c	USN	Illinois
APREA, Frank Anthony	COX	USN	
ARLEDGE, Eston	SM2c	USN	Louisiana
ARNAUD, Achilles	F3c	USN	Louisiana
ARNEBERG, William Robert	F2c	USN	
ARNOLD, Claude Duran Jr.	F3c	USN	Louisiana
ARNOLD, Thell	SC1c	USN	Arkansas
ARRANT, John Anderson	MM1c	USN	Florida
ARVIDSON, Carl Harry	CMMP	USN	Washington
ASHMORE, Wilburn James	S2c	USN	Louisiana
ATCHISON, John Calvin	PVT	USMC	Missouri
ATKINS, Gerald Arthur	HA1c	USN	Nebraska
AUSTIN, Laverne Alfred	S1c	USN	New York
AUTRY, Eligah T. Jr.	COX	USN	Arkansas
AVES, Willard Charles	F2c	USN	
AYDELL, Miller Xavier	WT2c	USN	Louisiana
AYERS, Dee Cumpie	S2c	USN	
BADILLA, Manuel Domonic	F1c	USN	
BAILEY, George Richmond	PFC	USMC	California
BAIRD, Billy Bryon	S1c	USN	Indiana
BAJORIMS, Joseph	S1c	USN	Illinois
BAKER, Robert Dewey	CMM	USN	
BALL, William V.	S1c	USN	

BANDY, Wayne Lynn	MUS2c	USN	Missouri
BANGERT, John Henry	FC1c	USN	
BARAGA, Joseph	SGT	USMC	Michigan
BARDON, Charles Thomas	S2c	USN	Oklahoma
BARKER, Loren Joe	COX	USN	Iowa
BARNER, Walter Ray	S2c	USN	Texas
BARNES, Charles Edward	Y3c	USN	Missouri
BARNES, Delmar Hayes	LTJG	USNR	California
BARNETT, William Thermon	S2c	USN	Arkansas
BARTLETT, David William	CPL	USMC	California
BARTLETT, Paul Clement	MM1c	USN	Texas
BATES, Edward Munroe Jr.	ENS	USNR	New York
BATES, Tobert Alvin	PHM3c	USN	Texas
BATOR, Edward	F1c	USN	New York
BAUER, Harold Walter	RM3c	USN	Kansas
BEATON, Freddie	PVT	USMC	California
BEAUMONT, James Ammon	S2c	USN	Texas
BECK, George Richard	S1c	USN	California
BECKER, Marvin Otto	GM3c	USN	Kansas
BECKER, Wesley Paulson	S1c	USN	Kansas
BEDFORD, Purdy Renaker	F1c	USN	Kentucky
BEERMAN, Henry Carl	CM3c	USN	Washington
BEGGS, Harold Eugene	F1c	USN	Missouri
BELL, Hershel Homer	FC2c	USN	Illinois
BELL, Richard Leroy	S2c	USN	California
BELLAMY, James Curtis	OS3c	USN	California
BELT, Everett Ray Jr.	PFC	USMC	Missouri
BENFORD, Sam Austin	BKR2c	USN	Minnesota
BENNETT, William Edmond Jr.	Y3c	USN	Illinois
BENSON, James Thomas	S1c	USN	Alabama
BERGIN, Roger Joseph	F2c	USN	Canada
BERKANSKI, Albert Charles	COX	USN	Pennsylvania
BERNARD, Frank Peter	SF2c	USN	

BERRY, Gordon Eugene	F2c	USN	Colorado
BERRY, James Winford	F2c	USN	California
BERTIE, George Allan Jr.	S2c	USN	Arizona
BIBBY, Charles Henry	F2c	USN	Alabama
BICKEL, Kenneth Robert	F1c	USN	Nebraska
BICKNELL, Dale Deen	S1c	USN	Washington
BIRCHER, Frederick Robert	RM3c	USN	Pennsylvania
BIRDSELL, Rayon Delois	F2c	USN	Missouri
BIRGE, George Albert	S1c	USN	New York
BISHOP, Grover Barron	MM1c	USN	Texas
BISHOP, Millard Charles	F3c	USN	Alabama
BISHOP, Wesley Horner Jr.	RM3c	USNR	New York
BLACK, James Theron	PVT	USMC	Alabama
BLAIS, Albert Edward	RM3c	USNR	New York
BLAKE, James Monroe	F2c	USN	Missouri
BLANCHARD, Albert Richard	COX	USN	Minnesota
BLANKENSHIP, Theron A.	S1c	USN	Alabama
BLANTON, Atticus Lee	SF3c	USN	Florida
BLIEFFERT, Richmond Frederick	S1c	USN	Washington
BLOCK, Ivan Lee	PHM2c	USN	New Mexico
BLOUNT, Wayman Boney	S1c	USN	Texas
BOGGESS, Roy Eugene	SF2c	USN	California
BOHLENDER, Sam	GM2c	USN	Colorado
BOLLING, Gerald Revese	S1c	USN	Arkansas
BOLLING, Walter Karr	F3c	USN	Kentucky
BOND, Burnis Leroy	CPL	USMC	Missouri
BONEBRAKE, Buford Earl	F2c	USN	Kansas
BONFIGLIO, William John	EM1c	USN	New York
BOOTH, Robert Sinclair Jr.	ENS	USNR	
BOOZE, Asbury Legare	BM1c	USN	Georgia
BORGER, Richard	CMMA	USN	California
BOROVICH, Joseph John	S1c	USN	California
BORUSKY, Edwin Charles	CPL	USMC	North Dakota

BOSLEY, Kenneth Leroy	EM3c	USN	Missouri
BOVIALL, Walter Robert	AMM2c	USN	Wisconsin
BOWMAN, Howard Alton	S2c	USN	Iowa
BOYD, Charles Andrew	CM3c	USN	Alabama
BOYDSTUN, Don Jasper	S2c	USN	Texas
BOYDSTUN, R. L.	S2c	USN	Texas
BRABBZSON, Oran Merrill	MUS2c	USN	New York
BRADLEY, Bruce Dean	S2c	USN	Illinois
BRAKKE, Kenneth Gay	F3c	USN	Washington
BRICKLEY, Eugene	PVT	USMC	Indiana
BRIDGES, James Leon	S1c	USN	Tennessee
BRIDGES, Paul Hyatt	S1c	USN	Arkansas
BRIDIE, Robert Maurice	F1c	USN	
BRIGNOLE, Erminio Joseph	S2c	USN	California
BRITTAN, Charles Edward	S2c	USN	California
BROADHEAD, Johnnie Cecil	F2c	USN	Alabama
BROCK, Walter Pershing	S1c	USN	Kentucky
BROMLEY, George Edward	SM3c	USN	Washington
BROMLEY, Jimmie	S1c	USN	
BROOKS, Robert Neal	ENS	USNR	Washington
BROOME, Loy Raymond	SM3c	USN	Oklahoma
BROONER, Allen Ottis	S1c	USN	Indiana
BROPHY, Myron Alonzo	F2c	USN	Vermont
BROWN, Charles Martin	S2c	USN	California
BROWN, Elwyn Leroy	EM3c	USN	Kansas
BROWN, Frank George	QM3c	USN	Oregon
BROWN, Richard Corbett	S1c	USN	California
BROWN, William Howard	S2c	USN	Oregon
BROWNE, Harry Lamont	CMMA	USN	California
BROWNING, Tilmon David	S1c	USN	West Virginia
BRUNE, James William	RM3c	USNR	Missouri
BRYAN, Leland Howard	S1c	USN	Texas
BRYANT, Lloyd Glenn	BM2c	USN	California
BUCKLEY, Jack C.	FC3c	USN	Kentucky

BUDD, Robert Emile	F2c	USN	Michigan
BUHR, Clarence Edward	S1c	USN	New Mexico
BURDEN, Ralph Leon	RM3c	USN	Ohio
BURDETTE, Ralph Warren	MUS2c	USN	New Jersey
BURKE, Frank Edmond Jr.	SK2c	USN	Tennessee
BURNETT, Charlie Leroy	S2c	USN	
BURNS, John Edward	F1c	USN	Pennsylvania
BUSICK, Dewey Olney	F3c	USN	Ohio
BUTCHER, David Adrian	F2c	USN	Washington
BUTLER, John Dabney	F1c	USN	Texas
BYRD, Charles Dewitt	S1c	USN	Tennessee
CABAY, Louis Clarence	S1c	USN	Illinois
CADE, Richard Esh	S2c	USN	Washington
CALDWELL, Charles Jr.	F3c	USN	Missouri
CALLAGHAN, James Thomas	BM2c	USN	Colorado
CAMDEN, Raymond Edward	S2c	USN	Oklahoma
CAMM, William Fielden	Y2c	USN	Arkansas
CAMPA, Ralph	S1c	USN	California
CAMPBELL, Burdette Charles	S1c	USN	California
CAPLINGER, Donald William	SC3c	USN	Ohio
CAREY, Francis Lloyd	SK3c	USN	New York
CARLISLE, Robert Wayne	S1c	USNR	Texas
CARLSON, Harry Ludwig	SK3c	USN	Connecticut
CARMACK, Harold Milton	F2c	USN	Colorado
CARPENTER, Robert Nelson	MATT1c	USN	Virginia
CARROLL, Robert Lewis	S1c	USN	
CARTER, Burton Lowell	S2c	USN	California
CARTER, Paxton Turner	WO (PYCLK)	USN	California
CASEY, James Warren	S1c	USN	
CASILAN, Epifanio Miranda	OS3c	USN	New York
CASKEY, Clarence Merton	S1c	USN	Washington
CASTLEBERRY, Claude W. Jr.	S1c	USN	Texas

CATSOS, George	F1c	USN	California
CHACE, Raymond Vincent	CSKP	USN	California
CHADWICK, Charles Bruce	MM2c	USN	Mississippi
CHADWICK, Harold	MATT1c	USN	California
CHANDLER, Donald Ross	PVT	USMC	Alabama
CHAPMAN, Naaman N.	S1c	USN	Nebraska
CHARLTON, Charles Nicholas	WT1c	USNR	California
CHERNUCHA, Harry Gregory	MUS2c	USN	New York
CHESTER, Edward	S1c	USN	Kansas
CHRISTENSEN, Elmer Emil	MM2c	USN	Wyoming
CHRISTENSEN, Lloyd Raymond	F1c	USN	Nebraska
CHRISTIANSEN, Edward Lee	BKR3c	USN	Wyoming
CIHLAR, Lawrence John	PHM3c	USN	Minnesota
CLARK, George Francis	GM3c	USN	Illinois
CLARK, John Crawford Todd	F3c	USN	California
CLARK, Malcolm	BKR3c	USN	Louisiana
CLARK, Robert William Jr.	FC3c	USN	Pennsylvania
CLARKE, Robert Eugene	S1c	USN	Kansas
CLASH, Donald	F2c	USN	Michigan
CLAYTON, Robert Roland	COX	USN	Missouri
CLEMMENS, Claude Albert	S1c	USN	Oklahoma
CLIFT, Ray Emerson	COX	USN	Missouri
CLOUES, Edward Blanchard	ENS	USN	New Hampshire
CLOUGH, Edward Hay	GM1c	USN	Nebraska
COBB, Ballard Burgher	S1c	USN	Texas
COBURN, Walter Overton	S1c	USN	Oklahoma
COCKRUM, Kenneth Earl	MM1c	USN	Indiana
COFFIN, Robert	SF3c	USN	Washington
COFFMAN, Marshall Herman	GMec	USN	Indiana
COLE, Charles Warren	SGT	USMC	Washington
COLE, David Lester	ENS	USNR	California
COLEGROVE, Willett S. Jr.	S2c	USN	Washington

COLLIER, John	F2c	USN	Oregon
COLLIER, Linald Long Jr.	BKR3c	USN	Texas
COLLINS, Austin	SF3c	USN	
COLLINS, Billy Murl	S1c	USN	California
CONLIN, Bernard Eugene	S2c	USN	Illinois
CONLIN, James Leo	F2c	USN	Illinois
CONNELLY, Richard Earl	CQMA	USN	California
CONRAD, Homer Milton Jr.	S1c	USN	Ohio
CONRAD, Robert Frank	S2c	USN	California
CONRAD, Walter Ralph	QM2c	USN	
COOPER, Clarence Eugene	F2c	USN	
COOPER, Kenneth Erven	F2c	USN	
CORCORAN, Gerard John	S1c	USN	New York
COREY, Ernest Eugene	PHM3c	USN	Washington
CORNELIUS, P. W.	SC3c	USN	
CORNING, Russell Dale	RM3c	USN	
COULTER, Arthur Lee	S1c	USN	Oklahoma
COWAN, William	COX	USN	Missouri
COWDEN, Joel Beman	S2c	USN	Oregon
COX, Gerald Blinton	MUS2c	USN	Illinois
COX, William Milford	S1c	USN	Kentucky
CRAFT, Harley Wade	CM3c	USN	Oregon
CRAWLEY, Wallace Dewight	COX	USN	Indiana
CREMEENS, Louis Edward	S1c	USN	Arizona
CRISCUOLO, Michael	Y2c	USN	California
CRISWELL, Wilfred John	S1c	USN	Indiana
CROWE, Cecil Thomas	GM2c	USN	Kentucky
CROWLEY, Thomas Ewing	LCDR (DC)	USN	California
CURRY, William Joseph	WT2c	USN	Oregon
CURTIS, Lloyd B.	S1c	USN	Missouri
CURTIS, Lyle Carl	RM2c	USN	Wisconsin
CYBULSKI, Harold Bernard	S1c	USN	
CYCHOSZ, Francis Anton	S1c	USN	Michigan

CZARNECKI, Stanley	F1c	USN	Michigan
CZEKAJSKI, Theophil	SM3c	USNR	Michigan
DAHLHEIMER, Richard Norbert	S1c	USN	Minnesota
DANIEL, Lloyd Naxton	Y1c	USN	Montana
DANIK, Andrew Joseph	S2c	USN	Ohio
DARCH, Phillip Zane	S1c	USN	Massachusetts
DAUGHERTY, Paul Eugene	Em3c	USN	Ohio
DAVIS, John Quitman	S1c	USN	Louisiana
DAVIS, Milton Henry	S1c	USN	Kansas
DAVIS, Murle Melvin	RM2c	USN	Ohio
DAVIS, Myrle Clarence	F3c	USNR	Iowa
DAVIS, Thomas Ray	SF1c	USN	California
DAVIS, Virgil Denton	PVT	USMC	Missouri
DAVIS, Walter Mindred	F2c	USN	Missouri
DAWSON, James Berkley	PVT	USMC	Kentucky
DAY, William John	S2c	USN	Washington
DE ARMOUN, Donald Edwin	GM3c	USN	California
DE CASTRO, Vicente	OS3c	USN	
DEAN, Lyle Bernard	COX	USN	
DELONG, Frederick Eugene	CPL	USMC	Ohio
DERITIS, Russell Edwin	S1c	USN	
DEWITT, John James	COX	USN	
DIAL, John Buchanan	S1c	USN	
DICK, Ralph R.	GM1c	USN	California
DINE, John George	F2c	USN	California
DINEEN, Robert Joseph	S1c	USN	Pennsylvania
DOBEY, Milton Paul Jr.	S1c	USN	Texas
DOHERTY, George Walter	S2c	USN	California
DOHERTY, John Albert	MM2c	USN	California
DONOHUE, Ned Burton	F1c	USN	
DORITY, John Monroe	S1c	USN	California
DOUGHERTY, Ralph McClearn	FC1c	USN	Massachusetts

DOYLE, Wand B.	COX	USN	Kentucky
DREESBACH, Herbert Allen	PFC	USMC	Illinois
DRIVER, Bill Lester	RM3c	USN	California
DUCREST, Louis Felix	S1c	USN	Louisiana
DUKE, Robert Edward	CCSTDA	USN	California
DULLUM, Jerald Fraser	EM3c	USN	Montana
DUNAWAY, Kenneth Leroy	EM3c	USN	Oklahoma
DUNHAM, Elmer Marvin	S1c	USN	
DUNNAM, Robert Wesley	PVT	USMCR	Texas
DUPREE, Arthur Joseph	F2c	USN	Missouri
DURHAM, William Teasdale	S1c	USN	North Carolina
DURIO, Russell	PFC	USMC	Louisiana
DUVEENE, John	1SGT	USMC	California
DVORAK, Alvin Albert	BM2c	USN	Minnesota
EATON, Emory Lowell	F3c	USN	Oklahoma
EBEL, Walter Charles	CTCP	USN	California
EBERHART, Vincent Henry	COX	USN	Minnesota
ECHOLS, Charles Louis Jr.	EM3c	USN	Tennessee
ECHTERNKAMP, Henry Clarence	S1c	USN	Michigan
EDMUNDS, Bruce Roosevelt	Y2c	USN	New Hampshire
EERNISSE, William Frederick	PTR1c	USN	California
EGNEW, Robert Ross	S1c	USN	Illinois
EHLERT, Casper	SM3c	USN	Wisconsin
EHRMANTRAUT, Frank Jr.	S1c	USN	Indiana
ELLIS, Francis Arnold Jr.	EM3c	USN	Canada
ELLIS, Richard Everrett	S2c	USN	Nebraska
ELLIS, Wilbur Danner	RM2c	USN	California
ELWELL, Royal	S1c	USN	Texas
EMBREY, Bill Eugene	F3c	USN	California
EMERY, Jack Marvin	ENS	USN	California
EMERY, John Marvin	GM3c	USN	North Dakota
EMERY, Wesley Vernon	SK2c	USN	Indiana
ENGER, Stanley Gordon	GM3c	USN	Minnesota

ERICKSON, Robert	S1c	USN	
ERSKINE, Robert Charles	PFC	USMC	Illinois
ERWIN, Stanley Joe	MM1c	USN	Texas
ERWIN, Walton Aluard	S1c	USN	Texas
ESTEP, Carl James	S1c	USN	Texas
ESTES, Carl Edwen	S1c	USN	Texas
ESTES, Forrest Jesse	F1c	USN	California
ETCHASON, Leslie Edgar	S1c	USN	Illinois
EULBERG, Richard Henry	FC2c	USN	Iowa
EVANS, David Delton	PVT	USMC	Louisiana
EVANS, Evan Frederick	ENS	USNR	California
EVANS, Mickey Edward	S1c	USN	Missouri
EVANS, Paul Anthony	S1c	USN	Illinois
EVANS, William Orville	S2c	USN	Idaho
EWELL, Alfred Adam	WT1c	USN	
EYED, George	SK3c	USN	Indiana
FALLIS, Alvin E.	PHM2c	USN	California
FANSLER, Edgar Arthur	S1c	USN	Oklahoma
FARMER, John Wilson	COX	USN	Tennessee
FEGURGUR, Nicolas San Nicolas	MATT2c	USN	Guam
FESS, John Junior	F1c	USN	California
FIELDS, Bernard	RM3c	USNR	
FIELDS, Reliford	MATT2c	USN	Florida
FIFE, Ralph Elmer	S1c	USN	California
FILKINS, George Arthur	COX	USN	Minnesota
FINCHER, Allen Brady	ACK	USMC	Texas
FINCHER, Dexter Wilson	SGT	USMC	Oregon
FINLEY, Woodrow Wilson	PFC	USMC	Tennessee
FIRTH, Henry Amis	F3c	USN	
FISCHER, Leslie Henry	S1c	USN	Washington
FISHER, Delbert Ray	S1c	USN	Wyoming
FISHER, James Anderson	MATT1c	USN	Virginia
FISHER, Robert Ray	S2c	USN	California

FISK, Charles Porter III	Y1c	USN	California
FITCH, Simon	MATT1c	USN	Texas
FITZGERALD, Kent Blake	PVT	USMC	Utah
FITZSIMMONS, Eugene James	F3c	USN	Illinois
FLANNERY, James Lowell	SK3c	USN	Ohio
FLEETWOOD, Donald Eugene	PFC	USMC	Iowa
FLOEGE, Frank Norman	MUS2c	USN	Illinois
FLORY, Max Edward	S2c	USN	Indiana
FONES, George Everett	FC3c	USN	Washington
FORD, Jack C.	S1c	USN	California
FORD, William Walker	EM3c	USN	Kentucky
FOREMAN, Elmer Lee	F2c	USN	Indiana
FORTENBERRY, Alvie Charles	COX	USN	Mississippi
FOWLER, George Parten	S2c	USN	Texas
FOX, Daniel Russell	LTCOL	USMC	California
FRANK, Leroy George	S1c	USN	Arkansas
FREDERICK, Charles Donald	EM2c	USN	Louisiana
FREE, Thomas Augusta	MM1c	USN	Texas
FREE, William Thomas	S2c	USN	Texas
FRENCH, John Edmund	LCDR	USN	Washington, D.C.
FRIZZELL, Robert Niven	S2c	USN	Alabama
FULTON, Robert Wilson	AMSMTH 1c	USN	Missouri
FUNK, Frank Francis	BM2c	USN	Missouri
FUNK, Lawrence Henry	S1c	USN	Wisconsin
GAGER, Roy Arthur	S2c	USN	Kansas
GARGARO, Ernest Russell	S2c	USN	
GARLINGTON, Raymond Wesley	S1c	USN	California
GARRETT, Orville Wilmer	SF2c	USN	Missouri
GARTIN, Gerald Ernest	S1c	USN	California

AUDETTE, William Frank	S1c	USN	Washington
AULTNEY, Ralph Martin	Em3c	USN	Illinois
AZECKI, Philip Robert	ENS	USNR	Wisconsin
EBHARDT, Kenneth Edward	S1c	USN	North Dakota
EER, Kenneth Floyd	S2c	USN	California
EISE, Marvin Frederick	S1c	USN	Wisconsin
EMIENHARDT, Samuel H. Jr.	MM2c	USN	Ohio
HOLSTON, Roscoe	Y2c	USN	Texas
IBSON, Billy Edwin	S1c	USN	West Virginia
IESEN, Karl Anthony	Y2c	USN	Iowa
ILL, Richard Eugene	S1c	USN	Nevada
IOVENAZZO, Michael James	WT2c	USN	Illinois
IVENS, Harold Reuben	Y3c	USN	
OBBIN, Angelo	SC1c	USN	California
OFF, Wiley Coy	S2c	USN	Oklahoma
OMEZ, Edward Jr.	S1c	USN	Colorado
OOD, Leland	S2c	USN	Illinois
OODWIN, William Arthur	S2c	USN	Colorado
ORDON, Peter Charles Jr.	F1c	USN	Colorado
OSSELIN, Edward Webb	ENS	USNR	Illinois
OSSELIN, Joseph Adjutor	RM1c	USN	Massachusetts
OULD, Harry Lee	S1c	USN	Illinois
OVE, Rupert Clair	S1c	USN	California
RANGER, Raymond Edward	F3c	USN	Iowa
RANT, Lawrence Everett	Y3c	USN	Missouri
RAY, Albert James	S1c	USN	Washington
RAY, Lawrence Moore	F1c	USN	Missouri
RAY, William James Jr.	S1c	USN	California
REEN, Glen Hubert	S1c	USN	Mississippi
REENFIELD, Carroll Gale	S1c	USN	Oregon
RIFFIN, Lawrence J.	PFC	USMC	Louisiana
RIFFIN, Reese Olin	EM3c	USN	Texas

GRIFFITHS, Robert Alfred	EM3c	USN	California
GRISSINGER, Robert Beryle	S2c	USN	Illinois
GROSNICKLE, Warren Wilbert	EM2c	USN	Iowa
GROSS, Milton Henry	CSKA	USN	California
GRUNDSTROM, Richard Gunner	S2c	USN	Iowa
GURLEY, Jesse Herbert	SK3c	USN	Illinois
HAAS, Curtis Junior	MUS2c	USN	Missouri
HADEN, Samuel William	COX	USN	Kansas
HAFFNER, Floyd Bates	F1c	USN	Illinois
HAINES, Robert Wesley	S2c	USN	California
HALL, John Rudolph	CBMP	USN	Arkansas
HALLORAN, William Ignatius	ENS	USNR	Ohio
HAMEL, Don Edgar	FLDMUS	USMCR	Illinois
HAMILTON, Clarence James	MM1c	USN	Washington
HAMILTON, Edwin Carrell	S1c	USN	
HAMILTON, William Holman	GM3c	USN	Oklahoma
HAMMERUD, George Winston	S1c	USN	North Dakota
HAMPTON, J. D.	F1c	USN	Kansas
HAMPTON, Ted W. Jr.	S1c	USN	Oklahoma
HAMPTON, Walter Lewis	BM2c	USN	Pennsylvania
HANNA, David Darling	EM3c	USN	Texas
HANSEN, Carlyle B.	MM2c	USN	
HANSEN, Harvey Ralph	S1c	USN	Wisconsin
HANZEL, Edward Joseph	WT1c	USN	Michigan
HARDIN, Charles Eugene	S1c	USN	Missouri
HARGRAVES, Kenneth William	S2c	USN	Washington
HARMON, William D.	PFC	USMC	Oregon
HARRINGTON, Keith Homer	S1c	USN	Missouri
HARRIS, George Ellsworth	MM1c	USN	Illinois
HARRIS, Hiram Dennis	S1c	USN	Georgia

HARRIS, James William	F1c	USN	Michigan
HARRIS, Noble Burnice	COX	USN	Missouri
HARRIS, Peter John	COX	USN	Nebraska
HARTLEY, Alvin	GM3c	USN	Oklahoma
HARTSOE, Max June	GM3c	USN	Missouri
HARTSON, Lonnie Moss	SM3c	USN	Texas
HASL, James Thomas	F1c	USN	Nebraska
HAVERFIELD, James Wallace	ENS	USNR	Ohio
HAVINS, Harvey Linfille	S1c	USN	
HAWKINS, Russell Dean	SM3c	USN	Illinois
HAYES, John Doran	BM1c	USN	California
HAYES, Kenneth Merle	F1c	USN	California
HAYNES, Curtis James	QM2c	USN	Idaho
HAYS, William Henry	SK3c	USN	Kansas
HAZDOVAC, Jack Claudius	S1c	USN	California
HEAD, Frank Bernard	CYA	USN	California
HEATER, Verrell Roy	S1c	USN	Oregon
HEATH, Alfred Grant	S1c	USN	Wisconsin
HEBEL, Robert Lee	SM3c	USNR	Illinois
HECKENDORN, Warren Guy	S1c	USN	
HEDGER, Jess Laxton	S1c	USN	California
HEDRICK, Paul Henry	BM1c	USN	California
HEELY, Leo Shinn	S2c	USN	Colorado
HEIDT, Edward Joseph	F1c	USN	California
HEIDT, Wesley John	MM2c	USN	California
HELM, Merritt Cameron	S1c	USN	Minnesota
HENDERSON, William Walter	S2c	USN	
HENDRICKSEN, Frank	F2c	USN	Michigan
HERRICK, Paul Edward	PVT	USMC	Wisconsin
HERRING, James Junior	SM3c	USN	Iowa
HERRIOTT, Robert Asher Jr.	S1c	USN	Texas
HESS, Darrel Miller	FC1c	USN	Utah
HESSDORFER, Anthony Joseph	MM2c	USN	Washington

HIBBARD, Robert Arnold	BKR2c	USN	
HICKMAN, Arthur Lee	SM3c	USN	
HICKS, Elmer Orville	GM3c	USN	Washington
HICKS, Ralph Dueard	PTR2c	USNR	Missouri
HILL, Bartley Talor	AOM3c	USN	California
HILTON, Wilson Woodrow	GM1c	USN	
HINDMAN, Frank Weaver	S1c	USN	Alabama
HODGES, Garris Vada	F2c	USN	Texas
HOELSCHER, Lester John	HA1c	USN	Nebraska
HOLLAND, Claude Herbert Jr.	S2c	USN	Alabama
HOLLENBACH, Paul Zepp	S1c	USN	New York
HOLLIS, Ralph	LTJG	USNR	California
HOLLOWELL, George Sanford	COX	USN	Arizona
HOLMES, Lowell D.	F3c	USN	Alabama
HOLZWORTH, Walter	MGYSGT	USMC	New Jersey
HOMER, Henry Vernon	S1c	USN	Michigan
HOPE, Harold W.	PVT	USMC	Illinois
HOPKINS, Homer David	S1c	USN	Michigan
HORN, Melvin Freeland	F3c	USN	Ohio
HORRELL, Harvey Howard	SM1c	USN	
HORROCKS, James William	CGMP	USN	Arizona
HOSLER, John Emmet	S1c	USN	Ohio
HOUSE, Clem Raymond	CWTP	USN	California
HOUSEL, John James	SK1c	USN	Missouri
HOWARD, Elmo	S1c	USN	Kentucky
HOWARD, Rolan George	GM3c	USN	Minnesota
HOWE, Darrell Robert	S2c	USN	Oregon
HOWELL, Leroy	COX	USN	Indiana
HUBBARD, Haywood Jr.	MATT2c	USN	Virginia
HUDNALL, Robert Chilton	PFC	USMC	Texas
HUFF, Robert Glenn	PVT	USMC	Texas
HUFFMAN, Clyde Franklin	F1c	USN	Ohio

HUGHES, Bernard Thomas	MUS2c	USN	Pennsylvania
HUGHES, Lewis Burton Jr.	S1c	USN	Alabama
HUGHES, Marvin Austin	PVT	USMCR	Texas
HUGHEY, James Clynton	S1c	USN	
HUIE, Doyne Conley	HA1c	USN	Missouri
HULTMAN, Donald Standly	PFC	USMC	Minnesota
HUNTER, Robert Frederick	S1c	USN	Ohio
HUNTINGTON, Henry Louis	S2c	USN	California
HURD, Willard Hardy	MATT2c	USN	Tennessee
HURLEY, Wendell Ray	MUS2c	USN	Indiana
HUVAL, Ivan Joseph	S1c	USN	Louisiana
HUX, Leslie Creade	PFC	USMC	Louisiana
HUYS, Arthur Albert	S1c	USN	Indiana
HYDE, William Hughes	COX	USN	Missouri
IAK, Joseph Claude	Y3c	USN	
IBBOTSON, Howard Burt	F1c	USN	California
INGALLS, Richard Fitch	SC3c	USN	New York
INGALLS, Theodore A.	SC3c	USN	New York
INGRAHAM, David Archie	FC3c	USN	
ISHAM, Orville Adalbert	CGMA	USN	Hawaii
ISOM, Luther James	S1c	USN	Alabama
IVERSEN, Earl Henry	S2c	USN	California
IVERSEN, Norman Kenneth	S2c	USN	California
IVEY, Charles Andrew Jr.	S2c	USN	California
JACKSON, David Paul Jr.	S1c	USN	Texas
JACKSON, Robert Woods	Y3c	USN	Iowa
JAMES, John Burditt	S1c	USN	Texas
JANTE, Edwin Earl	Y3c	USN	
JANZ, Clifford Thurston	LT	USN	California
JASTRZEMSKI, Edwin Charles	S1c	USN	Michigan
JEANS, Victor Lawrence	WT2c	USN	Oregon
JEFFRIES, Keith	COX	USN	Pennsylvania
JENKINS, Robert Henry D.	S2c	USN	Texas

JENSEN, Keith Marlow	EM3c	USN	Utah
JERRISON, Donald D.	CPL	USMC	California
JOHANN, Paul Frederick	GM3c	USN	Iowa
JOHNSON, David Andrew Jr.	OC2c	USN	Virginia
JOHNSON, Edmund Russell	MM1c	USN	California
JOHNSON, John Russell	RM3c	USN	Massachusetts
JOHNSON, Samuel Earle	CDR(MC)	USN	Alabama
JOHNSON, Sterling Conrad	COX	USN	Washington
JOLLEY, Berry Stanley	S2c	USNR	Idaho
JONES, Daniel Pugh	S2c	USN	Alabama
JONES, Edmon Ethmer	S1c	USN	Colorado
JONES, Floyd Baxter	MATT2c	USN	
JONES, Harry Cecil	GM3c	USN	Kansas
JONES, Henry Jr.	MATT1c	USN	California
JONES, Homer Lloyd	S1c	USN	Colorado
JONES, Hugh Junior	S2c	USN	California
JONES, Leland	S1c	USN	Tennessee
JONES, Quincy Eugene	PFC	USMC	Texas
JONES, Thomas Raymond	ENS	USNR	Louisiana
JONES, Warren Allen	Y3c	USN	Nebraska
JONES, Willard Worth	S1c	USN	Tennessee
JONES, Woodrow Wilson	S2c	USN	Alabama
JOYCE, Calvin Wilbur	F2c	USN	Ohio
JUDD, Albert John	COX	USN	Michigan
KAGARICE, Harold Lee	CSKA	USN	California
KAISER, Robert Oscar	F1c	USN	Missouri
KALINOWSKI, Henry	PVT	USMCR	Texas
KATT, Eugene Louis	S2c	USN	California
KEEN, Billy Mack	PVT	USMC	Texas
KELLER, Paul Daniel	MLDR2c	USN	Michigan
KELLEY, James Dennis	SF3c	USN	Oklahoma
KELLOGG, Wilbur Leroy	F1c	USN	Iowa
KELLY, Robert Lee	CEMA	USN	California
KENISTON, Donald Lee	S2c	USN	Ohio

KENISTON, Kenneth Howard	F3c	USN	Ohio
KENNARD, Kenneth Frank	GM3c	USN	Idaho
KENNINGTON, Charles Cecil	S1c	USN	Tennessee
KENNINGTON, Milton Homer	S1c	USN	Tennessee
KENT, Texas Thomas Jr.	S2c	USN	Arkansas
KIDD, Isaac Campbell	RADM	USN	
KIEHN, Ronald William	MM2c	USN	California
KIESELBACH, Charles Ermin	CM1c	USN	California
KING, Gordon Blane	S1c	USN	Tennessee
KING, Leander Cleaveland	S1c	USN	Texas
KING, Lewis Meyer	F1c	USN	
KING, Robert Nicholas Jr.	ENS	USNR	New York
KINNEY, Frederick William	MUS1c	USN	Washington
KINNEY, Gilbert Livingston	QM2c	USN	California
KIRCHHOFF, Wilbur Albert	S1c	USN	Missouri
KIRKPATRICK, Thomas Larcy	CAPT (CHC)	USN	Missouri
KLANN, Edward	SC1c	USN	Michigan
KLINE, Robert Edwin	GM2c	USN	New York
KLOPP, Francis Lawrence	GM3c	USN	Ohio
KNIGHT, Robert Wagner	EM3c	USN	Ohio
KNUBEL, William Jr.	S1c	USN	Missouri
KOCH, Walter Ernest	S1c	USN	Minnesota
KOENEKAMP, Clarence D.	F1c	USN	Washington
KOEPPE, Herman Oliver	SC3c	USN	Illinois
KOLAJAJCK, Brosig	S1c	USN	Texas
KONNICK, Albert Joseph	CM3c	USN	Pennsylvania
KOSEC, John Anthony	BM2c	USN	California
KOVAR, Robert	S1c	USN	Illinois
KRAHN, James Albert	PFC	USMC	North Dakota
KRAMB, James Henry	S1c	USN	New York
KRAMB, John David	MSMTH1c	USN	New York
KRAMER, Robert Rudolph	GM2c	USN	Indiana

KRAUSE, Fred Joseph	S1c	USN	Minnesota
KRISSMAN, Max Sam	S2c	USN	California
KRUGER, Richard Warren	QM2c	USN	California
KRUPPA, Adolph Louis	S1c	USN	Texas
KUKUK, Howard Helgi	S1c	USN	New York
KULA, Stanley	SC3c	USN	Nebraska
KUSIE, Donald Joseph	RM3c	USN	New York
LA FRANCEA, William Richard	S1c	USN	Michigan
LA MAR, Ralph B.	FC3c	USN	California
LA SALLE, Willard Dale	S1c	USN	Washington
LADERACH, Robert Paul	FC2c	USN	West Virginia
LAKE, John Ervin Jr.	WO (PYCLK)	USN	California
LAKIN, Donald Lapier	S1c	USN	California
LAKIN, Joseph Jordan	S1c	USN	California
LAMB, George Samuel	CSFA	USN	California
LANDMAN, Henry	AM2c	USN	Michigan
LANDRY, James Joseph Jr.	BKR2c	USN	Massachusetts
LANE, Edward Wallace	COX	USN	
LANE, Mancel Curtis	S1c	USN	Oklahoma
LANGE, Richard Charles	S1c	USN	California
LANGENWALTER, Orville J.	SK2c	USN	Iowa
LANOUETTE, Henry John	COX	USN	Connecticut
LARSON, Leonard Carl	F3c	USN	Washington
LATTIN, Bleecker	RM3c	USN	
LEE, Carroll Volney Jr.	S1c	USN	Texas
LEE, Henry Lloyd	S1c	USN	South Carolina
LEEDY, David Alonzo	FC2c	USN	Iowa
LEGGETT, John Goldie	BM2c	USN	Washington
LEGROS, Joseph McNeil	S1c	USN	Louisiana
LEIGH, Malcolm Hedrick	GM3c	USN	North Carolina
LEIGHT, James Webster	S2c	USN	California
LEOPOLD, Robert Lawrence	ENS	USNR	Kentucky

LESMEISTER, Steve Louie	EM3c	USN	North Dakota
LEVAR, Frank	CWTP	USNR	Washington
LEWIS, Wayne Alman	CM3c	USN	South Carolina
LEWISON, Neil Stanley	FC3c	USN	Wisconsin
LIGHTFOOT, Worth Ross	GM3c	USN	
LINBO, Gordon Ellsworth	GM1c	USN	Washington
LINCOLN, John William	F1c	USN	Iowa
LINDSAY, James E.	PFC	USMC	California
LINDSAY, James Mitchell	SF2c	USN	Colorado
LINTON, George Edward	F2c	USN	
LIPKE, Clarence William	F2c	USN	Michigan
LIPPLE, John Anthony	SF1c	USN	Iowa
LISENBY, Daniel Edward	S1c	USN	
LIVERS, Raymond Edward	S1c	USN	New Mexico
LIVERS, Wayne Nicholas	F1c	USN	New Mexico
LOCK, Douglas A.	S1c	USN	New York
LOHMAN, Earl Wynne	S1c	USN	
LOMAX, Frank Stuart	ENS	USN	Nebraska
LOMIBAO, Marciano	OS1c	USN	Philippines
LONG, Benjamin Franklin	CYP	USN	North Carolina
LOUNSBURY, Thomas William	S2c	USN	Illinois
LOUSTANAU, Charles Bernard	S1c	USN	Iowa
LOVELAND, Frank Crook	S2c	USN	Idaho
LOVSHIN, William Joseph	PFC	USMC	Minnesota
LUCEY, Neil Jeremiah	S1c	USN	New Jersey
LUNA, James Edward	S2c	USN	Oklahoma
LUZIER, Ernest Burton	MM2c	USN	
LYNCH, Emmett Isaac	MUS2c	USN	Washington
LYNCH, James Robert Jr.	GM3c	USN	Texas
LYNCH, William Joseph Jr.	S1c	USN	Texas
MADDOX, Raymond Dudley	CEMP	USN	California
MADRID, Arthur John	S2c	USN	California

MAFNAS, Francisco Reyes	MATT2c	USN	Guam
MAGEE, Gerald James	SK3c	USN	New York
MALECKI, Frank Edward	CYP	USN	California
MALINOWSKI, John Stanley	SM3c	USNR	Michigan
MALSON, Harry Lynn	SK3c	USN	Indiana
MANION, Edward Paul	S2c	USN	Illinois
MANLOVE, Arthur Cleon	WO(ELEC)	USN	California
MANN, William Edward	GM3c	USN	Washington
MANNING, Leroy	S2c	USN	Kentucky
MANSKE, Robert Francis	Y2c	USN	Iowa
MARINICH, Steve Matt	COX	USN	Utah
MARIS, Elwood Henry	S1c	USN	
MARLING, Joseph Henry	S2c	USN	Montana
MARLOW, Urban Herschel	COX	USN	Missouri
MARSH, Benjamin Raymond Jr.	ENS	USNR	Michigan
MARSH, William Arthur	S1c	USN	.
MARSHALL, Thomas Donald	S2c	USN	California
MARTIN, Hugh Lee	Y3c	USN	Utah
MARTIN, James Albert	BM1c	USN	Texas
MARTIN, James Orrwell	S2c	USN	California
MARTIN, Luster Lee	F3c	USN	Arkansas
MASON, Byron Dalley	S2c	USN	Idaho
MASTEL, Clyde Harold	S2c	USN	California
MASTERS, Dayton Monroe	GM3c	USN	Texas
MASTERSON, Cleburne E. Carl	PHM1c	USN	California
MATHEIN, Harold Richard	BMKR2c	USN	Illinois
MATHISON, Charles Harris	S1c	USN	Wisconsin
MATNEY, Vernon Merferd	F1c	USN	Wisconsin
MATTOX, James Durant	AM3c	USN	Florida
MAY, Louis Eugene	SC2c	USN	Kansas
MAYBEE, George Frederick	RM2c	USNR	California
MAYFIELD, Lester Ellsworth	F1c	USN	Colorado

MAYO, Rex Haywood	EM2c	USN	Florida
MEANS, Louis	MATT1c	USN	Texas
MEARES, John Morgan	S2c	USN	South Carolina
MENEFEE, James Austin	S1c	USN	Mississippi
MENO, Vicente Gogue	MATT2c	USN	
MENZENSKI, Stanley Paul	COX	USN	
MERRILL, Howard Deal	ENS	USN	Utah
MILES, Oscar Wright	S1c	USN	Arkansas
MILLER, Chester John	F2c	USN	Michigan
MILLER, Doyle Allen	COX	USN	Arkansas
MILLER, Forrest Newton	CEMP	USN	California
MILLER, George Stanley	S1c	USN	Ohio
MILLER, Jessie Zimmer	S1c	USN	Ohio
MILLER, John David	S1c	USN	
MILLER, William Oscar	SM3c	USN	Illinois
MILLIGAN, Weldon Harvey	S1c	USN	Texas
MIMS, Robert Lang	S1c	USN	Georgia
MINEAR, Richard J. Jr.	PFC	USMC	
MLINAR, Joseph	COX	USN	Pennsylvania
MOLPUS, Richard Preston	CMSMTHP	USN	California
MONROE, Donald	MATT2c	USN	Missouri
MONTGOMERY, Robert E.	S2c	USN	California
MOODY, Robert Edward	S1c	USN	Mississippi
MOORE, Douglas Carlton	S1c	USN	South Carolina
MOORE, Fred Kenneth	S1c	USN	Texas
MOORE, James Carlton	SF3c	USN	South Carolina
MOORHOUSE, William Starks	MUS2c	USN	Kansas
MOORMAN, Russell Lee	S2c	USN	California
MORGAN, Wayne	S1c	USN	California
MORGAREIDGE, James Orries	F2c	USN	Wyoming
MORLEY, Eugene Elvis	F2c	USN	Illinois
MORRIS, Owen Newton	S1c	USN	Alabama

MORRISON, Earl Leroy	S1c	USN	Montana
MORSE, Edward Charles	S2c	USN	Michigan
MORSE, Francis Jerome	BM1c	USN	California
MORSE, George Robert	S2c	USN	Montana
MORSE, Norman Roi	WT2c	USN	Virginia
MOSS, Tommy Lee	MATT2c	USN	Kentucky
MOSTEK, Francis Clayton	PFC	USMC	Idaho
MOULTON, Gordon Eddy	F1c	USN	California
MUNCY, Claude	MM2c	USN	California
MURDOCK, Charles Luther	WT1c	USN	Alabama
MURDOCK, Melvin Elijah	WT2c	USN	Alabama
MURPHY, James Joseph	S1c	USN	Arizona
MURPHY, James Palmer	F3c	USN	Ohio
MURPHY, Jessie Huell	S1c	USN	Louisiana
MURPHY, Thomas J. Jr.	SK1c	USN	Virginia
MYERS, James Gernie	SK1c	USN	Missouri
McCARRENS, James Francis	CPL	USMC	Illinois
McCARY, William Moore	S2c	USN	Alabama
McCLAFFERTY, John Charles	BM2c	USN	Ohio
McCLUNG, Harvey Manford	ENS	USNR	Pennsylvania
McFADDIN, Lawrence James	Y2c	USN	California
McGLASSON, Joe Otis	GM3c	USN	Illinois
McGRADY, Samme Willie Genes	MATT1c	USN	Alabama
McGUIRE, Francis Raymond	SK2c	USN	Michigan
McHUGHES, John Breckenridge	CWTA	USN	Washington
McINTOSH, Harry George	S1c	USN	Virginia
McKINNIE, Russell	MATT2c	USN	
McKOSKY, Michael Martin	S1c	USN	Oklahoma
McPHERSON, John Blair	S1c	USN	Tennessee
NAASZ, Erwin H.	SF2c	USN	Kansas
NADEL, Alexander Joseph	MUS2c	USN	New York
NATIONS, James Garland	FC2c	USN	South Carolina

NAYLOR, J. D.	SM2c	USN	Louisiana
NEAL, Tom Dick	S1c	USN	Texas
NECESSARY, Charles Raymond	S1c	USN	Missouri
NEIPP, Paul	S2c	USN	California
NELSEN, George	SC2c	USN	Washington
NELSON, Harl Coplin	S1c	USN	Arkansas
NELSON, Henry Clarence	BM1c	USN	Minnesota
NELSON, Lawrence Adolphus	CTCP	USN	California
NELSON, Richard Eugene	F3c	USN	North Dakota
NICHOLS, Alfred Rose	S1c	USN	Alabama
NICHOLS, Bethel Allan	S1c	USN	Washington
NICHOLS, Clifford Leroy	TC1c	USN	
NICHOLS, Louis Duffie	S2c	USN	Alabama
NICHOLSON, Glen Eldon	EM3c	USN	North Dakota
NICHOLSON, Hancel Grant	S1c	USN	
NIDES, Thomas James	EM1c	USN	California
NIELSEN, Floyd Theodore	CM3c	USN	Utah
NOLATUBBY, Henry Ellis	PFC	USMC	California
NOONAN, Robert Harold	S1c	USN	Michigan
NOWOSACKI, Theodore Lucian	ENS	USNR	New York
NUSSER, Raymond Alfred	GM3c	USN	
NYE, Frank Erskine	S1c	USN	California
O'BRIEN, Joseph Bernard	PFC	USMC	Illinois
O'BRYAN, George David	FC3c	USN	Massachusetts
O'BRYAN, Joseph Benjamin	FC3c	USN	Massachusetts
O'NEALL, Rex Eugene	S1c	USN	Colorado
O'NEILL, William Thomas Jr.	ENS	USNR	Connecticut
OCHOSKI, Henry Francis	GM2c	USN	Washington
OFF, Virgil Simon	S1c	USN	Colorado
OGLE, Victor Willard	S2c	USN	Oklahoma
OGLESBY, Lonnie Harris	S2c	USN	Mississippi
OLIVER, Raymond Brown	S1c	USN	California

OLSEN, Edward Kern	ENS	USNR	Kansas
OLSON, Glen Martin	S2c	USN	Washington
ORR, Dwight Jerome	S1c	USN	California
ORZECH, Stanislaus Joseph	S2c	USN	Connecticut
OSBORNE, Mervin Eugene	F1c	USN	Kentucky
OSTRANDER, Leland G.	PHM3c	USN	Minnesota
OTT, Peter Dean	S1c	USN	Ohio
OWEN, Frederick Halden	S2c	USN	Texas
OWENS, Richard Allen	SK2c	USN	Colorado
OWSLEY, Thomas Lea	SC2c	USN	Idaho
PACE, Amos Paul	BM1c	USN	California
PARKES, Harry Edward	BM1c	USN	California
PAROLI, Peter John	BKR3c	USN	California
PATTERSON, Clarence Rankin	PFC	USMC	
PATTERSON, Harold Lemuel	S1c	USN	Texas
PATTERSON, Richard Jr.	SF3c	USN	Connecticut
PAULMAND, Hilery	OS2c	USN	Philippines
PAVINI, Bruno	S1c	USN	California
PAWLOWSKI, Raymond Paul	S1c	USN	New York
PEARCE, Alonzo Jr.	S1c	USN	
PEARSON, Norman Cecil	S2c	USN	California
PEARSON, Robert Stanley	F3c	USN	Montana
PEAVEY, William Howard	QM2c	USN	Iowa
PECKHAM, Howard William	F2c	USN	Missouri
PEDROTTI, Francis James	PVT	USMC	Missouri
PEERY, Max Valdyne	S2c	USN	California
PELESCHAK, Michael	S1c	USN	Alabama
PELTIER, John Arthur	EM3c	USN	Ohio
PENTON, Howard Lee	S1c	USN	Alabama
PERKINS, George Ernest	F1c	USN	Rhode Island
PETERSON, Albert H. Jr.	FC3c	USN	New Jersey
PETERSON, Elroy Vernon	FC2c	USN	California
PETERSON, Hardy Wilbur	FC3c	USN	Washington

PETERSON, Roscoe Earl	S2c	USN	California
PETTIT, Charles Ross	CRMP	USN	California
PETYAK, John Joseph	S1c	USN	Tennessee
PHELPS, George Edward	S1c	USN	New York
PHILBIN, James Richard	S1c	USN	Colorado
PIASECKI, Alexander Louis	CPL	USMC	
PIKE, Harvey Lee	EM3c	USN	Georgia
PIKE, Lewis Jackson	S1c	USN	Georgia
PINKHAM, Albert Wesley	2c	USN	North Carolina
PITCHER, Walter Giles	GM1c	USN	California
POOL, Elmer Leo	S1c	USN	Indiana
POOLE, Ralph Ernest	S1c	USN	Ohio
POST, Darrell Albert	CMMA	USN	California
POVESKO, George	S1c	USN	Connecticut
POWELL, Jack Speed	PFC	USMC	California
POWELL, Thomas George	S1c	USN	Illinois
POWER, Abner Franklin	PVT	USMC	
PRESSON, Wayne Harold	S1c	USN	Ohio
PRICE, Arland Earl	RM2c	USN	Oregon
PRITCHETT, Robert Leo Jr.	S1c	USN	Louisiana
PUCKETT, Edwin Lester	SK3c	USN	Kentucky
PUGH, John Jr.	SF3c	USN	California
PUTNAM, Avis Boyd	SC3c	USN	Alabama
PUZIO, Edward	S1c	USN	Pennsylvania
QUARTO, Mike Joseph	S1c	USN	Connecticut
QUINATA, Jose Sanchez	MATT2c	USN	Guam
RADFORD, Neal Jason	MUS2c	USN	Nebraska
RASMUSSEN, Arthur Severin	CM1c	USN	California
RASMUSSON, George Vernon	F3c	USN	Minnesota
RATKOVICH, William	WT1c	USN	California
RAWHOUSER, Glen Donald	F3c	USN	Oregon
RAWSON, Clyde Jackson	BM1c	USN	Maryland
RAY, Harry Joseph	BM2c	USN	California
REAVES, Casbie	S1c	USN	Arkansas

RECTOR, Clay Cooper	SK3c	USN	Kentucky
REECE, John Jeffris	S2c	USN	Oklahoma
REED, James Buchanan Jr.	SK1c	USN	California
REED, Ray Ellison	S2c	USN	Oklahoma
REGISTER, Paul James	LCDR	USN	North Dakota
REINHOLD, Rudolph Herbert	PVT	USMC	Utah
RESTIVO, Jack Martin	Y2c	USN	Maryland
REYNOLDS, Earl Arthur	S2c	USN	Colorado
REYNOLDS, Jack Franklyn	S1c	USN	
RHODES, Birb Richard	F2c	USN	Tennessee
RHODES, Mark Alexander	S1c	USN	North Carolina
RICE, William Albert	S2c	USN	Washington
RICH, Claude Edward	S1c	USN	Florida
RICHAR, Raymond Lyle	S1c	USN	
RICHARDSON, Warren John	COX	USN	Pennsylvania
RICHISON, Fred Louis	GM3c	USN	California
RICHTER, Albert Wallace	COX	USN	
RICO, Guadalupe Augustine	S1c	USN	California
RIDDEL, Eugene Edward	S1c	USN	Michigan
RIGANTI, Fred	F3c	USN	California
RIGGINS, Gerald Herald	S1c	USN	California
RIVERA, Francisco Unpingoo	MATT2c	USN	Guam
ROBERTS, Dwight Fisk	F1c	USN	Kansas
ROBERTS, Kenneth Franklin	BM2c	USN	
ROBERTS, McClellan Taylor	CPHMP	USN	California
ROBERTS, Walter Scott Jr.	RM1c	USN	Missouri
ROBERTS, Wilburn Carle	BKR3c	USN	Louisiana
ROBERTS, William Francis	S2c	USN	
ROBERTSON, Edgar Jr.	MATT3c	USN	Virginia
ROBERTSON, James Milton	MM1c	USN	Tennessee
ROBINSON, Harold Thomas	S2c	USN	California
ROBINSON, James William	S2c	USN	California
ROBINSON, John James	EM1c	USN	Oregon
ROBINSON, Robert Warren	PHM3c	USN	West Virginia

ROBY, Raymond Arthur	S1c	USN	California
RODGERS, John Dayton	S1c	USN	Pennsylvania
ROEHM, Harry Turner	MM2c	USN	Illinois
ROGERS, Thomas Sprugeon	CWTP	USN	Alabama
ROMANO, Simon	OC1c	USN	Virginia
ROMBALSKI, Donald Roger	S2c	USN	Washington
ROMERO, Vladimir M.	S1c	USN	Virginia
ROOT, Melvin Leonard	S1c	USN	Ohio
ROSE, Chester Clay	BM1c	USN	Kentucky
ROSENBERY, Orval Robert	SF2c	USN	Illinois
ROSS, Deane Lundy	S2c	USN	New York
ROSS, William Fraser	GM3c	USN	New York
ROWE, Eugene Joseph	S1c	USN	New Jersey
ROWELL, Frank Malcom	S2c	USN	Texas
ROYALS, William Nicholas	F1c	USN	Virginia
ROYER, Howard Dale	GM3c	USN	Ohio
ROZAR, John Frank	WT2c	USN	California
ROZMUS, Joseph Stanley	S1c	USN	New Hampshire
RUDDOCK, Cecil Roy	S1c	USN	
RUGGERIO, William	FC3c	USN	
RUNCKEL, Robert Gleason	BUG1c	USN	
RUNIAK, Nicholas	S1c	USN	New Jersey
RUSH, Richard Perry	S1c	USN	Texas
RUSHER, Orville Lester	MM1c	USN	Missouri
RUSKEY, Joseph John	CBMP	USN	California
RUTKOWSKI, John Peter	S1c	USN	New York
RUTTAN, Dale Andrew	EM3c	USN	Florida
SAMPSON, Sherley Rolland	RM3c	USN	Minnesota
SANDALL, Merrill Deith	SF3c	USN	Illinois
SANDERS, Eugene Thomas	ENS	USN	New York
SANDERSON, James Harvey	MUS2c	USN	California
SANFORD, Thomas Steger	F3c	USN	
SANTOS, Filomeno	OC2c	USN	California
SATHER, William Ford	PMKR1c	USN	California

SAVAGE, Walter Samuel Jr.	ENS	USNR	Louisiana
SAVIN, Tom	RM2c	USN	Nebraska
SAVINSKI, Michael	S1c	USN	Pennsylvania
SCHDOWSKI, Joseph	S1c	USN	
SCHEUERLEIN, George Albert	GM3c	USN	Pennsylvania
SCHILLER, Ernest	S2c	USN	Texas
SCHLUND, Elmer Pershing	MM1c	USN	Nebraska
SCHMIDT, Vernon Joseph	S1c	USN	Minnesota
SCHNEIDER, William Jacob	PFC	USMC	
SCHRANK, Harold Arthur	BKR1c	USN	Texas
SCHROEDER, Henry	BM1c	USN	New Jersey
SCHUMAN, Herman Lincoln	SK1c	USN	California
SCHURR, John	EM2c	USN	Kansas
SCILLEY, Harold Hugh	SF2c	USN	Montana
SCOTT, A. J.	S2c	USN	
SCOTT, Crawford Edward	PFC	USMC	
SCOTT, George Harrison	PFC	USMC	
SCRUGGS, Jack Leo	MUS2c	USN	California
SEAMAN, Russell Otto	F1c	USN	Iowa
SEELEY, William Eugene	S1c	USN	Connecticut
SEVIER, Charles Clifton	S1c	USN	California
SHANNON, William Alfred	S1c	USN	Idaho
SHARBAUGH, Harry Robert	GM3c	USN	Pennsylvania
SHARON, Lewis Purdie	MM2c	USN	California
SHAW, Clyde Donald	S1c	USN	Ohio
SHAW, Robert K.	MUS2c	USN	Texas
SHEFFER, George Robert	S1c	USN	Indiana
SHERRILL, Warren Joseph	Y2c	USN	Texas
SHERVEN, Richard Stanton	EM3c	USN	North Dakota
SHIFFMAN, Harold Ely	RM3c	USN	Michigan
SHILEY, Paul Eugene	S1c	USN	Pennsylvania
SHIMER, Melvin Irvin	S1c	USN	
SHIVE, Gordon Eshom	PFC	USMC	California

SHIVE, Malcolm Holman	RM3c	USNR	California
SHIVELY, Benjamin Franklin	F1c	USN	Michigan
SHORES, Irland Jr.	S1c	USN	Alabama
SHUGART, Marvin John	S1c	USN	Colorado
SIBLEY, Delmar Dale	S1c	USN	New York
SIDDERS, Russell Lewis	S1c	USN	Ohio
SIDELL, John Henry	GM2c	USN	Illinois
SILVEY, Jesse	MM2c	USN	Texas
SIMENSEN, Carleton Elliott	2LT	USMC	
SIMON, Walter Hamilton	S1c	USN	New Jersey
SIMPSON, Albert Eugene	S1c	USN	
SKEEN, Harvey Leroy	S2c	USN	Arizona
SKILES, Charley Jackson Jr.	S2c	USN	Virginia
SKILES, Eugene	S2c	USN	
SLETTO, Earl Clifton	MM1c	USN	Minnesota
SMALLEY, Jack G.	S1c	USN	Ohio
SMART, George David	COX	USN	Montana
SMESTAD, Halge Hojem	RM2c	USN	Minnesota
SMITH, Albert Joseph	LTJG	USN	Virginia
SMITH, Earl Jr.	S1c	USN	Missouri
SMITH, Earl Walter	FC3c	USN	Florida
SMITH, Edward	GM3c	USN	Illinois
SMITH, Harry	S2c	USNR	California
SMITH, John A.	SF3c	USN	Ohio
SMITH, John Edward	S1c	USN	California
SMITH, Luther Kent	S1c	USN	Tennessee
SMITH, Mack Lawrence	S1c	USN	Arkansas
SMITH, Marvin Ray	S1c	USN	Texas
SMITH, Orville Stanley	ENS	USN	Oklahoma
SMITH, Walter Tharnel	MATT2c	USN	Mississippi
SNIFF, Jack Bertrand	CPL	USMC	
SOENS, Harold Mathias	SC1c	USN	California
SOOTER, James Fredrick	RM3c	USN	
SORENSEN, Holger Earl	S1c	USN	New Mexico

SOUTH, Charles Braxton	S1c	USN	Alabama
SPENCE, Merle Joe	S1c	USN	Tennessee
SPOTZ, Maurice Edwin	F1c	USN	Illinois
SPREEMAN, Robert Lawrence	GM3c	USN	Michigan
SPRINGER, Charles Harold	S2c	USN	California
STALLINGS, Kermit Braxton	F1c	USN	North Carolina
STARKOVICH, Charles	EM3c	USN	Washington
STARKOVICH, Joseph Jr.	F2c	USN	Washington
STAUDT, Alfred Parker	F3c	USN	Washington
STEFFAN, Joseph Philip	BM2c	USN	Illinois
STEIGLEDER, Lester Leroy	COX	USN	Ohio
STEINHOFF, Lloyd Delroy	S1c	USN	California
STEPHENS, Woodrow Wilson	EM1c	USN	Washington
STEPHENSON, Hugh Donald	S1c	USN	New York
STEVENS, Jack Hazelip	S1c	USN	Texas
STEVENS, Theodore R.	AMM2c	USN	California
STEVENSON, Frank Jake	PFC	USMC	New York
STEWART, Thomas Lester	SC3c	USN	Arkansas
STILLINGS, Gerald Fay	F2c	USN	
STOCKMAN, Harold William	FC3c	USN	Idaho
STOCKTON, Louis Alton	S2c	USN	California
STODDARD, William Edison	S1c	USN	Louisiana
STOPYRA, Julian John	RM3c	USN	Massachusetts
STORM, Laun Lee	Y1c	USN	California
STOVALL, Richard Patt	PFC	USMC	
STRANGE, Charles Orval	F2c	USN	
STRATTON, John Raymond	S1c	USN	Indiana
SUGGS, William Alfred	S1c	USN	Florida
SULSER, Frederick Franklin	GM3c	USN	Ohio
SUMMERS, Glen Allen	Y1c	USN	Washington
SUMMERS, Harold Edgar	SM2c	USN	Ohio
SUMNER, Oren	S2c	USN	New Mexico
SUTTON, Clyde Westly	CCSTDP	USN	California

SUTTON, George Woodrow	SK1c	USN	Kentucky
SWIONTEK, Stanley Stephen	FLDCK	USN	Illinois
SWISHER, Charles Elijah	S1c	USN	California
SYMONETTE, Henry	OC1c	USN	California
SZABO, Theodore Stephen	PVT	USMCR	
TAMBOLLEO, Victor Charles	SF3c	USN	Maryland
TANNER, Russell Allen	GM3c	USN	Washington
TAPIE, Edward Casamiro	MM2c	USN	California
TAPP, Lambert Ray	GM3c	USN	Kentucky
TARG, John	CWTP	USN	California
TAYLOR, Aaron Gust	MATT1c	USN	California
TAYLOR, Charles Benton	EM3c	USN	Illinois
TAYLOR, Harry Theodore	GM2c	USN	Indiana
TAYLOR, Robert Denzil	COX	USN	Iowa
TEELING, Charles Madison	CPRTP	USNR	California
TEER, Allen Ray	EM1c	USN	California
TENNELL, Raymond Clifford	S1c	USN	Texas
TERRELL, John Raymond	F2c	USN	Arkansas
THEILLER, Rudolph	S1c	USN	California
THOMAS, Houston O'Neal	COX	USN	Texas
THOMAS, Randall James	S1c	USN	West Virginia
THOMAS, Stanley Horace	F3c	USN	
THOMAS, Vincent Duron	COX	USN	California
THOMPSON, Charles Leroy	S1c	USN	Illinois
THOMPSON, Irven Edgar	S1c	USN	Ohio
THOMPSON, Robert Gary	SC1c	USN	California
THORMAN, John Christopher	EM2c	USN	Iowa
THORNTON, George Hayward	GM3c	USN	Mississippi
TINER, Robert Reaves	F2c	USN	Texas
TISDALE, William Esley	CWTP	USN	California
TRIPLETT, Thomas Edgar	S1c	USN	California
TROVATO, Tom	S1c	USN	California
TUCKER, Raymond Edward	COX	USN	Indiana

TUNTLAND, Earl Eugene	S1c	USN	North Dakota
TURNIPSEED, John Morgan	F3c	USN	Arkansas
TUSSEY, Lloyd Harold	EM3c	USN	North Carolina
TYSON, Robert	FC3c	USN	Louisiana
UHRENHOLDT, Andrew Curtis	ENS	USNR	Wisconsin
VALENTE, Richard Dominic	GM3c	USN	California
VAN ATTA, Garland Wade	MM1c	USN	California
VAN HORN, James Randolf	S2c	USN	Arizona
VAN VALKENBURGH, Franklin	CAPT(CO)	USN	Minnesota
VARCHOL, Brinley	GM2c	USN	Pennsylvania
VAUGHAN, William Frank	PHM2c	USN	
VEEDER, Gordon Elliott	S2c	USN	Idaho
VELIA, Galen Steve	SM3c	USN	Kansas
VIEIRA, Alvaro Everett	S2c	USN	Rhode Island
VOJTA, Walter Arnold	S1c	USN	Minnesota
VOSTI, Anthony August	GM3c	USN	California
WAGNER, Mearl James	SC2c	USN	California
WAINWRIGHT, Silas Alonzo	PHM1c	USN	New York
WAIT, Wayland Lemoyne	S1c	USN	
WALKER, Bill	S1c	USN	Texas
WALLACE, Houston Oliver	WT1c	USN	Arkansas
WALLACE, James Frank	S1c	USN	Wisconsin
WALLACE, Ralph Leroy	F3c	USN	Oregon
WALLENSTIEN, Richard Henry	S1c	USN	
WALTERS, Clarence Arthur	S2c	USN	California
WALTERS, William Spurgeon Jr.	FC3c	USN	New Mexico
WALTHER, Edward Alfred	FC3c	USN	
WALTON, Alva Dowding	Y3c	USN	Utah
WARD, Albert Lewis	S1c	USN	Oklahoma
WARD, William E.	COX	USN	Illinois

WATKINS, Lenvil Leo	F2c	USN	Kentucky
WATSON, William Lafayette	F3c	USN	Florida
WATTS, Sherman Maurice	HA1c	USN	Arkansas
WATTS, Victor Ed	GM3c	USN	Texas
WEAVER, Richard Walter	S1c	USN	Nevada
WEBB, Carl Edward	PFC	USMC	
WEBSTER, Harold Dwayne	S2c	USN	Colorado
WEEDEN, Carl Alfred	ENS	USN	Colorado
WEIDELL, William Peter	S2c	USN	Minnesota
WEIER, Bernard Arthur	PVT	USMC	Illinois
WELLER, Ludwig Fredrick	CSKP	USN	California
WELLS, Floyd Arthur	RM2c	USN	
WELLS, Harvey Anthony	SF2c	USN	California
WELLS, Raymond Virgil Jr.	S1c	USN	Missouri
WELLS, William Bennett	S1c	USN	Missouri
WEST, Broadus Franklin	S1c	USN	South Carolina
WEST, Webster Paul	S1c	USN	Arkansas
WESTCOTT, William Percy Jr.	S1c	USN	Indiana
WESTERFIELD, Ivan Ayers	S1c	USN	California
WESTIN, Donald Vern	F3c	USN	Oregon
WESTLUND, Fred Edwin	BM2c	USN	California
WHISLER, Gilbert Henry	PFC	USMC	
WHITAKER, John William Jr.	S1c	USN	Louisiana
WHITCOMB, Cecil Eugene	EM3c	USN	Michigan
WHITE, Charles William	MUS2c	USN	
WHITE, James Clifton	F1c	USN	Texas
WHITE, Vernon Russell	S1c	USN	South Carolina
WHITE, Volmer Dowin	S1c	USN	Mississippi
WHITEHEAD, Ulmont Irving Jr.	ENS	USN	Connecticut
WHITLOCK, Paul Morgan	S2c	USN	Texas
WHITSON, Ernest Hubert Jr.	MUS2c	USN	California
WHITT, William Byron	GM3c	USN	Kentucky

WHITTEMORE, Andrew Tiny	MATT2c	USN	Tennessee
WICK, Everett Morris	FC3c	USN	Oregon
WICKLUND, John Joseph	S1c	USN	Minnesota
WILCOX, Arnold Alfred	QM2c	USN	Iowa
WILL, Joseph William	S2c	USN	Colorado
WILLETTE, Laddie James	S2c	USN	Michigan
WILLIAMS, Adrian Delton	S1c	USN	Louisiana
WILLIAMS, Clyde Richard	MUS2c	USN	Oklahoma
WILLIAMS, George Washington	S1c	USN	Virginia
WILLIAMS, Jack Herman	RM3c	USNR	South Carolina
WILLIAMS, Laurence A.	ENS(AV)	USNR	Ohio
WILLIAMSON, Randolph Jr.	MATT2c	USN	
WILLIAMSON, William Dean	RM2c	USNR	California
WILLIS, Robert Kenneth Jr.	S1c	USN	Louisiana
WILSON, Bernard Martin	RM3c	USNR	New York
WILSON, Comer A.	CBMP	USN	Alabama
WILSON, Hurschel Woodrow	F2c	USN	Ohio
WILSON, John James	S1c	USN	California
WILSON, Neil Mataweny	CWO (MACH)	USN	California
WILSON, Ray Milo	RM3c	USNR	Iowa
WIMBERLY, Paul Edwin	GM3c	USN	Tennessee
WINDISH, Robert James	PVT	USMC	Missouri
WINDLE, Robert England	PFC	USMC	Illinois
WINTER, Edward	WO (MACH)	USNR	Washington
WITTENBERG, Russell Duane	PVT	USMC	
WOJTKIEWICZ, Frank Peter	CMMP	USN	California
WOLF, George Alexanderson Jr.	ENS	USNR	Pennsylvania
WOOD, Harold Baker	BM2c	USN	Colorado
WOOD, Horace Van	S1c	USN	Texas

WOOD, Roy Eugene	F1c	USN	Arizona
WOODS, Vernon Wesley	S1c	USN	Texas
WOODS, William Anthony	S2c	USN	New York
WOODWARD, Ardenne Allen	MM2c	USN	California
WOODY, Harlan Fred	S2c	USN	
WOOLF, Norman Bragg	CWTP	USN	Alabama
WRIGHT, Edward Henry	S2c	USN	Illinois
WYCKOFF, Robert Leroy	F1c	USN	New Jersey
YATES, Elmer Elias	SC3c	USN	Nebraska
YEATS, Charles Jr.	COX	USN	Illinois
YOMINE, Frank Peter	F2c	USN	Illinois
YOUNG, Eric Reed	ENS	USN	Colorado
YOUNG, Glendale Rex	S1c	USN	
YOUNG, Jay Wesley	S1c	USN	Utah
YOUNG, Vivan Louis	WT1c	USN	Virginia
ZEILER, John Virgel	S1c	USN	Colorado
ZIEMBRICKE, Steve A.	S1c	USN	New York
ZIMMERMAN, Fred	Cox	USN	North Dakota
ZIMMERMAN, Lloyd McDonald	S2c	USN	Missouri
ZWARUN, Michael Jr.	S1c(S2c)	USN	New Jersey

USS *ARIZONA* SURVIVORS

DECEMBER 7, 1941

UNITED STATES NAVY

Charles A. Amacher, Sea1c

John D. Anderson, BM2c

Walter F. Bagby, SF3c

Kasten A. Ball, F1c

Galen O. Ballard, F1c

DeWayne Barth, BM1c

Edward F. Bass, F2c

William N. Baumeister, ACMM

Harvey H. Becker, GM2c

Edwin W. Bemis, Sea1c

Earl D. Bennett, GM3c

George A. Berdollt, FC3c

Leroy A. Bird, CTC

Estelle Birdsell, MM1

Daniel T. Birtwell, Lt. Comdr.

Edward R. Bodey, BM2c

Andrew J. Bowen, Jr., CMM

Harry F. Bradshaw, Sea1c

John Braydis, Sea1c

Gene R. Brown, Sea1c

Robert J. Browning, Sea2c

John F. Bruce, GM3c

Lauren F. Bruner, FC3c

Martin B. Bruns, Y2c

Herbert V. Buehl, F3c

Jimmie C. Burcham, Sea1c

Leland Burk, GM3c

William J. Bush, Ens

Ralph D. Byard, CCStd

Frank M. Campbell, Ens

George K. Campbell, CTC

Ray C. Carlson, Sea2c

Carl M. Carson, Sea1c

Edwin R. Chandler, Sea1c

Noel B. Chapman, Sea2c

William R. Chappell, Sea1c

Harlan C. Christiansen, Sea2c

Gordon P. Chung-Hoon, Lt.

Marion H. Clouser, GM1c

George W. Coburn, Sea1c

Charles W. Coker, Lt.

Clyde J. Combs, Sea1c

Daniel J. Condon, Lt(jg)

Louis A. Conter, QM3c

Lonnie D. Cook, Sea1c

Lloyd E. Coole, Sea1c

Norman W. Coplin, Sea1c

Ralph V. L. Corbin, Sea1c

Lyle R. Cornelius, Sea2c

Ray C. Cosby, Sea1c

John M. Cox, Jr., Lt. Comdr.

Francis B. G. Cozad, Sea2c

Lee R. Crothers, BM1c

Henry M. Cruz, MAtt1c

Donald A. Culp, Sea2c

Anthony F. Czarnecki, MM1c

Alfred E. Daniel, GM1c

James A. Dare, Ens.

Carl E. Davis, GM3c

Elvin C. Davis, Sea1c

Henry D. Davison, Ens.

William E. Dean, BM1c

John D. Dearing, WT2c

Deward Decker, Cox

Joseph C. Deserano, Mldr1c

William C. A. Dickerson, RM2c

Merle E. Dickinson, GM3c

Clarence J. Dobson, GM3c

John A. Doherty, CGM

Timothy A. Donegan, Prtr1c

John W. Doucett, GM3c

Henry B. Duncan, FC3c

Tommie W. Duncan, BM2c

Kenneth E. Edmondson, Cox

Paul H. Egan, FC3c

Merle Elkins, Sea1c

Lawrence E. Elliott, MM1c

George W. Ellis, SC1c

James R. Enos, Sea2c

Weldon V. Eskew, MM1c

John W. Evans, Sea1c

Elmer E. Eversole, Sea1c

Lawrence O. Eyman, Sea1c

Francis M. Falge, Lt.

Lawrence A. Farquhar, FC2c

Paul H. Faulkner, Sea1c

Lawrence E. Fay, GM3c

Nathaniel Felton, MAtt1c

Jennings P. Field, Ens.

William R. Finger, SM1c

Harry L. Fitch, Ens.

Guy S. Flanagan, Jr., Ens.

Wendell L. Flannery, Cox

Dale F. Flory, WT2c

James L. Forbis, Cox

James P. Foster, Jr., Sea1c

Ralph E. Fowler, BM1c

Robert D. Fowler, Sea2c

Glen Frazier, CGM

Everett E. Frye, Sea1c

Samuel G. Fuqua, Lt. Comdr.

William F. Gallagher, CEM

Jerome H. Garfield, Ens.

Walter J. Gaskins, Sea1c

Harold W. Gaut, Sea1c

Ellis H. Geiselman, Comdr.

Claud C. Gibson, Sea1c

Arthur B. Gilbert, Sea1c

Charles M. Gillem, Sea1c

Charles E. Gillenwater, Sea1c

David W. Gillespie, Sea1c

Richard C. Glenn, Ens.

William J. Goldsberry, Sea1c

Donald E. Gordon, GM2c

William E. Goshen, Sea1c

Leon Grabowsky, Ens.

Donald A. Graham, AMM1c

James V. Gray, Sea1c

Clay D. Green, Jr., Sea1c

James W. Green, GM3c

George E. Grim, GM1c

Charles W. Guerin, Jr., Sea1c

Andrew Guna, BM1c

Howard G. Haerling, BM1c

Raymond J. Haerry, Cox

Elsworth F. Hamilton, ACMM

James E. Hamilton, Sea1c

Vernon Hand, Sea1c

Paul E. Hargis, Y3c

Oliver V. Harr, MM1c

Allen B. Harrell, Sea1c

Henry S. Harris, Sea1c

John D. Harris, Sea1c

James W. Hart, F1c

Alfred J. Hartland, Sea1c

Richard Hauff, GM3c

Douglas Hein, Ens.

Robert H. Heinz, Sea1c

Robert M. Hendon, CGM

John W. Henry, Ens.

Clarendon R. Hetrick, Sea1c

Richard H. Hill, Y2c

John H. Hinton, CSM

Clarence O. Hjelle, Sea2c

Fred M. Holland, Sea1c

Roy W. Holmes, Sea1c

Alfred J. Homann, Lt.

Woodrow R. Hooks, Sea2c

Clifford C. Hooper, RM2c

John P. Howatt, Ens.

James C. Hughes, Sea1c

Lester D. Hull, Sea1c

Milton T. Hurst, AMM3c

Edward F. Hutchins, Lt.

Peter Huzar, WT1c

Charles E. Hyslope, F1c

Donald Inselman, Sea1c

Edward J. Janikowski, Cox

Warren E. Jeffers, Sea1c

Donald R. Johnson, Sea1c

Neil F. Johnson, Cox

Brooxey J. Johnston, Jr., GM3c

Hubert H. Jones, CWT

Joe F. Karb, CWT

C. H. Keener, GM3c

Carl E. Keffer, Sea1c

Bruce K. Kelley, Lt. Comdr

Guy D. Kirk, Sea1c

Walter M. Kissinger, MM1c

Harold J. Kuhn, Sea1c

Stanley R. Kurtz, Sea1c

James D. Lancaster, Sea1c

Ralph W. Landreth, GM2c

Glenn H. Lane, RM3c

Joseph K. Langdell, Ens.

Thomas H. Lawrence, Sea1c

James L. Lawson, GM3c

Leonard G. Lawson, Sea1c

Lindsay R. Leighton, WT1c

Louis Lencses, GM3c

George B. Lenning, Ens.

Curtis J. Leopard, BM1c

William E. Lewis, Lt.(jg)(MC)

Jack L. Lindsey, Sea1c

Russell A. Lott, Sea1c

Steven J. Lukasavitz, Sea1c

Donald E. MacQueen, Ens.

Billy B. Mainwaring, F3c

John Malaski, Sea1c

Everett A. Malcolm, Ens.

Joseph Mancuso, Sea1c

Charles C. Mann, Lt.

Harry B. Marcum, CEM

Edward J. Marks, Cox

Kleber S. Masterson, Lt.

Herbert Mattlage, Ens.

John H. McCarron, GM2c

Don E. McDonald, Sea1c

Charles W. McFall, GM1c

Kenneth K. McKenna, SM1c

Earle T. Melvin, CFC

John H. Metcalf, Sea2c

Thomas W. Migliaccio, Sea2c

Harvey H. Milhorn, GM3c

Jim D. Miller, Ens.

Donald H. Millikin, Sea2c

James H. Mini, Lt.(jg)

Stanley R. Mode, EM1c

Rolland E. Mommer, BM2c

Thomas D. Murdock, CY

Clay H. Musick, Sea1c

Jack C. Mylan, SM2c

Grady L. Nelson, Jr., Sea2c

Bobby E. Newell, Sea2c

John E. Nichols, RM1c

Stanley J. Niemara, Sea1c

Edward F. J. O'Brion, Sea1c

Harold E. Olip t, GM3c

Vernon J. Olsen, Sea1c

William D. Osborne, Jr., Sea1c

Robert H. Osmond, FC3c

Vernon M. Osterberg, Ens.

Clarence W. Otterman, GM2c

Paul R. Owen, Sea1c

Patrocinio Pablo, OS1c

Louis J. Pacitti, GM3c

William Parker, Sea1c

Earl H. Pecotte, GM2c

William J. Peil, BM2c

Seth H. Perry, Sea2c

Berwyn R. Phipps, SF2c

George D. Phraner, Sea2c

George F. Pittard, Lt.

Robert L. Pitz, Sea1c

Francis L. Pollack, SC3c

Stanley H. Port, Jr., Cox

Ernest M. Posey, MM1c

Howard K. Potts, Cox

Alfred A. Pousson, Sea2c

Richard W. Probst, Sea1c

Louis A. Puckett, Comdr. (SC)

William R. Purvis, F3c

Wallace F. Quillin, Sea1c

Carl F. Rahn, Jr., Sea1c

John W. Rampley, GM3c

Millard A. Ramsdell, Ens.

Everett O. Reid, MM1c

Eldon R. Reifert, Cox

Maurice D. Rider, BM1c

William H. Ridley, RM3c

Earl W. Riner, GM3c

Lewis P. Robinson, Sea1c

John P. Rourke, Sea1c

Welton D. Rowley, Lt. Comdr.

Fred L. Ruhlman, Lt.

Jack I. Sadler, Sea2c

Joseph S. Sadowski, Sea1c

Elmer L. Sanders, GM1c

Robert I. Sargent, Jr., Sea2c

Herman L. Schafer, Jr., Ens.

Anthony R. Schubert, Ens.

William J. Schumacher, WT1c

Robert F. Seeley, Sea2c

John J. Shaffer III, Lt.

Ernest M. Shawn, GM3c

Joseph Shebak, Sea1c

Martin L. Shew, MM2c

Claude W. Simmons, Jr., Sea1c

Clyde C. Smith, CEM

Harold F. Smith, BM2c

Roscoe B. Smith, GM3c

William H. Smith, Jr., Cox

Rutherford H. Snow, WT1c

Thomas W. Stanborough, Jr., Sea1c

Don H. Starks, MM1c

Bernald H. Stoffer, AMM1c

Donald G. Stratton, Sea1c

Herbert R. Strong, Cox

Jean M. Stuart, Sea1c

Aubry R. Sullivan, Cox

Laurence E. Tagtmeyer, Ch Gun

Murray L. Tapp, Sea2c

Stanley M. Teslow, GM2c

Steven J. Thoma, EM3c

Norman Thompson, Mach

Glenwood O. Trantham, BM1c

Vernon A. Travioli, Sea2c

Edward D. Tucker, BM2c

Richard N. Turner, Jr., Sea1c

Edmund L. Urbaniak, Ch Carp

Edward L. Van Winkle, F2c

Keith L. Velia, Sea2c

James A. Vessels, GM3c

Daniel Vidal, Matt1c

Vincent J. Vlach, Jr., Y1c

Charles A. Von Spreckelsen, Ptr2c

Robert E. Wagner, Sea1c

Rudolph L. Wagner, CBM

James E. Walker, QM2c

Homan L. Walsh, Ens. (SC)

James R. Ward, Sea1c

Kenneth T. Warriner, Sea2c

Russell W. Warriner, Sea1c

Joseph H. Washington, Matt1c

Howard L. Watson, BM1c

Richard D. Weaver, BM1c

Frank Welch, Jr., Ens.

Oree C. Weller, Sea2c

Harold L. Wells, Sea1c

Eddie C. Welter, Sea1c

Edward L. Wentzlaff, AOM2c

Mark A. West, CMM

Clinton H. Westbrook, Sea1c

Thomas A. White, BM2c

John F. Williams, GM3c

Charles L. Wilson, Sea1c

Harold G. Wilson, Jr., F2c

James L. Wise, Sea1c

Edward A. Zadik, Sea2c

UNITED STATE MARINES

John M. Baker, Sgt

Edward J. Braham, PFC

Frank R. Cabiness, PFC

Edward J. Carter, PlatSgt

James E. Cory, Pvt1c

John P. Coursey, 1stLt.

Lamar S. Crawford, Pvt1c

John H. Earle, Jr., Capt.

Kenneth D. Goodman, Pvt1c

Charles L. Hardy, Pvt

Russell J. McCurdy, Pvt

Earl C. Nightingale, Cpl

Alan Shapley, Maj

Michael Soley, Cpl

Donald G. Young, Pvt1c

APPENDIX D

FUNERAL SERVICES OF *ARIZONA* MEN
ABOARD THE USS *ARIZONA*

Stanley M. Teslow   GM2C   April 12, 1982
(Funeral urn dropped into the U.S.S. *Arizona*)
Donald H. Millikin   S2C   March 19, 1984
(Interment by U.S. Navy Explosive Ordnance Disposal)
Ralph Crippen   Y1C   July 8, 1987
(ashes scattered) Captain's Yeoman on the *Arizona,* 1937
William J. Peil   BM2C   November 22, 1988
(Interment by U.S. Navy Explosives Ordnance Disposal)
Robert L. Pitz   S1C   December 7, 1989
(Interment by U.S. Navy Explosives Ordnance Disposal)
Harold E. Oliphant   GM3C   August 1, 1990
(Interment by U.S. Navy Explosives Ordnance Disposal)
James C. Hughes   S1C   March 2, 1991
(ashes scattered) S1C Hughes was assigned to the Naval Hospital but served on a temporary detail to the U.S.S *Arizona* on December 7, 1941.
Guy S. Flanagan Jr.   ENS   May 13, 1992
(Interment by U.S. Navy Explosives Ordnance Disposal)
Lyle R. Cornelius   S2C   July 11, 1992
(Interment by U.S. Navy Explosives Ordnance Disposal)
Paul H. Egan   FC3C   January 12, 1993
(Interment by U.S. Navy Explosives Ordnance Disposal; Wit-

nessed by Resource Manager Kendall Thompson and Volunteer Jim Adams, NPS)

Grady Lee Nelson Jr.   S2C   December 7, 1993
(Interment by Resource Manager Jim Adams and Volunteer USMC Staff Sergeant Todd Hall, NPS)

Kenneth Norton   S1C   June 5, 1995
(ashes scattered) S1C Norton was in Maui conducting gunnery exercises for the fleet on December 7, 1941.

Harold W. Gaut   S1C   June 9, 1995
(Interment by Resource Manager Jim Adams and Volunteer USMC Staff Sergeant Todd Hall, NPS)

Norman W. Coplin   S1C   December 7, 1996
(Interment by Ranger Jim Adams, Chief Ranger Randy Wester, and Volunteers USMC Captain Bob Venema and USMC Staff Sergeant Todd Hall, NPS)

James W. Green   GM3C   December 7, 1996
(Interment by Ranger Jim Adams, Chief Ranger Randy Wester, and Volunteers USMC Captain Bob Venema and USMC Staff Sergeant Todd Hall, NPS)

Frank M. Campbell   ENS   December 7, 1996
ENS Campbell had just left the USS *Arizona* in a whaleboat to attend Catholic church services shortly before the bombings began.
(Interment by Ranger Jim Adams, Chief Ranger Randy Wester, and Volunteers USMC Captain Bob Venema and USMC Staff Sergeant Todd Hall, NPS)

Jack I. Sadler   S2C   October 6, 1998
(ashes scattered)

Richard Foley   FN2   November 3, 1998
(ashes scattered) FN2 Foley served aboard the USS *Arizona* in peacetime during the interwar period between World War I and World War II.

John Mitchell   Unknown July 13, 1999

(ashes scattered) Mr. Mitchell was "a sailor" aboard the USS *Arizona* in peacetime during the interwar period between World War I and World War II. He served in the U.S. Navy for less than three years.

Don Harrison Starks   MM1C   July 13, 1999

(Interment by Curator Deborah King and Volunteer Dick Capps, NPS)

Francis M. Falge   LT   April 26, 2000

Lt. Falge was attending Mass in Kailua with his wife and three sons at the time of the attack.

(Interment by Superintendent Kathy Billings, Curator Deborah King, and Volunteer Dick Capps, NPS)

Lewis P. Robinson   S1C   December 7, 2000

S1C Robinson was returning to the *Arizona* from a dockside pier. With the USS *Arizona* destroyed, the "shore boat" proceeded to the USS *Maryland,* where he crewed the antiaircraft director.

(Interment by Superintendent Kathy Billings, Curator Deborah King, and Ranger Eric Andersen)

APPENDIX E

SHIP CASUALTIES OF JAPAN IN WORLD WAR II

Of the attacking Japanese fleet that initiated the war against the United States on December 7, 1941, all ships ended up on the bottom of the sea by the war's end *except* one midget submarine.

CARRIERS

Kaga, Akagi, Hiryu, and *Soryu*—sunk at Midway, June 4–, 1942

Shokaku—sunk near Yap Island, June 19, 1944

Zuikaku—sunk at Battle of Cape Engano, October 20, 1944

BATTLESHIPS

Hiei—sunk off Savo Island (Solomons), November 13, 1942

Kirishima—sunk off Savo, November 15, 1942

CRUISERS

Chikuma—badly damaged off Samar (Philippines) and then scuttled, October 25, 1944

Tone—bombed and sunk at Kure (Japan), July 24, 1945

LIGHT CRUISERS

Abukuma—sunk by aircraft off Philippines, October 27, 1944

DESTROYERS

Akigumo—sunk off Philippines, April 11, 1944

Arare—sunk off Kiska, July 5, 1942

Hamakaze—sunk off Japan, April 7, 1945

Isokaze—sunk off Japan, April 7, 1945

Kagero—sunk off Rendova, May 8, 1943

Kasumi—sunk off Japan, April 7, 1945

Shiranui—sunk off Panay, October 27, 1944

Tanikaze—sunk off Philippines, June 9, 1944

Urakaze—sunk off Formosa, November 21, 1944

SUBS

I-1—wrecked off Guadalcanal, January 29, 1943

I-2—sunk April 7, 1944 off New Hanover

I-3—sunk off Guadalcanal, December 2, 1942

I-4—sunk December 25, 1942

I-5—sunk off Guam, July 19, 1944

I-6—missing off Saipan, June 30, 1944

I-7—sunk off Kiska, July 5, 1943

I-8—sunk off Okinawa, March 31, 1945

I-9—sunk off Kiska, June 13, 1944

I-15—sunk off San Cristobal, November 2, 1942

I-16—sunk off Cape Alexander, May 19, 1944

I-17—sunk off Noumea, August 19, 1943

I-18—sunk off San Cristobal, February 11, 1943

I-19—sunk off Makin, November 25, 1943

I-20—missing from August 30, 1943 (i.e., sunk around this time)

I-21—sunk off Tarawa, November 27, 1943

I-22—missing from October 5, 1942

I-23—missing off Oahu, February 15, 1942

I-24—sunk off Attu, June 10, 1943

I-25—missing from September 20, 1943

I-68—sunk off New Hanover, July 27, 1943

I-69—sunk at Truk, April 4, 1944

I-70—sunk off Oahu, December 10, 1941 (FIRST RETAL-IATION)

I-71—sunk off Buka Island, February 1, 1944

I-72—sunk November 10, 1942

I-73—sunk off Midway January 27, 1942

I-74—sunk off Truk, April 12, 1944

I-75—sunk off Jaluit, February 4, 1944

TANKERS

Kenyo Maru—sunk off Palau, January 14, 1944

Kokuyo Maru—sunk in Sulu Sea, July 30, 1944

Koykuto Maru—sunk at Manila, September 21, 1944 (raised and returned to service 1951, scrapped 1963!)

Nihon Maru—sunk January 16, 1944

Shinkoku Maru—Sunk off Truk, February 17, 1944

Toei Maru—sunk off Truk, January 18, 1943

Toho Maru—sunk Makassar Strait, March 29, 1943

MIDGET SUBS

Four sunk, one (HA-19) beached and captured

One raised in 1963 and now displayed at Eta Jima, Japan

BIBLIOGRAPHY

Adams, Val. "That Sunday 25 Years Ago, I Was on a Tower Overlooking Pearl Harbor . . ." *Esquire,* December 1966.

Agawa, Hiroyuki. *The Reluctant Admiral: Yamamoto and the Imperial Navy.* Tokyo: Kodansha International, 1983.

Brown, David. *Warship Losses of World War Two.* Annapolis, Maryland: Naval Institute Press, 1995.

Cohen, Stan. *East Wind Rain.* Missoula, Montana: Pictorial Histories Publishing Company, 1991.

Collier, Richard. *The Road to Pearl Harbor: 1941.* New York: Atheneum, 1981.

"The Day the Arizona Died." *Santa Fe Reporter,* December 7, 1983.

"The Search for the Titanic Is Over but Now a Rush for the Gold Has Begun." *Smithsonian* 17, no. 5 (August 1986).

Delgado, James P. "Recovering the Past of USS Arizona: Symbolism, Myth and Reality." *Historical Archaeology* 26, no. 4 (1992): 69–80.

Gould, Richard A., ed. *Shipwreck Anthropology.* Albuquerque, New Mexico: UNM Press, 1983.

Jasper, Joy Waldron, ed. *Historic Shipwrecks: Issues in Management.* Washington D.C.: National Trust for Historic Preservation, 1988.

Jasper, Joy Waldron. "Fifty Years Later the Arizona Rests Peacefully." *Underwater USA* (December 1991).

Kimmett, Larry, and Margaret Regis. *The Attack on Pearl Harbor: An Illustrated History* Seattle, Washington: Navigator Publishing, 1991.

Lenihan, Daniel J., ed. *Submerged Cultural Resources Study: USS Arizona Memorial and Pearl Harbor National Historic Land-*

mark. Santa Fe, New Mexico: National Park Service, Submerged Cultural Resources Unit, 1989.

Lott, Arnold S. ed., and Robert F. Sumrall. *USS Arizona (BB39), Ship's Data.* Annapolis, Maryland: Leeward Publications, 1978.

Lowry, Lt. Cmdr. R. G., Royal Navy. *The Origins of Some Naval Terms and Customs.* London: Sampson Low, Marston & Co., Ltd, n.d.

Manchester, William. *Goodbye, Darkness: A Memoir of the Pacific War,* Little, Brown & Company, 1980.

Prange, Gordon W. *At Dawn We Slept: The Untold Story of Pearl Harbor.* New York: Penguin Books, 1981.

Prange, Gordon W., Donald M. Goldstein, and Katherine V. Dillon. *Miracle at Midway.* New York: McGraw Hill, 1982.

Raymer, Commander Edward C. *Descent into Darkness: Pearl Harbor, 1941, a Navy Diver's Memoir.* Novato, California: Presidio Press, 1996.

Slackman, Michael. *Remembering Pearl Harbor: The Story of the USS Arizona Memorial.* Honolulu: Arizona Memorial Museum Association, 1986.

Stern, Rob. *U.S. Battleships in Action, Part 2.* Carrollton, Texas: Squadron/Signal Publications, 1984.

Stillwell, Paul. *Battleship Arizona: An Illustrated History.* Annapolis, Maryland: Naval Institute Press, 1991.

Sulzberger, C. L. *World War II.* New York: American Heritage Press, 1985.

Toland, John. *Infamy.* Garden City, New York: Doubleday & Co, 1982.

Wallin, Homer. *Pearl Harbor: Why, How, Fleet Salvage and Final Appraisal.* Washington D.C. 1968.

Weintraub, Stanley. *Long Day's Journey into War: December 7, 1941.* New York: Dutton, 1991.

ACKNOWLEDGMENTS

Our deepest appreciation and admiration to the men of the USS *Arizona.* Heartfelt thanks to the survivors who granted interviews and unburdened their hearts of long-locked memories of December 7, 1941: John Anderson, Galen Ballard, Ralph Byard, Jimmie Burcham, Jim Foster, William Goshen, Jim Lawson, Vern Olsen, John Rampley, and Clint Westbrook.

We appreciate the cooperation and assistance of the National Park Service (NPS), particularly from former Superintendent of the *Arizona* Memorial Gary Cummins, superintendent Kathy Billings, and staff divers Kendell Thompson, Randy Wester, Daniel A. Martinez, Deborah Ling, and Eric Andersen. Thanks also to the archaeologists and staff of the NPS Submerged Cultural Resources Center in Santa Fe, New Mexico, particularly Larry Murphy, SCR chief, and Dan Lenihan.

We acknowledge significant contributions also from Richard A. Gould of Brown University; Burl Burlingame of the *Hawaii Star Bulletin;* Dr. Edward Tabor Linenthal of the University of Wisconsin at Oshkosh; Edwin C. Bearss, former Chief Historian of the National Park Service; James Charlton of the Washington NPS office; Dr. Carmine Prioli of the University of North Carolina, Chapel Hill; and many thanks to Stanley Weintraub for his timely assistance.

Special appreciation to the three volunteers who worked with Jim Adams: submariner Lieutenant Jerry Peterson USN, and two Marines, Master Sergeant Todd Hall and

Captain Bob Venema. "Quite a team," Adams says, "and we spoke and felt alike when it came to the *Arizona*."

Very special thanks and gratitude to our fine editor, Truman Talley, for his insightful comments and suggestions, his unfailing patience, and most of all for believing in the book from the beginning.

A huge debt of gratitude to our literary agent, Sam Fleishman, whose scholarship, acumen, compassion, and creativity render him truly unique.

Joy Waldron Jasper gives deepest thanks for their unstinting love and encouragement to her parents, Carl and Agnes Johnson, to her children, Ellen Roots McBride, Logan McCook Roots, and April Roots Prewitt, and to the most special man in her life, her husband, Mark Jasper.

INDEX